Language, Race, and P(in Schools

In this edited collection, authors from various academic, cultural, racial, linguistic, and personal backgrounds use critical discourse analysis as a conceptual framework and method to examine social inequities, identity issues, and linguistic discrimination faced by historically oppressed groups in schools and society. *Language, Race, and Power in Schools* unravels the ways and degrees to which these groups have faced and resisted oppression and draws on critical discourse analysis to examine how multiple forms of oppression intersect. This volume interrogates areas of discrimination and injustice and discusses possibilities of developing coalitions and concerted efforts across the lines of diversity.

Pierre W. Orelus is Associate Professor of Curriculum and Instruction, New Mexico State University, USA.

Routledge Research in Education

For a full list of titles in this series, please visit www.routledge.com

Language, Race, and Power in Schools

A Critical Discourse Analysis

Edited by Pierre W. Orelus

Routledge
Taylor & Francis Group

LONDON AND NEW YORK

First published 2017
by Routledge

2 Park Square, Milton Park, Abingdon, Oxfordshire OX14 4RN
52 Vanderbilt Avenue, New York, NY 10017

Routledge is an imprint of the Taylor & Francis Group, an informa business

First issued in paperback 2018

Copyright © 2017 Taylor & Francis

The right of Pierre W. Orelus to be identified as editor of this work has been asserted by him in accordance with sections 77 and 78 of the Copyright, Designs and Patents Act 1988.

Library of Congress Cataloguing in Publication Data
A catalog record for this book has been requested.

ISBN: 978-1-138-69049-3 (hbk)
ISBN: 978-0-367-19587-8 (pbk)

Typeset in Sabon
by Apex CoVantage, LLC

Contents

Foreword

We live in perilous times. We are on our way to the highest levels of inequality we have ever had in the United States and across the world. We have a new global "casino capitalism," a form of capitalism based on bets that have little to do with producing anything of real value to people. Global warming threatens the very existence of human beings and civilization. Violent extremism in the name of ideology is spreading across the world. Environmental degradation and violence are leading to massive flows of immigration and displaced people. The Internet is now so vital to the operations of our governments, businesses, and infrastructure—and so thoroughly interconnected—that hackers could bring on a disaster as big as or bigger than the detonation of a nuclear weapon, leaving whole cities without light, water, or safety.

The bad news here is this: Business as usual cannot go on. Tinkering at the edges of school and society in the name of "reform," without addressing these major problems and their interconnections with each other, is like Nero fiddling while Rome burns.

The good news here is this: Business as usual cannot go on. It was business as usual that brought us this mess, so the fact that we will be forced to end it now is good news, if we can take advantage of this climatic moment in human history and direct change down positive pathways.

We academics have to begin to think bigger thoughts and seek impact, not just citations. We have to interrogate racism, classicism, gender discrimination of all sorts, and all other forms of injustice but without destroying—indeed, by creating—possibilities for coalitions and concerted efforts across the lines of diversity. We have to start offering solutions and not just critique. And solutions are going to require new categories, new collaborations, and new forms of knowing, being, and activism.

Critical discourse analysis names a variety of different approaches to research on, and interventions in, the functioning of talk, text, activity, and identity at work in the world to produce, reproduce, and change society, culture, institutions, history, our notions of humanness, and our place as humans in the wider world. Like so much of academics, discourse analysts have placed themselves in well-protected silos. Such silos are part of business as usual and part of what needs to end if we are to move forward and not meet our fate without having put up any real fight.

Why is discourse analysis crucial? Because it is talk and text in all their complex relationships with each other and with objects, tools, places and spaces, ways of acting and interacting, and ways of believing and valuing in and across history that brought us to this tipping point. Unless we understand how we got here and how we can talk ourselves out of this mess, we are doomed. Yes, talk our way out—communication, interaction, and collaboration in the service of a new world, not a utopia surely, but a place where we can be better people, better to each other, and better to our mother, the Earth.

We are down to the basics here. It is a portentous time for those of us who study how people "talk the talk" and "walk the walk" and, so too, how we humans can talk new talk and walk a new walk, even something of a dance. It is the worst of times and the best of times to be an academic.

Dear reader, let Pierre W. Orelus's enticing collection of chapters—*Language, Race, and Power in Schools: A Critical Discourse Analysis*—be not just training for the mind but an invitation for you to collect your thoughts, begin to build your own theories and coalitions, and prepare yourself for action and collaboration.

James Paul Gee
Mary Lou Fulton Presidential Professor
of Literacy Studies
Regents' Professor

Acknowledgments

This book would not have been a reality without the genuine contribution of all contributors involved in it. I wish to thank them all for their knowledge, experience, expertise, and inspiration. Second, my deepest gratitude goes to the staff at Routledge, namely Christina Chronister and Katherine Tsamparlis, who were very understanding, patient, and supportive from the beginning to the end. Third, I want thank Professor James Gee, who graciously agreed to write the foreword supporting this book project. Finally, thank you to my wife and my daughter, who were extremely supportive and patient throughout the process of writing this book. As always, you two are my rock and will always be!

1 Introduction

Language, Race, and Power in Schools

Pierre W. Orelus

A Critical Discourse Analysis

Educators and students, particularly linguistically and culturally diverse students, are facing a challenging era. Inequities are pervasive and happening nearly everywhere. For example, in schools, various forms of inequities—often language-, race-, class-, and gender-based—often occur and shape student-student and teacher-student interactions and unequal power relations. These structural inequities often lead to resource and opportunity gaps between affluent and nonaffluent students. These gaps, in turn, influence the learning and academic outcomes of students and their future professional lives.

What happens in schools is often a reflection of what is happening in society. This is to say that these forms of inequities are intrinsically linked to a long history of discrimination against certain groups in schools and society at large. For instance, while privileged students have well-prepared and adequately supported teachers at their schools, students from linguistically and racially marginalized groups and poor socioeconomic backgrounds tend to attend schools that have ill-prepared teachers and lack resources needed to enhance student learning.

There are numerous scholars addressing a wide range of social justice issues in schools and society at large (Adams et al., 2012; North, 2009). This book touches on similar issues and concerns. Specifically, this edited volume draws on critical discourse analysis (CDA) to critically examine crucial educational, linguistic, racial, and socioeconomic issues facing students and teachers in many schools and communities around the world, particularly the United States. This book demonstrates ways and the degree to which CDA can and has been used as a theoretical tool to analyze various ways in which inequities might have affected multilingual, multiracial, and multicultural groups, including students and educators of color.

This book gathers an eclectic multilingual, multicultural, and multiracial group of progressive scholars and educators around the world who draw on discourse analysis as well as on their professional and personal experiences to point out the manner in which factors, such as language, race, and class, influence the learning experience and academic achievement of linguistically and culturally diverse students as well as teaching practices of educators, including educators of color. The section that follows examines CDA as a conceptual framework informing this volume.

CDA: An Overview

What is CDA? Rogers (2011) states, "Critical discourse analysis is a problem-oriented and transdisciplinary set of theories and methods that have been used in educational research" (p. 1). CDA is not a new, emerging critical approach. It can be traced back to the time of Plato (2008). It has evolved over time and has been taken on by many critical scholars with different foci and from different fields and disciplines, such as sociolinguistics (Gumperz, 1982; Labov, 1972); systemic functional linguistics (Fairclough, 2003); linguistics (Gee, 2011); critical ethnography of communication (Blommaert, 2001; Collins & Blot, 2003); ethnography of communication (Gumperz & Hymes, 1964; Scollon & Scollon, 2004); linguistic anthropology (Hymes, 1996); social semiotics (Kress, 2009; Lemke, 2002; van Leeuwen, 2008); education (Rogers, 2011); philosophy (Foucault, 1977); sociology (Du Bois, 1903); and narrative research (Bruner, 1991; Ochs & Capps, 1996). Classroom researchers have also drawn on CDA to study classroom interactions between students and teachers as well as interactions between students and students (Bloome et al., 2005).

Many of these scholars have used CDA to critically examine many forms of "social wrongs" (Gee, 2011) and offer alternatives to these wrongs. Like many critical and analytical tools, CDA has provided scholars with a window to deconstruct and unmask what is often constructed in texts as normal and sacred. In other words, CDA has proven to be a vital tool allowing critical scholars to unveil the root causes of social inequality normalized through texts. By texts, I am not only referring to written texts but also oral and visual texts. As Fairclough (1995) states,

> A rather broader conception has become common within discourse analysis, where a text may be either written or spoken discourse, so that, for example, the words used in a conversation (or their written transcription) constitute a text. In cultural analysis, by contrast, texts do not need to be linguistic at all; any cultural artifact—a picture, a building, a piece of music—can be seen as a text.
>
> (p. 4)

Analyzing meanings embedded in texts, particularly the ways and contexts in which these meaning are constructed, is central to the work of CDA scholars. Meanings are not constructed in a vacuum. Ideology and power play fundamental roles in the way meanings are constructed and the purposes and interests they serve. Rogers (2011) states, "Because systems of meaning are caught up in political, social, racial, economic, religious, and cultural formations which are linked to socially defined practices that carry more or less privilege and value in society, they cannot be considered neutral" (p. 1). Along the same lines, Fairclough contends,

> While it is true that the forms and content of texts do bear the imprint of ideological processes and structures, it is not possible to 'read off' ideologies from texts. This is because meanings are produced through interpretations of texts and texts are open to diverse interpretations, and because ideological processes appertain to discourses as whole social events-they are processes between people-not to the texts which are produced, distributed and interpreted as moments of such events.
>
> (p. 71)

In this context, ideology is defined and used here from a Gramscian perspective. Gramsci (1971) defines ideology as being "a conception of the world that is implicitly manifest in art, in law, in economic activity and in the manifestations of individual and collective life" (p. 328). Fairclough argues that "[f]or Gramsci, ideology is tied to action, and ideologies are judged in terms of their social effects rather than their truth values" (p. 76). Similarly, Hall (1988) maintains that Gramsci sees "the field of ideologies in terms of conflicting, overlapping, or intersecting currents or formations" (pp. 55–56).

Leading CDA figure James Gee (2011) examines the way language, ideology, and power interweave to influence the social construction of meanings. Gee has also looked at how these concepts have shaped discourses, particularly dominant discourses. Specifically, Gee unravels how dominant discourses have been used to shape, reshape, and maintain the power structure, which seem to have served the interests of the powerful. Fairclough (2011) and Kress (2009) also address the power issue in their work. For example, Fairclough talks about different types of power. He argues that there is power to, power over, and power behind. He contends that CDA can help us figure out how these types of power manifest themselves through social and political practices.

Power is often perceived and talked about in negative terms. This is due to the fact that people historically have used power, whether it be political, socioeconomic power or both, to oppress others (Freire, 2010). Blommeart contends, "[T]he deepest impact of power everywhere is inequality, as power differentiates and selects, includes and excludes" (p. 2). By contrast, I argue that rather than using power over people, it can and should be used with people. That is, power can be used collectively to equally distribute social goods as a way to combat inequities.

As an analytical tool, CDA can help us dissect and dig deep into texts wherein many forms of inequities of power are normalized for the preservation of the status quo. Through the deconstruction of texts, a language of possibility might emerge, and those who have been marginalized can use such a language to take necessary steps toward human freedom and liberation. In some way, CDA can be an emancipatory tool depending on how it is used.

Another central concept to CDA is language. Language is used to construe meanings. In addition, language has been used as a political tool to dehumanize people, like many contributors to this volume pointed out in their chapters. Oppressed groups have also used their languages to resist and change their conditions. Hence, from a critical standpoint, language is not innocent; it is ideologically loaded and intrinsically connected to power. Gee (2011) maintains, "[C]ritical discourse analysis argues that language-in-use is always part and parcel of, and partially constitutive of, specific social practices, and that social practices always have implications for inherently political things like status, solidarity, the distribution of social goods, and power" (cited in Rogers, 2011, p. 28). Examining language use through a CDA lens is critically important, for doing so might help us deconstruct power as broadly conceived as well as meanings entrenched in texts.

CDA is a theoretical tool that can be used to critically analyze inequities in schools and in society as a whole. Specifically, CDA can and has been used to examine institutional racism, linguicism, classism, sexism, and the effects of these "isms" on people, particularly historically marginalized groups. Authors in this volume have drawn on CDA to analyze what Gee calls *figured world and situated meanings.* According to Gee, "[a] figured world is a picture of a simplified world that captures what is taken to be typical or normal. What is taken to be typical or normal, of course, varies by context and by people's sociocultural affiliations" (cited in Rogers, 2011, p. 42). Gee goes on to say,

> When people "figure" a world, that is, imagine what the world looks like from a certain perspective of what is "normal" or "typical", they are imaging pictures of Discourses or aspects of Discourses at work in the world. They are imaging typical identities and activities within typical environments.
>
> (cited in Rogers, 2011, p. 43)

Regarding situated meanings, Gee goes on to note, "Situated meanings arise because particular language forms take on specific or situated meanings in specific different contexts of use" (cited in Rogers, 2011, p. 25). Theoretically, these two concepts guide this volume.

Situating CDA in a Multilingual, Multiracial, and Multicultural Context

As demonstrated, CDA has greatly influenced many scholars and researchers across various fields and disciplines. CDA is transcending and represents a paradigmatic shift in the way many scholars see, understand, and interpret texts, among other things. CDA can and has enabled many scholars to read "the word and the world" (Freire & Macedo, 1987) through textual analysis. Because of its cross-border and interdisciplinary focus and nature, CDA can be and has been used in many disciplines and fields. Many scholars have used CDA to unpack how competing and antagonistic forms of ideology are often embedded in texts (written, visual, oral, etc.) and driven by many hidden interests. By carefully reading, analyzing, and interpreting the scholarly work on ideology by sociolinguists, linguists, and scholars who use CDA as their theoretical lenses guiding their analysis, one can, for example, better comprehend ways and the degree to which ideology shapes texts and its role in shaping meanings and influencing people's minds, behavior, and actions.

Despite its profound influence, theoretical appeal, and useful application to various fields, CDA, like many groundbreaking theoretical frameworks, is not immune to criticism. One of the criticisms is the degree to which the field has been driven by the ideas and scholarly work of European male scholars. Indeed, CDA has been dominated by European male sociolinguists, linguists, and scholars from various fields. As such, the contribution of this volume to the field lies in the diverse body of scholars that it brings— both well-established and emerging scholars—who have drawn on CDA to examine issues facing historically oppressed groups, including linguistically and culturally diverse students and educators of color. These scholars look at and use CDA from a multicultural and multilingual epistemology.

This edited volume aims to show ways and the extent to which CDA can be incorporated in the analysis of crucial issues facing linguistically, culturally, and racially diverse groups, particularly students and educators of color. Using a CDA framework, contributors to this volume have captured in their analysis the ontological, linguistic, cultural, racial, and socioeconomic lived experiences of historically marginalized groups, particularly students of color. All in all, authors in this book show how CDA can be utilized in the analysis of important sociolinguistic, linguistic, educational, racial, an socioeconomic issues facing multiracial, multilingual, and multiracial people, in particular students and educators of color. Their analysis will contribute to the growing scholarship in CDA through particularly a multicultural, multilingual, and multiracial lens.

Contextualizing the Book

How was this book conceptualized? The idea of producing this book emerged from a doctoral seminar course on emancipatory discourse that I taught three years ago. After teaching this doctoral seminar course, I decided that I would make this long-contemplated book project become a reality, particularly as there does not seem to be many published books of this kind. In this seminar class, I had the most engaging doctoral students— most of whom with years of experiences teaching and working with linguistically and culturally diverse students, including English language learners

(ELLs) and bilingual students here in the United States and other parts of the world, like Africa, Europe, and Asia. They were from different countries and brought with them a wealth of experience and wisdom to the seminar class. I, as the instructor, engaged them in heated and rich conversations that revolved around CDA of language, ideology, power, and race. We read, analyzed, and discussed various forms of written, oral, and visual texts that talked about these issues.

Since the main focus of the seminar was on discourse and emancipation, we had extensive discussions about CDA and emancipatory discourse drawing on the work of Blommaert (2001), Gee (2011, 2012), Fairclough (2003), Fairclough & Fairclough (2012), Fanon (1963), Freire (1970, 2003), and Memmi (1965). This seminar class was designed in ways that created space for students to dialogue with and challenge one another on issues previously mentioned. Space was also created in this seminar so that students' voices, entrenched in their lived, educational, and professional experiences, could be heard and, more importantly, taken into account. In class, students often shared stories about their academic, personal, and professional lives connected to their own learning and teaching experiences. This book draws on CDA to make an urgent appeal for equity and fairness in schools and society at large.

This book consists of a collection of 12 essays written by respected educators and scholars. As the content analysis of their respective chapters show, they are genuinely concerned with social justice issues aforementioned. Relevant examples drawn from professional and personal experiences and observations are used throughout their individual chapters to expose various forms of social injustices to which historically oppressed groups, principally students and educators of color, have been subjected and the manner in which these injustices might have limited their life chances and opportunities.

I have always wanted to write a book that creates space for, and honors students' voices rooted in, their lived and professional experiences as well as in their unofficial and subjugated knowledge and wisdom. I contemplated various book projects during the last five years or so. At first, I wanted to do an empirical study exploring what has inspired students to become teachers since I have been primarily working with preservice teachers. I attempted to conduct this study, without much success. I then decided to pursue this book project whose content fundamentally reflects voices of social justice scholars and educators using CDA as their theoretical lens to examine and expose inequities—often language-, race-, class-, and gender-based—occurring in schools and society at large. These scholars and educators propose alternative solutions to these social wrongs.

Backgrounds of Contributors

The contributors come from different walks of life. Their socioeconomic status varies from working-class to middle-class backgrounds. Their religious backgrounds vary from being Catholics to Protestants. While some are native speakers of English and Chinese, others speak Spanish and Polish as their native tongue; their racial and ethnic backgrounds range from being Whites, Latina/os, Afro-Latina/os, Asians, and Indians (from India) to being Blacks, and they are predominantly females.

Moreover, they are from different countries around the world, such as Mexico, Poland, Argentina, Jamaica, Columbia, China, India, Venezuela, Spain, and the United States. Many of them were first-generation college students and immigrants from diverse backgrounds. Their different characteristics and backgrounds reflected a great of level diversity in the seminar class. Regardless of their various backgrounds, they all shared something in common: They all talked about at least one form of oppression they, family members, their friends, and their students have been battling against.

I have had mentored many of these students in some capacity. Many were specially invited to participate in this book primarily because of their knowledge, critical consciousness, and impressive critical and courageous stance on sociolinguistic, linguistic, social justice, and educational issues that we explored in depth during the seminar and what they have accomplished professionally since. They were all eager to participate in this book project when I invited them. Their authentic voices echoing through their narratives are voices that need to be heard and taken seriously in the academy and beyond. Through their narratives one can feel a deep sense of hope for the creation of a school system and society where people's diverse sociolinguistic, cultural, racial, linguistic, and historical backgrounds are not seen as a problem but rather something unique and precious to embrace, honor, and respect.

Book Organization

This book is composed of three different sections yet connected. Each section contains four chapters. The first section sheds light on identity issues, as broadly defined, and linguistic discrimination historically oppressed groups have faced and resisted in schools and in society. The second section contains writings that unravel the ways and the degree to which historically marginalized groups, including women and people of color, have faced and resisted various forms of language-, class-, race-, and gender-based oppression. Last, writings in the third section examine the manner in which multiple forms of oppression intersect and influence the learning of students from historically underprivileged backgrounds.

Audience

Given its interdisciplinary scope, this book can be used in language, CDA, literacy, and education courses as well as multicultural education courses. Moreover, the narrative of scholars in this book can be inspiring to multilingual, multicultural, and multiracial students and social justice educators who are battling social wrongs in schools and society at large (Gee, 2011). Last, but not least, this book might hold relevance to sociolinguists and linguists.

Outline of Chapters

Section One

In Chapter 1, the author starts from a personal experience of how she was downgraded by her fourth grade head teacher to indicate that language is heavily loaded with ideology and hidden power and how "Big D" discourse can affect "small d" discourse as defined by Gee (1999). The author further explores the concept of "Big D" and "small d" in discourse analysis and argues that language is part of discourse. The author goes on to maintain that since it is through discourse that we get most of our knowledge, it is of great importance that we not only do peripheral discourse analysis but do CDA as well. In relating CDA to her career as an English as a foreign language (EFL) teacher, the author maintains that both "Big D" and "small d" need to be incorporated in discourse analysis. The analysis of "small d" has to be put into the context of "Big D" so as to make it meaningful and insightful. From there, the author points out that teachers' discourses can be either positive or negative in the process of students' identity exploring and agency developing in school settings. Finally, the author concludes that her journey from the East City Gate to the East of the Pacific is not only a travel through time and space but also a journey of emancipation through CDA.

The second chapter explores the potential of media as a mechanism that venues emancipatory discourses to catapult democratic ideological transformation and social change. Using CDA along with the argumentation theory (Blommaert, 2012), the author analyzes a video featuring a young college student of color who critically questions the myth hidden in the ideology that seems to equate schooling to success. By doing so, she aims at illuminating relationships among the structures of the "orders of discourse" (Fairclough & Fairclough, 2012, p. 80) and various narratives revolved around the often assumed automatic socioeconomic advantages associated with schooling. As a way to counteract oligarchic power, she calls on those interested in the field of education to become aware of the power invested in their voices to dismantle hegemonic structures in social media as forms of discourse that prevent change and transformation in education operating in contemporary, digital-oriented, diverse societies.

Chapter 3 uses CDA as a conceptual framework to investigate ways and the extent to which ideology and power represented in the discourse of war and weapons are influencing American public opinion. As a reference point, it uses the American celebrity and gun rights advocate Mr. Charlton Heston's 1998 National Rifle Association (NRA) address. The chapter proposes the composition and rhetoric teachers need to introduce the discourse of war and weapons in their classrooms and to develop curriculum based on the following participatory action research (PAR) paradigm. Implemented in the classroom, this process offers opportunities for students to investigate and deconstruct social discourse. Finally, the chapter suggests that achieving personal and social emancipation is possible if teachers start the dialectical process in class in deconstructing embedded hegemony in the social discourse.

Chapter 4 uses discourse as a pilgrimage to trace the temporal and spatial situatedness of the author's journey through an autobiographical inquiry. It posits contested narratives between silenced voices of opposition and official discourse and argues for a commitment and action to rise above oppression. Through the localities of two countries, Argentina and the United States, the practiced and lived experiences of self as a student and teacher evolve. Discourse proceeds from history and stories, thus deriving identities of individuality and collectivity. This historicity manifests in distinct scales of temporality that constitute the framework to comprehend sociolinguistic performances that assist in understanding the mediated relation of self to locality and subjective experience. The conclusion stresses the fluidity of a lived experience and the ever-evolving reflective process toward self-trust and a temporal love.

Section Two

Chapter 5 explores the lack of criticality in the standard curriculum and how a conscious educator can create change in the urban setting and beyond. The author argues that although the New York City (NYC) landscape has been labeled a cultural melting pot, it is the ideal place to challenge issues of inequities and engage students from diverse backgrounds concerning injustices to expose and strive to uproot these inequities. It is also a place where many schools mainly focus on the importance of standardized testing to a point where culture, social justice, and creating critical consciousness are ignored. This chapter focuses on a student/teacher's experience in one of NYC's largest public schools. This student/teacher attempts to bring criticality to my classroom and my school. After spending two years creating student-centered films on issues, such as racism, stereotyping, the third world, and understanding the power of hegemony, a transformation ensued, and students became actively engaged in challenging injustices around them.

In Chapter 6, the author draws on the fields of rhetoric, feminist studies, and CDA with attention to emotional expression within the classroom for nontraditional students and role in which comforts at such expression can contribute to nontraditional student retention. The author argues that the classroom community is shaped by the ways in which the teacher and peers respond to emotional expression. Utilizing Pegeen Reichert Powell's *Retention and Resistance: Writing Instruction and Students Who Leave*, the author emphasizes the need to revisit the label "nontraditional student" for replacement by the term "learner." She contends that what is most important is positive reception of shared emotional expressions and attention to retaining the students in the classroom as a way of making their time enrolled valuable. To this end, the author offers recommendations for the learner, teacher, and classroom community to encourage the public expression of private emotion by all learners. Finally, she explains her wishes to continue this research so as to continue the discussion of the need for the classroom to present as a safe place for sharing.

Chapter 7 examines the various interpretations and assumptions that have influenced the author's concept of identity. Identity is one of the most complex conceptions of human nature. It is constructed, shaped, and reformulated within varying social, cultural, emotional, and psychological realms. Based on social identity components such as class, race, ethnicity, and gender, first, the author briefly discusses her upbringing in her home country and how this shaped some of the core ideas that she has on identity. Then, she focuses on the international experiences that have contributed to her construction of identity as a teacher, learner, and cultural crosser in different locations. Using pivotal ideas from CDA (Gee, 2011), the author examines the connection between language and identity while explaining that the experiences she has accumulated living in diverse countries, rather than any consistent ideology, have shaped her notion of identity. She concludes that her own current concept of identity has been influenced by sociocultural, economic, and emotional events that have enhanced her perceptions on this issue and refined her understanding of societal power dynamics.

In Chapter 9, the author uses comparative discourse analysis of the works and interviews of two African authors, Chimamanda Ngozi Adichie and Ngugi Wa Thiong'o, to increase understanding of varying opinions regarding owning the English language by people from the continent of Africa. Because the author has been teaching English in Africa for the past 28 years and has been preparing others to teach English the latter half of that time, she describes her position based on experiences she has had in various countries in East Africa. After decades of teaching English to speakers of other languages, she began to see more clearly the questions people have about whether English, a language that had its beginnings through colonialism, should be taught in Africa. Thus, the analysis is a springboard for further investigation into questions of English. The author argues that one cannot overlook how English was historically introduced into most countries of Africa, but one can also go further to explore the meanings people are making today because of English language access. After the analysis of differing opinions about the English language in Africa, readers can look at their own contexts and make personal decisions about English language use, remembering that their decisions will affect those around them.

Section Three

Drawing on the work of sociocultural and postcolonial theorists, Chapter 9 explores accentism. Accentism is accent-based discrimination often connected to one's nonstandard accent along with one's linguistic and social class backgrounds, nationality, and country of origin. To illuminate how this form of accent-based discrimination has occurred, the author provides a historical overview of the way many varieties of accents labeled as non-standard or "foreign" emerged and have been looked down upon, discriminating against those who spoke and continue to speak with these accents. Further, the author demonstrates the way and the extent to which accentism has affected the cultural life, the learning process, the identity, and the subjective and material conditions of marginalized groups, particularly for linguistically and culturally diverse students. Finally, the author proposes alternative ways to challenge and counter accentism that linguistically and culturally diverse students have faced in schools and in society at large.

In Chapter 10, the authors use CDA to unveil the workings of power in their situated experiences as women with multiple identities. The main purpose of this chapter is to contribute to a process of societal transformation in ways that break with the constraining effects of sexism, racism, classism, and heterosexism in women's and girl's lives. Through the analysis of their own stories, the authors attempt to demonstrate that the way people choose to tell their stories helps them not only display who they are to others but also co-construct the range of identities that come together at different facets of "this is who I am."

Chapter 11 principally aims at shedding light on the notions of discourse and emancipation leading to the life story of the author, who lived in Poland under the Communist regime in the 1970s and 1980s. The Communist discourse is presented and analyzed from the perspective of the author's own experiences and lenses. The author observes injustices and oppression occurring in her native land, following the historical and political events, and talks about the political shifts and the reasons for the shifts in Poland leading to emancipation of the country from the Communist regime. The author also undergoes an individual transformation through her personal experience as an immigrant in the United States and her work with people pushed to the margins of society: people with learning disabilities, homeless individuals, and refugees. She experiences changes in her Polish discourse leading to political emancipation and later a voluntary change of discourse from the Polish to the American discourse, providing empowering personal liberation through experience and formal institutional education.

Informed by CDA, the last chapter examines how ELLs are viewed in the curriculum. Primarily, the author notes the importance regarding immigration and bilingualism throughout history. Next, she presents a comparison between school and technical knowledge in reference to developing curriculum (Apple, 2004). Seeing the curriculum as colonizer brings the discussion to look closer at the hidden curriculum exercised in schools, which reproduces an ideological hegemony (Apple, 2004). She also analyzes the deficit thinking model further, linked to explain culturally and linguistically diverse and nonmainstream students' school failure (Valencia, 2010). Two other attitudes are presented that neglect linguistic and cultural diversity: "colorblindness" (Nieto, Bode, Kang, & Raible, 2007) and "cultural neutrality" (Ladson-Billings, 2000). Finally, she makes a strong case for considering bi(multi)lingualism as the norm.

Conclusion

Many scholars have addressed language, race, power, student learning, and identity issues in their work (Banks, 2007; Grant & Sleeter, 2011; Nieto & Bode, 2011; Sleeter & Cornbleth, 2011). However, more work is needed to further examine these crucial issues. It is within this spirit that this book was conceptualized and written. As noted at the outset, this book draws on CDA to examine many forms of inequities taking place in schools and society at large. This book aims to create awareness around these issues for transformative social change. This book is primarily designed for social justice educators, teachers, teacher practitioners, and parents concerned about and interested in fighting against social inequality, prejudices, and bigotry in schools and society at large. This book aims to have a deep influence on students, teachers, and readers from various backgrounds, inspiring them to collectively denounce and battle to eradicate linguistic, educational, racial, and socioeconomic inequities occurring in schools and society at large.

References

Adams, M., Blumenfeld, W., Castania, C. R., Hackman, H., Peters, M., & Zúñiga, X. (2012). *Readings for diversity and social justice.* New York: Routledge.
Banks, J. (2009). *The Routledge international companion to multicultural education.* New York: Routledge.
Bloome, D., Power Carter, S., Morton Christian, B., Otto, S., & Shuart-Faris, N. (2005). *Discourse analysis and the study of classroom language and literacy events: A microethnographic perspective.* Mahwah, NJ: Lawrence Erlbaum Associates.
DuBois, W. E. B. (1903/1990). *The souls of black folks.* New York: Vintage Books.
Fairclough, N. (1989). *Language and power.* London: Longman.
Fairclough, N. (1992). *Discourse and social change.* Cambridge, UK: Polity Press.
Fairclough, N. (1995). *Critical discourse analysis: The critical study of language.* London: Addison Wesley Publishing Company.
Fairclough, N. (2003). *Analysing discourse: Textual analysis for social research.* New York: Routledge.
Fairclough, I., & Fairclough, N. (2012). *Political discourse analysis: A method for advanced students.* New York: Routledge Taylor and Francis Group.
Fanon, F. (1963). *Wretched of the earth.* New York: Grove Press, Inc.

Fanon, F. (1967). *Black skin white masks*. New York: Grove Press, Inc.

Foucault, M. (1972). *The archeology of knowledge and the discourse on language*. New York: Pantheon Books.

Freire, P. (2010). *Education for critical consciousness*. New York: Continuum, Inc.

Gee, J. (1991). A linguistic approach to narrative. *Journal of Narrative and Life History*, 1(1), 15–39.

Gee, J. (2004). *Situated language and learning: A critique of traditional schooling*. London: Routledge.

Gee, J. (2010). *How to do discourse analysis: A toolkit*. New York: Routledge.

Gee, J. (2011a). *How to do discourse analysis: A tool kit*. New York: Routledge.

Gee, J. (2011b). Discourse analysis: What makes it critical? In R. Rogers (Ed.), *An introduction to critical discourse analysis* (2nd edition) (pp. 23–45). New York: Routledge.

Gee, J. (2012). *Social linguistics and literacies: Ideology in discourses* (4th edition). New York: Routledge.

Gramsci, A. (1971). *Selections from the prison notebooks*. (Q. Hoare and G. Nowell Smith, Ed. and Trans.). UK: Lawrence & Wishart.

Grant, C., & Sleeter, C. (2011). *Doing multicultural education for achievement and equity*. New York: Routledge.

Gumperz, J. (1982). *Discourse strategies*. Cambridge, UK: Cambridge University Press.

Gumperz, J., & Hymes, D. (Eds.). (1964). The ethnography of communication. *American Anthropology*, 66(6), 1–34.

Hall, S. (1982). The rediscovery of 'ideology': Return of the repressed in media studies. In M. Gurevitch, T. Bennet, J. Curan and J. Woollacott (Eds.), *Culture, society and the media* (pp. 56–90). London/New York: Methuen.

Halliday, M. K. K. (1978). *Language as social semiotic: The social interpretation of language and meaning*. Baltimore: University Park Press.

hooks, b. (2010). *Teaching critical thinking: Practical wisdom*. New York: Taylor & Francis.

Hymes, D. (1974). *Foundations of sociolinguistics*. Philadelphia: University of Pennsylvania Press.

Hymes, D. (1996). *Ethnography, linguistics, narrative inequality: Toward an understanding of voice*. New York: Taylor & Francis.

Kress, G. (2009). *Multimodality: A social semiotic approach to contemporary communication*. London: Taylor & Francis.

Kress, G., & van Leeuwen, T. (2006). *Reading images: The grammar of visual design*. New York: Routledge.

Labov, W. (1972). *Sociolinguistic patterns*. Philadelphia: University of Pennsylvania Press.

Lemke, J. L. (2002). Travels in hypermodality. *Visual Communication*, 1(30), 299–325.

Nieto, S., & Bode, P. (2011). *Affirming diversity: The sociopolitical context of multicultural education* (6th edition). New York: Pearson.

North, C. (2009). *Teaching for social justice: Voices from the front lines*. Denver, CO: Paradigm Publisher.

Orelus, P. (2011). *Rethinking race, class, language, and gender: A dialogue with Noam Chomsky and other leading scholars*. Lanham, MD: Rowman & Littlefield.

Rogers, R. (Ed.). (2011). *An introduction to critical discourse analysis* (2nd edition). New York: Routledge.

Scollon, R., & Scollon, S. (1981). *Narrative, literacy, and face in interethnic communication*. Norwood, NJ: Ablex.

Sleeter, C., & Cornbleth, C. (2011). *Teaching with vision: Culturally responsive teaching in standards-based classrooms*. New York: Teachers College Press.

van Dijk, T. (1993). Principles of critical discourse analysis. *Discourse & Society*, 4(2), 249–283.

van Dijk, T. (2008a). *Discourse in context: A sociocognitive approach*. Cambridge, UK: Cambridge University Press.

van Dijk, T. (2008b). *Discourse and practice: New tools for critical discourse analysis*. New York: Oxford University Press.

2 From East City Gate to the East of the Pacific

My Pedagogical Journey Through CDA

Lihua Zhang

Discourse analysis is a term quite familiar to language teachers, especially teachers working with English majors in colleges or universities. However, traditionally, discourse analysis has been dealing with mostly, if not completely, "anecdotal reflections on written or oral texts" (Gee, 2009, p. 2). Having been a teacher of English as a foreign language (EFL) in China for over 25 years, I am not alien to such anecdotal reflections of discourse analysis. However, it was the first time that I had been struck by the concept of CDA while pursuing my doctoral study in the United States. The impact of CDA was so powerful that during my deciphering process of CDA, I experienced time travel back to my early years of schooling. Naturally, the focus of this chapter is on the impact of CDA, which led to my critical reflections as both a teacher and a learner.

In this chapter, I am following James Paul Gee's (1999) critical conceptualization of discourse as my theoretical framework in analyzing my pedagogical emancipatory journey through CDA in EFL teaching and teacher education. Specifically, I employ James Paul Gee's (1999) "Big D" and "small d" concepts in which the "Big D" discourse refers to language plus "other stuff" and the "small d" discourse means "the language in use" (p. 17). Gee argued that "making visible and recognizable who we are and what we are doing always involves a great deal more than 'just language'" (p. 17). Thus, he proposed the differentiation terms of the "Big D" and the "small d" discourses. For convenience, words like "language" and "discourse" will be used interchangeably referring either to the concept of "Big D" or "small d" discourse or both depending on specific context.

I start the chapter with the historical moment of my fourth grade classroom anecdote. From there, I discuss the importance for educators to do CDA and the interwoven relationship of language (discourse), ideology, and power. I argue that discourse not only penetrates every corner of the educational setting but also functions as either an empowerment or disempowerment to students' agency depending on what discourse is promoted and how discourse is presented in the micro and macro educational settings. Most importantly, I highlight my pedagogical emancipation as the climax of CDA.

Story of the East City Gate

The East City Gate was a place where I spent most of my childhood years. The beautiful sceneries of nature and the ancient-old bedtime stories of my grandparents are always the main themes of my sweetest childhood memories. However, there is one occurrence that always pops up in the middle of the nostalgic moment and brings a discord to the harmony and peace of mind at the time. Sometimes I can't help asking myself why I just cannot forget that particular incident that happened in one of my fourth grade classrooms. It seems that I have to live with that occurrence all my life.

One day in particular, when I was listening attentively to my fourth grade head teacher's instruction, I suddenly saw her facial expression change drastically with anger. I then heard her scold one "misbehaved" classmate, a boy who lived outside the East City Gate, by saying: "There is not a single good person among you people who live outside the East City Gate!" I felt so ashamed and upset at her words because my family was also living outside the East City Gate at that time. Unfortunately, by location, I was included among one of those "no good persons" in her mind. The untypical fourth grade classroom scenario always comes clearly into view each time I am engaged in conversations on matters related to education, be it in formal classroom or at private settings. The fourth grade incident would pop up in my mind just like movie snapshots. It was kind of strange that I really could not remember what the misbehavior was, but I just could not forget the behavior and the words of my fourth grade head teacher.

East City Gate: The Symbolic Discourse

In the old times, the cities in China used to have four walls with one gate at each side for people to come in and out. The ones who lived within the city walls were mostly the rich or what we nowadays call middle- and upper-class people. Those who lived outside the city walls were mostly the working class or the poor who earned a living through hard physical labor. So the city walls were like dividers set in people's minds. After the downfall of the Qing Dynasty in the turn of the 20th century, there were barely any physical city walls in my hometown; however, the invisible walls remained in people's minds. What's more, although people were mingling by then, those who lived outside the East City Gate were still mostly farmers and workers. I remember clearly that some of my classmates who lived outside the East City Gate, including the one being reprimanded by my fourth grade head teacher, used to wear clothes that did not fit their figures appropriately. Since teenage boys grow faster, mothers usually made clothes bigger than the boys' actual sizes so that the clothes could be worn for a longer time. However, these oversize outfits, plus the sometimes unsanitary faces that resulted from dirt and sweat after break-time playing, created funny looks for the young boys. Such appearances contrasted sharply with the image of my fourth grade, middle-class head teacher, who lived inside the East City Gate and who always dressed herself cleanly and neatly. I would readily recognize her otherwise elegant posture if not for her often over-serious facial expression and her cold attitude toward those of us who lived outside the East City Gate. In retrospect, I see the East City Gate, the physical, historical wall that separated people by classes, as a symbolic discourse that created an invisible gap between us fourth grade working-class children and my middle-class head teacher. In that particular fourth grade class, I learned something that was not intended in the official school curriculum. Yet, what I took from my fourth grade head teacher's discourse was much more than a fourth grade child could digest at that moment. The impact was huge, and the memory was full of humiliation.

Language, Power, Ideology: The Triad of Discourse

The fourth grade incident has been an anguishing experience in my schooling. When I was still in my adolescent years, I disliked this teacher, and I could even feel a bit of hatred inside me. Although she had other behaviors or ways of dealing with students who I did not feel comfortable with, this incident brought all my negative emotions to a climax. When I got older and became a teacher, I could see my negative emotions gradually dissolve since I was able to see that incident from a positive perspective. Even though I was still not able to understand why my fourth grade head teacher was so harsh on us by making those hurtful remarks, I was able to use it as a learning experience to remind myself that as a teacher, I should never make hurtful or insulting comments to my students in the classroom. However, it was not until I learned CDA that I was able to make sense as to why my fourth grade teacher had engaged in that malicious talk. Obviously, by employing language in such an insulting way, my female, middle-class, fourth grade teacher was exercising power over my working-class classmates. Her language was the manifestation of her ideology, insinuating that working-class children living outside the East City Gate were doomed to be failures of future life and thus they were not worthy of education. The negative power generated by her middle-class ideology and manifested by her abusive language sent out the message of hopelessness, the consequence of which was devastating to the self-esteem and agency seeking of us fourth grade teenagers.

Language, power, and ideology are the triad of discourse. They intertwiningly exist in almost all human interactions. According to Blommaert (2005), there are two types of ideology categories. The first one is related to symbolic representations of personal discourses, such as socialism, Marxism, and so on, whereas the second type of ideology refers to the societal norms and practices. In this chapter, I mainly employ the second type of ideology when discussing the interwoven relationships among language, power, and ideology. Blommaert (2005) maintained that ideology "penetrates the whole fabric of societies or communities and results in normalized, naturalized patterns of thought and behavior" (p. 159). To me, ideology is something deeply embedded in people's minds. An iceberg is a metaphorical example that could be used to show what ideology entails. I argue that language is the upper part of an iceberg, whereas ideology is the part that is under the surface of the sea level. Consequently, we are very apt to be negligent of the underwater part of an iceberg but see only the upper part of it. However, how can we know exactly where the underwater iceberg is if we do not see its upper part above water? Obviously, we need to identify the upper part of an iceberg and then go underneath the water to locate the hidden part of the iceberg. Similarly, language (discourse), in its broadest sense, is like the upper part of an iceberg. In other words, the language people use in everyday life always reflects their ideologies, which resemble the underwater part of an iceberg. Whether one is aware of it or not, one's ideology is very apt to exercise two modes of power: empowerment and disempowerment. By making that vicious talk, my fourth grade teacher was using her language generated by her ideology to disempower all those who lived outside the East City Gate. Illuminating my fourth grade story with critical analysis, I see the impact of school discourse on students' psychological well-being and cognitive development. I realized the importance of critical reflections on teachers' discourses both inside and outside the classroom. I believe that only when teachers contemplate teacher-student interactions through critical lenses are they able to see the delicate, interwoven relationships among language, power, and ideology in the process of students' agency development.

Furthermore, language is more than verbal expressions. According to Blommaert (2005), language comprises "all forms of meaningful semiotic human activity seen in connection with social, cultural, and historical patterns and developments of use" (p. 3). In this sense, language can be manifested in different forms: verbal, nonverbal, and other semeiotics. Referring back to my East City Gate story, while my fourth grade teacher made her scolding comments, her facial expressions, the cold tone filled with disgusting and anger, together with those insulting and hurtful words, sent the message to us that people who lived outside East City Gate were not worthy of any respect or dignified treatment. Such language functioned as disempowerment for most of us at a young age. I do not know how my other classmates felt at that moment, but I know how that specific occurrence in the fourth grade classroom has haunted me from time to time and made my heart laden with indignity and sorrow.

Agiro (2012) argued that "throughout their educational experiences, students are subjected to values that are by products of schooling; interaction with teachers or parents, texts, and other students are not purely academic, and therefore cause students to experience 'educationally significant' leanings outside of official curriculum" (p. 212). This is especially true with my fourth grade story. The indignity of inhabiting at the outside of the East City

Gate and the sense of failure were exactly the "educationally significant" experiences that we learned outside our official fourth grade curriculum. Therefore, I strongly feel the need to critically reflect on teachers' discourses so as to improve teacher-student interactions, to develop students' sense of agency, and to help construct students' own identities.

Language, Power, Ideology: The Critical Pedagogic Lens

Blommeart (2005) argued that "language is always produced by someone to someone else, at a particular time and place, with a purpose and so forth" (p. 39). Likewise, Tijk (2013) maintained that we obtain our knowledge of the world from three sources: from our experiences in the world, from discourse, and from the inference of both our experience and the discourse. This echoes with the sociocultural perspective that "view[s] individuals and their cognitive and emotional development as constituting and constituted by their social milieu" (Swain & Deters, 2007, p. 823). In real world, most of our knowledge comes from our interactions with each other through family discourse, school discourse, social discourse, and interactional discourse. Inevitably in social interactions, we are not only immersed in vast occurrences of discourse but are also affected either positively or negatively by them. For example, babies begin to know the world from both experiencing the world around them and hearing their parents talking to them and around them. Later, when they grow up, they go to school and start their formal education. At this time, their understanding, even though still coming from their experiencing with the world, mostly comes from the written or spoken discourses they encounter at school or in social settings. The discourses they encounter may be the "Big D" or the "small d" or both (Gee, 1999). Thus, evaluating discourse from a critical pedagogic lens will provide teachers with divergent perspectives to their professional practices, especially when they are interacting with students from diverse social, cultural, and economic backgrounds. Teachers with a critical pedagogic lens are more able to develop an awareness of the overt and covert knowledge (Apple, 2004) taught in school and thus will be more sensitive to the issue of hidden curriculum (Anyon, 1980; Apple, 2004) exercised in their classrooms or in their schools. Moreover, they may be able to appreciate students' funds of knowledge (Gonzalez, Moll, & Amanti, 2013) and celebrate the diversity among their students. In terms of EFL teaching, teachers with critical lenses will be more aware of the fact that language teaching actually involves multidisciplinary knowledge. A qualified, effective EFL teacher should always know more than just the structural knowledge of the language to be taught (Tijk, 2013). EFL teachers need to have vast knowledge about the language so that they can understand the discourse of the language (Tijk, 2013). Thus a critical understanding of discourses in the school settings can help EFL teachers understand language and discourse better. As a result, they will not narrow down their teaching practices to merely sub-disciplinary activities.

Language and Education: The "Big D"

According to Trappes-Lomax (2008), language can be a means of education and a goal of education. For example, if we use Chinese language to teach Chinese students school subjects, we are using the language as a means of education. However, if we use Chinese language in teaching Chinese students Chinese language arts, the language can be both a means and a goal of education. When we use English as an instructional language with Chinese students in the English classroom, English functions mostly as a goal of education. Of course, most learners can experience these two situations co-concurrently. It is really hard to make a clear cut between the means and ends of language in education. However, it is critical that we be more sensitive in discourse selection when language is employed as a means of education. As an EFL educator, I would like to take up both roles of the English language as a means of education as well as a goal of education in my teaching practice and in my interaction with students.

Language is dynamic, power laden, and power given. We can either be oppressed or empowered by the language we have. By assuming my role in using the English language as a means of education, I would employ my knowledge of "Big D" discourse. Putting the language back into life would be a first step to get students to understand that language is not an isolated school subject that has to be learned, memorized, and tested. A good example of putting language in the "Big D" discourse is illustrated in the following story:

A Japanese visiting scholar who is quite proficient in both oral and academic English language was once involved in a car accident in the United States. When the police questioned him, he said, "I looked around, and I didn't see any car." The police then refuted him by saying, "[Y]ou didn't see any car, does not mean there was no car" (personal conversation, December 21, 2013). Right away the Japanese scholar realized that there was a mistake in his English expression. Isolated, his "small d" discourse is grammatically perfect. However, putting it in the "Big D" context of the car accident, his "small d" discourse is very problematic. Then the police questioned the other party of the accident, who was a native speaker, and let him go first. As a result, the Japanese was judged as the guilty party and given a ticket, even though it was not his fault at all. When the police later found out that it was the other party, not the Japanese, who was guilty of this car accident, he told this Japanese visiting scholar that when he went to court, he should not admit his guilt and should argue with the judge for his innocence. Obviously, possessing the use of the English language and the proper use of it in this car accident context was critical. A more appropriate English expression for the Japanese in this context could be: "I looked around but I saw no car." Miscommunication that results in a misunderstanding and failure of the officer's judgment could happen in any other instance if the visitor cannot clearly express him- or herself in the language of the country he or she is in. So, language empowers people if they know how to use it according to the context, considering not only syntax but also pragmatics and semiotics. In view of this, it is ideal that EFL teachers situate their "small d" teaching within the context of the "Big D." Otherwise, learners may have good knowledge accumulation of the English language but still feel powerless in real-life situations.

Second, helping students to be culturally sensitive should also be an important part of the "Big D" discourse. By culturally sensitive, I mean as EFL teachers, we must connect "small d" discourse (language items) with "Big D" discourse (social cultural context) and constantly remind learners that real-life communication always requires more than language itself. In Gee's (1999) terms, "Big D" is language plus other stuff. In fact, language and culture are deeply interconnected. A metaphorical expression of such a relationship can be best illuminated in a Chinese idiom that goes like this: if there is no oxhide, then what is the worth of having the furs of the ox? Culture, in a certain sense, is like the oxhide, whereas, language is similar to the fur of the ox. Therefore, teaching English separately from the culture would be like helping students to collect a handful of furs without knowing where to put them. Consequently, students lose the complete picture of the ox. A lack of social cultural knowledge in English language learning inevitably results in learners' inadequacy in cross-cultural communication.

Third, understanding the "Big D" discourse enables us to put our teaching in a bigger context and to understand the nuances of students' different linguistic repertoires, learning behaviors, and academic performances. It is very important that teachers put the nuances of student behaviors in a bigger social cultural context so that they do not make judgmental mistakes and abuse their authoritative power entailed by their roles as teachers. For example, if my fourth grade head teacher did not overlook her students' different social economic status, or conversely, she recognized her students' prior knowledge and appreciated their funds of knowledge (Gonzalez, Moll, & Amanti, 2013), the incident would become just another scenario, and the memory of my fourth grade teacher would be a different story. In school settings, there are numerous other factors that may affect students' learning. Without a keen awareness of the "Big D" discourse, teachers are very apt to develop a deficit thinking (Valencia, 2010) modality. Consequently, teachers tend to focus too much on the subject matter teaching, unaware of the fact that " when we emphasized subject matter too much," we "lost sight of the development of the child and of his social context, society" (Dewey, 1919, p. 191).

Language and Education: The "Small D"

According to Gee (1999), the "small d" discourse is the "language in use" (p. 17). Such being the case, the discourses that teachers use when interacting with students both inside and outside of the classroom play a critical role in their identity building and agency developing. For example, the discourse that my fourth grade teacher used on that particular day's instruction was enormously damaging to my classmates and me, who were still cognitively immature and who were still in the stage of building our identities in our personal and social lives. Although I should not hold my fourth grade teacher solely responsible for most of my elementary classmates' failure to continue schooling education after eight grade, I am pretty sure that what she did had a negative impact on them. Some of them even dropped out earlier than eighth grade. Many years later when I became a teacher, especially when I have gone this far in my academic journey, I can tell that if my fourth grade classmates were inspired and valued by teachers or someone else in their lives early on, most of them would have been able to achieve more later on. Some of them were really smart, and they actually performed better than me in some of the school subjects. I do not understand why they decided not to continue schooling after eighth grade. Sometimes I have the impulse to revisit them and investigate the root causes that led to their dropping out of school at a young age.

Even though I do not know for sure why most of my fourth grade classmates dropped out of school after eighth grade, I know for myself that I owe my education for my being fortunate in having a caring family and a couple of inspiring teachers in my schooling experience. I feel so grateful to my first grade teacher, who gave me a public praise in class for the good grade that I earned on the final exam despite the fact that I was on a sick leave for about a month that semester. I am also indebted to my seventh grade Chinese language art teacher because if he had not discovered and identified publicly my talents in Chinese language arts, I would not have known early on where my strength was and may not have been as successful as to be able to continue my doctoral study in the United States. In fact, I feel I am so lucky in having a handful of caring and supportive teachers all the way through my education. These caring teachers are the propelling force that moved me forward. Their positive discourses have obviously offset those negative discourses of my fourth grade teacher. When I contemplate from time to time on my past schooling experience, I am amazed at how miraculous my teachers' positive "small d" discourse had impacted me. In the meantime, it is also very poignant to find how hurtful my fourth grade teacher's negative "small d" discourse was. The wound may have been healed with time; the scar has not disappeared. Since "small d" is so "small," it is very likely that most of us just let them pop out of our mouths without giving them a second thought. However, as teachers and educators, we really have to be very careful with our "small d" discourses because they will have a long-lasting effect on the shaping of students' agency and identity. Rarely do teachers intend to hurt their students or damage their students' self-esteem; however, due to ignorance of CDA, they make inadvertent mistakes. Perhaps, the charm of CDA to us educators lies in that it emancipates us by providing a critical lens to reflect on our pedagogy and our "Big D" and "small d" discourses in school settings.

My Pedagogical Emancipation Through CDA

According to Raelin (2008), discourse is "the carrier of emancipation" (p. 4). To me, emancipatory discourse is one step further of CDA. It is the goal of CDA. Since language embodies power, and such power can either serve as an oppressive force or an emancipatory force, we have to be very critical when employing language as a major means of interaction with our students in school settings. I believe if we EFL teachers could have a better understanding of the relationships among language, power, ideology, and the differentiation between "Big D" and "small d" discourse, we would not only embark on a journey of self-emancipation but also would be able to help our students start their journeys of emancipation. Therefore, a better understanding of the importance of "Big D" and "small d" is of great significance for anyone who is inspired to be a true sense educator, who keeps democracy and social justice as the core of their pedagogical creed.

In the process of studying CDA, I constantly make connections between CDA and my pedagogical practices as an EFL teacher and teacher educator. The more I understand the dynamics between the "Big D" and the "small d" discourses, the more I feel the importance of a critical lens in my pedagogical practice. I am relieved to find that the study of CDA, especially the critical analysis of "Big D" and "small d" discourses, brings me both personal and professional emancipation.

Coming Out of the Ivory Tower

With CDA I have been able to emancipate myself from my past ideology of seeing education as a neutral act. I now fully realize that I cannot teach in an ivory tower. Such an awareness brings me what I called a painful pleasure. On one hand, the painful experience comes from the realization of how my good-intentioned malpractices might have affected my students negatively and what might have been the consequences of those inappropriate teacher ideologies. However, on the other hand, it also gives me pleasure. Owing to this realization, I am able to elevate myself to a new platform, where I have seen a broader picture of education and my role as an educator. I understand better that school curricula can "never be neutral but represents what is thought to be important and necessary knowledge by those who are dominant in a society" (Nieto, 1996, p. 93). In retrospect, I can see that the main reason most of my classmates who lived outside the East City Gate were not able to move up in academic learning was partially due to the hidden curriculum of the school, which devalued their world knowledge. If they had been able to receive the discipline of hope (Kohl, 1998), in which their prior knowledge of the world outside the classroom had been celebrated, they might have achieved quite differently.

Kosik (1976) maintained, "One always has a certain understanding of reality that precedes explication" (p. 36). Unfortunately, our schools seldom give attention to students' prior fund of knowledge (Moll et al., 1992) on which they build students' understanding of reality. Instead, most schools are in favor of instilling students with the "legitimate" ideology and content of learning (Apple, 2004). Therefore, it is the educators' job to help students develop their skills in finding out such power relations and become critical learners. If teachers understand that students come to school with their stories to tell and value their students' prior knowledge, their perceptions, and their imaginations of the world, there would not have been so many students who dropped out of school at an early age. As an EFL educator, I know that my future efforts should go toward "changing the schools through redoing the curriculum (Kohl, 1998, p. 17)," especially the curriculum of EFL teacher preparation programs in China. I strongly believe that if we want to empower students, we need to empower teachers first "since adolescents rarely notice hegemonic influences without being taught to see them" (Apple, 2004, cited in Agiro, 2012, p. 212).

Putting My "Small D" in the "Big D"

With CDA, I am able to understand that education is more than teaching the subject matter. This is because, first of all, subject matter is static, whereas learners are quite dynamic. Each individual learner is unique, and they bring into the learning process diverse personal backgrounds and cultural heritages. Second, if we take EFL teaching as both a means and a goal of education, we will understand that focusing our teaching mainly on the subject matter (English) can be rather simplistic and problematic. Both my master's and doctoral studies have provided me with valuable knowledge and refreshed perspectives for becoming an effective EFL teacher and teacher educator. The multi-intelligence theory (Gardner, 2011), the constructivism of Vygotsky (1978) and his famous Zone of Proximal Development (ZPD), and so on, have had such a huge impact on me that reflecting on my past practices, I am shameful of what I have done to my students, even though the misdeeds were out of good intentions. I came to understand that to be a good EFL teacher, having the content area knowledge itself is far from enough. Our students are not empty vessels waiting for us to pour into what we perceive as important knowledge for them. I realized that the curriculum I chose before was typically content centered with little or no consideration of the learners, who came into the classroom with their unique cultures and diversified backgrounds, which are indispensable parts of the curriculum. More specifically, I came to understand that we need to have an enormous knowledge to understand discourse (Tijk, 2003). In other words, to be an effective EFL teacher, it is not good enough just knowing the grammar and the vocabulary. We need to know much more than just the surface structure of the language if we wish to understand better English discourse, be it verbal or textual.

Understanding the Significance of "Small D" Discourse

In the school setting, where a large percent of teacher-student interactions are carried out through spoken language, it is vital that we teachers monitor our ways of talking to our students. According to Hatch (1992, p. 3), classroom communication is a very problematic medium because it is going to affect either positively or negatively students' identity building and agency developing. Apart from affecting students' identity building, teacher's discourse also matters when it comes to academic learning since most of the teacher's instruction in class is done through his/her oral communication with the students. By making sense of what the teacher is saying to them, students have to make use of what they already know because "speech makes available to reflection the process by which they relate the new knowledge to old (Barnes, cited in Hatch, 1992, p. 2)"; however, "this possibility depends on the social relationship, the communication system that the teacher sets up (Hatch, 1992, p. 2)." Referring back to my fourth grade teacher's discourse, we are able to see how negatively her discourse has affected her students not only in terms of their identity building but also in academic learning. When the teacher was making the remark "There is no good person among you guys who live outside the East City Gate," she was actually shutting the door for learning since her downgrading discourse left us with no hope of future success in life. In other words, no matter how hard we tried, we were not going to make good people out of ourselves because, in her mind, our home locations determined our destinies.

Examining Educational Practice Through a Critical Lens

With CDA, I am able to observe and examine educational practice through a critical lens. For example, most overseas Chinese students have encountered moments of frustration when they first arrived in a foreign land where English is the major communication tool both for everyday and school life. The sadness lies in that most Chinese students have had more than 12 years of English learning all the way through primary school to college. Why, after so many years of English learning, are our students still struggling with the language? Quite a great number of people attribute this phenomenon to the lack of English learning environments in China. I do not blame them for such thinking. It is true that we do not have optimal English learning environments compared with English as a second language (ESL) learners in native English-speaking countries such as the UK or United States. However, is this the sole factor, or is it the most crucial factor that leads to the ineffectiveness of English teaching and learning? Do we overexaggerate the need of a native English learning environment? If we attach too much importance to this factor, we are very likely to lead ourselves to a state of disempowerment because we can never have a native English-speaking environment in China. As a matter of fact, if we critically examine our EFL teaching curriculum, observe EFL teaching practices in the classrooms, and make in-depth inquiry into EFL learners' English learning experiences, we are able to understand that other than learning environments, there are numerous other factors in play behind the phenomenon of ineffective EFL teaching and learning in China. If we probe still further, we may see that the EFL teacher preparation programs are also partly to blame because they are not doing their jobs well enough in educating competent EFL teachers (Zhang, 2013; Zhou, 2009). Thus, there is a vicious circle of EFL teaching and learning. It is always wise to go through the superficial phenomenon to the deep root of a problem. To do this, we have to empower ourselves with CDA. With this critical lens, we are able to find the fundamental issues and come up with better solutions. Thus, to improve EFL teaching and learning, we need to prepare our future EFL teachers to be reflective educators rather than simply doing the job as technocrats. Dewey (1933) argued that reflective thinking "emancipates us from merely impulsive and merely routine activity" (p. 17). What is lacking in China's EFL teacher preparation curriculum is exactly the development of this reflective, critical-thinking ability in EFL teacher candidates.

Owing to CDA, I am able to refocus my research from studying the language phenomenon itself to EFL teacher preparation curriculums. If we do not start from the bottom, we will continue to do the surface work. Therefore, I will exert more research effort to examine critically EFL teacher preparation curriculums. I believe that once we emancipate teachers from the routinized teaching activities, we are then able to help students embark on their journeys of emancipation.

The Journey to the East of the Pacific

I bet that in her wildest imagination my fourth grade teacher had never ever thought of me, a girl who lived outside the East City Gate, could be able to go this far to the East of the Pacific and pursue both a master's and doctoral degree in the United States, which boasts to have the best education in the world. Sometimes, I have the impulse to visit and tell her how her words had hurt me and my classmates, many of whom did not have a chance to go on with academic learning. I would like to ask her: "Did you have any hope for us? Did you value our ideas or our stories?" However, now I do not hate my fourth grade teacher anymore because I believe that if she had had the educational knowledge to guide her, she would have known how to perform properly as an elementary school teacher, and that if she had known CDA, she might have behaved quite differently, I am sure.

Dewey (1919) maintained that "education means growth" (p. 185). I feel so blessed that I have been able to learn so much in the field of education. If

I were not armed with this knowledge, I perhaps would still be performing in the wrong way while in the meantime feeling myself to be the innocent. Therefore, I feel that my journey from the East City Gate to the East of the Pacific is not only a geographic distance but also a symbolization of my intellectual growth. I am now confident that one day when I take my journey back to the East City Gate, I will become a true sense educator with enhanced perspectives on education and new expertise in teaching. More importantly, I am confident in becoming a caring educator who makes social justice the core of education, puts learners at the center of school curriculum, and values each learner as a unique, individual being. I would like to share what I have learned and experienced at the East of the Pacific with my colleagues in China. I especially wish to share my transformational journey through CDA, which gives me the critical lens to reexamine my past professional experiences and reinvent my ambition for and confidence in my future career as an EFL teacher educator.

References

Agiro, C. P. (2012). Comparative critical discourse analysis of student and teacher editions of secondary Christian American literature textbooks. *Journal of Research on Christian Education, 21*(3), 211–234.

Anyon, J. (1980). Social class and the hidden curriculum of work. *Journal of Education, 162*(1), 67–92.

Apple, M. (2004). *Ideology & curriculum.* New York: RoutledgeFalmer.

Blommaert, J. (2005). *Discourse: A critical introduction.* Cambridge: Cambridge University Press.

Dewey, J. (1919). The misuse of subject matter. In R. W Clopton & Ou, Tsuin-Chen (Eds. & Trans.), *John Dewey: Lectures in China, 1919–1920.* Honolulu: The University Press of Hawaii.

Dewey, J. (1933). *How we think: A restatement of the relation of reflective thinking to the educative process.* Washington, DC: Heath and Company.

Dijk, V. T. (2013). *Discourse and knowledge.* Retrieved from https://www.youtube.com/watch?v=sxfc-WJRKEM

Gardner, H. (2011). *Frames of mind: The theory of multiple intelligences.* New York: Basic Books.

Gee, J. P. (1999). *An introduction to discourse analysis: Theory and method.* New York: Routledge.

Gee, J. P. (2009). *Discourse analysis: What makes it critical.* Retrieved from http://www.jamespaulgee.com/node/11

Gonzalez, N., Moll, L. C., & Amani, C. (Eds.). (2013). *Funds of knowledge: Theorizing practices in households, communities, and classrooms.* New York: Routledge.

Hatch, E. (1992). *Discourse and language education.* New York: Cambridge Language Teaching Library.

Kohl, H. (1998). *The discipline of hope: Learning from lifetime of teaching.* New York: The New York Press.

Kosik, K. (1976). *Dialectics of the concrete: A study on problems of man and world.* Boston, MA: D. Reidel Publishing Co.

Moll et al. (1992). Funds of knowledge for teaching: Using a qualitative approach to connect homes and classrooms. *Theory into Practice, 31*(2), 132–141.

Nieto, S. (1996). *Affirming diversity: The sociopolitical context of multicultural education.* Longman Publisher.

Raelin, J. A. (2008). Emancipatory discourse and liberation. *Management Learning, 39*(5), 519–540.

Swain, M., & Deters, P. (2007). "New" mainstream SLA theory: Expanded and enriched. *The Modern Language Journal, 91, Focus Issue,* 820–836.

Trappes-Lomax, H. (2008). *The Handbook of applied linguistics.* John Wiley & Sons, Ltd. Retrieved from http://dx.doi.org/10.1002/9780470757000.ch5

Valencia, R. R. (2010). *Dismantling contemporary deficit thinking: Educational thought and practice.* New York: Routledge.

Vallance, E. (1983). Hiding the hidden curriculum: An interpretation of the language of justification in nineteenth century education reform. In H. Giroux & D. Purpel (Eds.), *The hidden curriculum and moral education* (pp. 9–27). Berkeley, CA: McCutchan Press.

Vygotsky, L. (1978). *Mind and society.* Cambridge, MA: Harvard University Press.

Waters, A. (2009). Ideology in applied linguistics for language teaching. *Applied Linguistics, 30*(1), 138–143.

Zhang, L. (2013). *Curriculum effectiveness: A critical study on 4 EFL teacher preparation programs in China.* Final research project for EDUC 698. Doctoral Program at NMSU.

Zhou, W. (2009). A study on pre-service EFL teacher education in basic education in China. *Journal of Foreign Language Learning Theory and Practice, 1,* 1–16–19.

3 Emancipatory Discourses on Ideology, Power, and the Media
A CDA

Susana Ríos

The purpose of this chapter is to explore the application of critical discourse analysis (CDA) to the potential of the media as a mechanism that venues emancipatory discourses to catapult ideological transformation and democratic social change. Discourse, ideology, and power in the media, as oppressive systems, maintain the status quo and control people's ideologies and their perspectives. This chapter analyzes and critiques the discourse of Suli Breaks—a young male in the media—on his position regarding school and education through CDA, an approach that helps reveal the linkages among discourse, ideology, and power.

By using a dialectical theory of argument, which is a postcolonial analytical framework that allows us to evaluate speech as a practical argument (Fairclough & Fairclough, 2012), this chapter examines the ways and the degree to which discursive oppressive systems in social media produce reasons for action to human agency. More specific, the structure of "practical argumentation" (Fairclough & Fairclough, 2012, p. 87) deals with making judgments that inform a certain trend of action based on practical arguments, resulting in decisions that can be implemented into actions.

This chapter is organized in two parts. The first part contains my personal contingencies (the origin of my interest in this topic), the background of Suli Breaks, and the background of sociological and technological contingencies in relation to ideology, power, and the media in a contemporary context. The conceptual framework of this study draws on CDA and linking concepts such as discourse and ideology to help understand various aspects of the phenomena under study (Maxwell, 2012). I provide the definitions of these key interrelated concepts embedded throughout the chapter before delving into Part 2. The second part unveils the structural analysis of Suli Breaks' critical discourse based on premises of coherence and cohesion across the beginning, the middle, and the end of the poem. I conclude by evaluating Suli Breaks' critical language awareness and claims for action in relation to power. To this end, I present my positions on the media as a funnel for emancipatory discourses.

Part 1: The Background

Author's Contingencies

I began this exploration based on a hunch of curiosity regarding the application of CDA on the use of the media and its power to develop emancipatory discourse. My intention was to approach the objects of my curiosity by developing "more skill and methodological rigor" (Freire, 1998, p. 82) in search for new knowledge through the application of critical pedagogy and critical discourse analysis. As defined by Kincheloe (2010), epistemology is the "branch of philosophy that analyses the nature of knowledge and what we believe to be true" (p. 15). Driven by "epistemological curiosity" (Freire, 1998, p. 83), which is a routinary thinking process that entails asking questions searching for the truth of things and events that happen around you (Ríos, YouTube Video, 2012), I decided to investigate the hidden agenda of a video that I watched during my doctoral course work. The video is titled *Why I Hate School But Love Education | Spoken Word* (Breaks, 2012) and was published by Suli Breaks in 2012 in London, England (see the video at http://www.youtube.com/watch?v=y_ZmM7zPLyI). As a concerned scholar in the education field, I chose this video because it adheres to a dichotomy between higher education and contemporary school through the perspective of a young adult male. This chapter is the result of that epistemological curiosity journey.

Breaks' YouTube video caught my attention not only for its controversial title but for the massive views it had received. I then found myself wanting to know more about Suli Breaks, highlighting my search with the following.

Suli Breaks' Background

Suli Breaks, the author of the video under analysis, has risen in popularity as a spoken word artist in the contemporary European world. Breaks, who considers himself an expressionist, is a young man from London, England, who shares his poetry and coveys his personal experiences about school and education through social media in controversial yet charismatic ways (Breaks, 2014). With a law degree from the University of Sheffield and fueled by a distrust in the current educational system, Breaks decided to pursue a career in poetry. He anchored his fame and unprecedented fan base on using the power of social media to spread his word to the world. With an unprecedented number of subscribers to his YouTube channel, Breaks' video *Why I Hate School But Love Education | Spoken Word* is what provided him with a much anticipated breakthrough (Breaks, 2014). With a portfolio of motivational speeches, workshops, and conferences about his transcendental poetry and projects, Breaks (2014) takes ideas and makes them accessible to every person in social media. He inspires and provokes people to rethink and reconstruct their own realities in their own terms.

With such material at hand, I explore the hidden role of the media as a tool of power that manipulates or exhorts thought and human action. Consequently, I focus my attention to both the sociological and technological contingencies in relation to power that contextualize this study in contemporary sociocultural times.

Sociological Context: Power in Society

Ramanathan and Hoon (2015) refer to power as an association between "the act of controlling and constraining the contributions of the non-powerful participants in the society as this encounter usually takes place between the powerholder and the powerless" (p. 62). People inherit the rules and norms immersed in the society they are born into. They are expected to act in accordance to the language, values, ideologies, traditions, and culture that have been appropriated in that particular territory and likely to follow prescribed behaviors and manufactured ways of thinking. These societal impositions drive individuals to code the world based on their particular interpretations of reality in ways that satisfy their needs. Also important is that individuals not only inherit these social behaviors but, consciously or not, participate in the construction of new rules, making them creators and re-creators of new social order ruling, which is the process of codifying the world and acting upon it. Implied in any society is that its constituents will follow these rules, and any deviation from the status quo will be rapidly corrected by carefully crafted mechanisms of rule enforcement made by institutions in power in the societal ring (Hall, 1987).

Frantz Fanon (2008) reminds us that society crafts hallucinatory challenges that impede consciousness of dominant themes and awareness of possibilities of change in the social structure. This phenomenon is operationalized by using various interrelated manifestations of group power. Different types of power differ among each other based on the resources it uses to produce action (van Dijk, 2007), oppressive or liberatory. Money for the rich, knowledge and information for those in the realm of education, and force for the military and mafia are, for example, a few representations of power in society. Furthermore, exercising group power means not only to control content but also to control "the structures of text and talk" (van Dijk, 2007, p. 356) in terms of gender, class, race, and language. These societal issues hinder societies with unequal opportunities for all: sports programs that accept boys only, policy officers who stop only men of color while driving nice cars at certain times of the day, or industries that only hire women at the *maquiladoras* (manufacturing facilities) so that they can pay less and provide them with no benefits.

As an ideological sociopolitical power, global media drives propaganda and molds the way people behave, speak, and respond to environmental and societal stimuli embedded in commercialism. There is little reason to believe that power in society would not be disturbingly aligned to media power. The following is a modest exploration of the later.

Technological Context: Media Power

As explained by Ramanathan and Hoon (2015), "the most crucial aspect where power and domination are exercised is in the life of the public through media" (p. 63). In parallel, Altheide (2011) reminds us that "the institutional media forms not only help shape and guide content and numerous everyday life activities, but also the audience-as-actors normalize these forms and use them as reality maintenance tools" (p. 121). Radical transformations have occurred in new media technologies that influence the growth of human communications and epitomize the role of media power. According to Kincheloe (2010), "[t]he knowledge economy of cyberspace interfaces with contemporary modes of social organization, continuing technological innovation, and emerging culture industries" (p. 203). Research in social networking such as Facebook, Twitter, and other similar applications, as part of the new media wave, must direct their attention to the structures of power organically embedded in these technologies (Loehwing & Motter, 2012).

New media has acquired unprecedented power in the construction of ideological messages. It has changed and continues to change the way people think, feel, and act upon education (Coombs, 2010) and offers new communicative practices and methods of identity, community, and culture formation. In their work *Manufacturing Consent*, Edward S. Herman and Noam Chomsky (1988, 2002) document their arguments about the manipulation of information in the news media. Herman and Chomsky (2002) assert that most television stations and book publishers are owned by a "global media [commercial] system" (p. xiv) that dominates and controls the national culture and politics.

In their "propaganda model" which serves as a framework to analyze what dominates and controls truth and reality, they appointed five successive filters that act as a tunneling system that directs biased information to the masses. These filters are: (1) size, ownership, and profit orientation of the mass media; (2) the advertising license to do business; (3) sourcing mass-media news; (4) flak and the enforcers; and (5) anticommunism as a control mechanism (Herman and Chomsky, 2002). In conjunction, these filters serve as the machinery that reshapes information that may threaten or compromise the interests of large corporate elites before they go public. As Herman and Chomsky (2002) put it, "These five filters narrow the range of news that passes through the gates, and even more sharply limit what can become 'big news', subject to sustained new campaigns" (p. 31). In other words, crafted to consent totalistic truth, mainstream media acts as the global channel through which veiled information is made available to the public. The ultimate purpose of global media is to deliver information that guards the interests and image of corporations and government by retelling reality and world facts through their own biased voices and for-profit agendas.

Having presented the origin of the study, Suli Breaks' background, and the sociological and technological contexts in relation to power, I turn my attention to CDA as the conceptual framework of this study to help me understand "the hidden power dimensions and [the] effects" (Blommaert, 2005, p. 33) of Breaks' discourse. To begin, the following is an exploration of the concept of CDA.

CDA

Post-Second World War developments gave place to CDA, which "was founded on the premises that linguistic analysis could provide a valuable additional perspective for existing approaches to social critique" (Bloomaert, 2005, p. 22). As a branch of discourse analytical research (van Dijk, 2007) or as a perspective of discourse analysis (Jansen, 2008), CDA tries to explain communication by dissecting how the social interaction and social structures of a discourse "enacts, confirm, legitimate, reproduce, or challenge relations of power and dominance in society" (van Dijk, 2007, p. 353). In other words, CDA is an approach that helps us understand the relationships and linkages among language (discourse), ideology (cognition), and power (hegemony) and attempts to unveil the interests behind discursive practices with the goal to create social change (emancipation). Also, as a starting point to CDA, social theory helps bridge "from 'non-critical' to 'critical' discourse analysis" (Bloomaert, 2005, p. 30), where discourse is viewed as a social phenomenon.

The definitions that follow of the linking concepts of discourse and ideology to CDA appear pertinent in the discussion to help explore "*how* and *why* discourse cumulatively contributes to the reproduction of macro-structures and highlights the traces of cultural and ideological meaning" (Ramanathan & Hoon, 2015, p. 57).

Discourse

Fairclough and Fairclough (2012) define discourses "as ways of representing the world [that] do not only describe what social reality is but also what it should be" (p. 103). Further, van Dijk (2007) mentions that there are different types of discourse: those in the micro and macro level of analysis. When we analyze daily language use, verbal interactions, and communication, we are analyzing the micro level in discursive social order. Analyzing the inequalities, conflict, and dominance among social groups relates to a macro level of analysis in discursive social order.

A contemporary theorist, Michel Foucault challenged some assumptions of sociological criticism. He argued that we cannot have access to the past unless we go through its "discursive formations," which are the ways of how other people in the past have made sense of the world around them (Quin, 2003, p. 103). When communicating, people draw from beliefs, common sense, background knowledge, and experiences to produce utterances. With this in mind, Blommaert (2005) points out that "acts of communication produce *indexical* meaning" (p. 11). Thus, when these utterances "in connection with social, cultural and historical patterns" (Blommaert, 2005, p. 3) interact in the form of language, questions, communications, ideas, dialogs, or arguments, discourse occurs and is shared among groups through various indexes of meanings. To illustrate, he explains that a word such as *sir* not only refers to a male person but also indexes a social status. Next, I define the notion of ideology considering that discourse is "historical and ideological" (Blommaert, 2005, p. 160).

Ideology

Bloomaert (2005) defines ideology as a "specific set of symbolic representations" (p. 158) in forms of discourse, terms, arguments, images, or stereotypes that serve a purpose to a specific group of people. Ideology has the particular power to blindfold public mind and action by imposing a belief (Ramanathan & Hoon, 2015) through the injection of ideas created under unique institutional and historical conditions that serve the interests of the bourgeois.

In a society where hegemonic structures support the ideology of the colony, Memmi (1965) contends that the colonized experience a need for change. Memmi explains how the conscious destitution of self-identity, culture, and language from the colonized is a practice in the phenomenon of assimilation that positions the colonized closer to an emulation of the colonizer. In efforts to assimilate the identity and culture of the colonizer, the colonized lose focus of their own ideologies until in one way or another they recognize that revolt is the only way to dismantle the colonial structure wrapped in hegemonic practices. Concurrently, Fairclough and Fairclough (2012) explain that the theory of ideology is concerned with how the interests, beliefs, and concerns of dominant social groups enact and affect social life.

Having concluded with the background of the study, its contingencies, and definitions of main concepts, I now turn to the main body of the CDA identified as Part 2 of the study.

Part 2: The Analysis

CDA focuses on analyzing how sentences build a text, if they make sense, and if they have unity. To describe the properties of written text, cohesion and coherence are two main concepts evident in written discourse analysis. In the context of this chapter, coherence is defined as the "grammatical and semantic patterns that connect various parts of discourse into a structured and meaningful whole" (Bloomaert, 2005, p. 251). Cohesion refers "to the surface relations between sentences that create a text, i.e. to create connected sentences within a sequence" (Azzouz, 2009, p. 18).

In this section, I analyze Suli Breaks' discourse by presenting extracts of his speech from his video *Why I Hate School But Love Education ‖ Spoken Word*. I present the structural discourse analysis based on premises in the poem according to coherence (relationship between parts) and cohesion (looking at specific words or ideas between parts). The focus here is on the discovery of structural features of language in use "operating at higher levels than the single sentence" (Blommaert, 2005, p. 2).

Structural Discourse Analysis

Fairclough and Fairclough (2012) point out that as a complex speech act, argumentation is the social and rational activity that pursues the justification of a claim, with the goal to persuade the debater of the acceptance or rejection of such claim. Reality could be represented in different ways such as circumstances and goals through discourse. These "representations enter as premises in arguments" (Fairclough & Fairclough, 2012, p. 86) urging individuals to act in certain ways rather than other ways dependent on their reasoning and set of circumstantial scenarios.

The theory of argument is an analytical framework that I use to evaluate Suli Breaks' speech as a practical argument from the properties of his text by looking at the circumstantial premises, goal premises, value premises, and a claim for action. The discourse analysis is presented in three sections to honor the sequence of the events in the video. I analyze some beginning, middle, and ending excerpts of Breaks' speech from the YouTube video in the sections that follow: (1) A Problem: Why a degree?, (2) Ideological Background: Institutionalized Schooling, and (c) Breaks' Proposal: Reflection.

A Problem: Why a Degree? What follows is an excerpt of the beginning of Suli Breaks' discourse.

So you want to get a degree . . . Why?
Let me tell you what society will tell you:

> Increases your chances of getting a job
> Provides you with an opportunity to be successful
> Your life will be a lot less stressful
> Education is the key

Now let me tell you what parents will tell you:

> Make me proud
> Increases the chances of getting a job
> Provides you with an opportunity to be successful
> Your life will be a lot less stressful
> Education is the key

Now let's look at the statistics:

> Steve Jobs net worth $7 billion RIP
> Richard Branson net worth $4.2 billion
> Oprah Winfrey net worth $2.7 billion
> Mark Zuckenberg, Henry Ford, Steven Spielberg, Bill Gates, now here
>   comes the "coup de grace"

Blommaert (2005) asserts that narrative in sociolinguistics and anthropology is a function of language and a mode of human communication where an experience is made social. With a focus on coherence, this section provides an analysis of Breaks' narrative in regard to understanding the relationship between parts or sentences of his discourse. The background at the beginning of the video shows the exterior staircase of the main entrance at the premises of Waltham Forest College. In here, Breaks explains that according to *society* and *parents*, a degree increases the chances of getting a job and being successful; thus, people's life stress levels reduce. Here, Breaks blurs the personality of those representing the word *society* to perhaps passively avoid a directional connotation with teachers or other educational instructors. Breaks also provides statistics of people who have been successful in life and whose net worth profits reach a scale in billions despite their lack of higher education. He organizes this information in sequential order from the highest net worth value to the lowest value, evidencing a monetary value premise.

Blommaert (2005) reminds us that when language is used, speakers orient "towards the immediate result of their actions . . . [and also to] . . . higher-level, non-immediate complexes of perceived meaningfulness" (p. 73). In other words, the speakers orient toward "orders of indexicality" (p. 73), which are "[s]tratified patterns of social meanings often called 'norms' or 'rules', to which people orient when communicating" (Blommaert, 2005, p. 253). To exemplify, in this beginning part of the discourse Breaks exposes heavily oriented societal ideologies about education based on narrow exceptional statistics and problematizes "going to school to get a degree" by stratifying the concepts of "society," "parents," and "statistics" and by attributing different indexical meanings to each of them. Breaks orients towards an order of indexicality that belongs to the groupness of valuing money over education (value premise). By doing so, he positions the "statistics" index at a higher value level over the "society" and "parental" indexes.

In the first two paragraphs, Breaks presents what other people would say about school, framing the context of action toward success. According to Breaks, "society" and "parents" delineate a course for action favoring the concept of "education as the key" to success. However, he shares advice statements in regard to education that are too broad and that cannot be generalized because of their lack of context and validity to other diverse sociocultural spheres.

Acting as if people have internalized ruling beliefs and imposed ideas, when in reality they have not, is the beginning of an ideological process called orthopraxy, which "uses coercion as an instrument of hegemonization" (Bloomaert, 2005, p. 169). In a study conducted with a group of Latin American parents with children attending an Anglo-dominant institution in Canada, Bernhard et al. (1998) examine their experiences and roles as supporters of their children's education. The study had the goal to understand the parents' perspectives on the ethno-cultural disadvantages that had been institutionally imposed on them. The relationships of power became evident, and the parents realized their capabilities to transform that situation through their actions. The findings of the study show that parents understood their positions as constituted by the system, began supporting each other, started to speak up, and began to customize the educational programs of their children. The parents' advice given to their children changed and was based on their personal cultural view of the educational system (Bernhard et al., 1998). In other words, they found a way to counteract orthopraxy.

Returning to Breaks' discourse analysis, he failed to consider that parental advice about schooling is different from country to country and region to region with various ethnic, linguistic, and cultural differences and with different access to power structures as related to education. For power to cause influence, it needs channels such as politics, education, science, or the media to transport forms of discourse from dominant structures to those in less favorable circumstances to access these channels. Breaks makes use of resources to reject the utterance of "education is the key" for success by referring to narrow statistical data of some people in the world who have accrued financial success without obtaining a professional degree.

Further, Breaks uses the name Steve in colloquial language as an example to refer to Steven Paul Jobs. Jobs, who went through rough times and struggled with formal schooling in his academic life, became the cofounder of Apple in 1976. His revolutionary products such as the Macintosh computer, iPod, iPhone, and iPad have changed the way education runs in contemporary classrooms around the globe. In his efforts to convince the audience that "uneducated" people have become successful without a degree (goal premise), Breaks establishes an imaginary correlation between monetary profit and ontological success. Nevertheless, for Jobs to build a $7 billion network, he was moved based on values to make great products (Biography Channel, n.d.). As stated in his authorized biography, Jobs "reinforced [his] sense of what was important—creating great things instead of making money, putting things back into the stream of history and of human consciousness as much as [he] could" (Metz et al., 2011).

What Breaks presents as universal advice in reference to education is a claim that is not only based on exceptional global statistics, but perhaps is also an effort to contextualize a space in the form of power. In here subjective meaning could be attributed and applicable only to his closest contemporary societal surroundings. To this end, careful considerations must take place before appropriating, adopting, or institutionalizing media messages as total reality. Due to the lack of analytic perspectives from the masses, consented truth ends up ruling the lives of many people whose interests contrast to the ideology the media proclaims.

Next, I present some of the excerpts that belong to the middle part of Breaks' discourse in the video regarding his ideology about schooling.

Ideological Background: Institutionalized Schooling

> Looking at these individuals [the ones stated in the previous excerpt] what's your conclusion? Neither of them in being successful, never graduated from a higher learning institution . . .

> Let's look at the statistics: Jesus, Muhammed, Socrates, Malcolm X, Mother Theresa, Spielberg, Shakespeare, Beethoven, Jesse Owens, Muhammed Ali, Sean Carter, Michael Jeffrey Jordan, Michael Joseph Jackson. Were either of these people unsuccessful or uneducated? . . .

> See? If education is the key then school is the lock. Because it rarely ever develops your mind to the point where it can perceive if red is green and continues to go when someone else said stop because as long as you follow the rules and you pass the exams you are cool . . .

> Proverbs 17:16 "It does a fool no good to spend money in education." Why? "Because he has no common sense." George Bush need I say more? Education is about inspiring one's mind, not just filling their head. And take this from me because I'm an "educated man" myself who only came to this realization of the countless nights at the library with a can of Red Bull keeping me awake till dawn and another can in the morn'. Falling sleep in between piles of books which probably equated to the same amount I had spent on my rent . . .

> And then after three years of the mental suppression and frustration, my "proud mother" didn't even turn up to my graduation . . .

In the preceding excerpts from the middle of the poem, Breaks presents an ideological circumstantial premise that positions institutionalized school as a problem, claiming that many uneducated people have succeeded in terms of monetary stability. Drawing on this premise, he questions the utility of obtaining a degree without understanding the meaning behind it. In this light, "[c]ontemporary discursive practices condition our current educational climate" (Anderson, Aronson, Ellison, & Fairchild-Keyes, 2015, p. 339). In his attempt to convince others that school is not the key for success, Breaks positions the experience of going to school and getting a degree as a problem, implying that is lengthy and costly. This positions institutionalized schooling at the core of the ideological circumstantial premise.

Fanon (2008) claims that "intellectual alienation is a creation of bourgeois society" (p. 199). The purpose of power is to control the ideas and actions of the colonized by using intellectual tools such as persuasion and dominance to cover hidden agendas of personal and collective interests. Therefore, social groups with influential discourses are highly positioned to control ideas and actions of others immersed in structures with considerable less power (van Dijk, 2007). Breaks, who self-denominates as educated and possesses a law degree, uses media as a medium to share the ideology that being uneducated does not correlate with not being able to become successful and that the journey of school may not be the route to attain such goal, presenting a contradictory utterance.

In his speech, Breaks immerses this instance of language in pretextuality, which are the contexts that influence the language long before it is produced as utterances. Defined by Bloomaert (2005), pretextuality are "[t]he features that people bring along when they communicate: complexes of resources, degrees of control over genres, styles, language varieties, codes, and so on that influence what people can actually do when they communicate" (p. 254). In Breaks' speech these contexts relate to multimillionaire celebrities and known people around the world who share the commonality of not holding a professional degree, presetting a hegemonic framework to define success. Much of this is related to Antonio Gramsci's concept of hegemony, where ideology turns arbitrary living into normal and regular conditions by saturating the consciousness of the classes through pervasive powerful means (Gramsci, 1971).

Popps (2010) recommends that "[i]t is important that scholars, critics, and civil libertarians examine how groups use media to construct, maintain, and exercise power over visual culture" (p. 512). Under the value premise, "persuasive definitions" (Fairclough & Fairclough, 2012, p. 92) are embedded, acting as a direction to guide the audience to a conclusion that money determines success. Following Blommaert's (2005) approach focused on discourse, it appears that the context of Breaks' social world is dominated by the rule of "money equals success" and adopts a reaction against school by suggesting to know your motives and reassess what you aim for since school "rarely ever develops your mind" (2:04). As Blommaert (2005) points out, this type of reaction indicates the "*adherence* to something else" (p. 78) that affects how we perceive ideology and identity. This "something else" is what I call the hidden agenda of discourse, where a heavy orientation against school is based on mere personal experiences.

With a focus on cohesion, this part of the analysis involves identifying a specific link, words, or ideas between sentences or parts within the narrative that Blommaert (2005) presents as being "always structured into units, segments, episodes" (p. 84). While background music raises a climax, Breaks' speech suggests that school is the issue but not education. In addition to these excerpts, he points out, with the use of a metaphor, that in a family tree, hard work and education are related, while school may be a distant cousin. He goes on to argue that seeing things through the glasses of others will only perpetuate the status quo. I argue that being part of a society comes with costs that some people must be willing to pay to continue to be part of it, as it is when working for a company or enterprise to earn a living. The linkage of this voluntary participation is the endorsement of individuals to condescend to manufactured reality based on other people's lenses. This invisible contract sustains and recreates societal hegemonic systems and mechanisms of power.

A society comprised with human activity behaves and acts according to structures of power. Groups with power or simply dominant groups use it to impose norms, behaviors, habits, and ideologies upon subordinate groups who are expected to conform, comply, or obey unquestionably. Once acquired by societal consensus, these norms, behaviors, habits, and ideologies of what is acceptable or required in a society become some natural *modus operandi* (ways of practice) and everyday *modus vivendi* (standards of living).

In the same thread of ideas, Breaks elicits descriptions of schooling as an intellectual tool that calls for societal alienation and reproduction of the status quo where individuals follow other people's dreams and ideas but never their own. Therefore, he calls for reevaluating education and rethinking actions and beliefs. His claim of action cautions not to be encapsulated in a system that imposes upon people to comply, to become standard, or to be a symbiotic product of a society. In this last part of the narrative, Breaks presents a persuasive position against school since he views it as a system that is not necessary to undergo to become successful. However, his discourse is not cohesive because he contradicts himself by saying that he is an educated man.

Blommaert (2005) points out that "[s]ynchronisation creates a particular point from which one speaks, a point in history often crystallised in particular epistemic stances or ways of speaking" (p. 134). As a tool of power, synchronization crystalizes utterances from different levels or orders and encapsulates them within a context of origin and within a particular point in history. The utterances that Breaks presents about school are the results of his own educational journey, which might have been lengthy, painful, costly, and worthy or not. However, such a journey helped him acknowledge the agency of his emancipatory voice and became "an educated man." Without an education, he may not have been able to articulate what he did so artistically in his narrative.

With a focus on coherence analysis, Breaks successfully webs the themes of education, ideology, and power by the middle of his narrative. Breaks' discourse switches across orders of indexicality, causing confusion at times to understand his intended meaning because most of his narrative is built on utterances that negatively portray the school experience. At the end of his speech, Breaks challenges individuals who are working for other reasons than money. He also attempts to persuade the audience to ask themselves why they are doing what they are doing, this time with a higher speech tone.

Headquartered in ideological premises, media supports manufactured consent. By using the media, Breaks positions going to school to get a degree as a questionable way of becoming successful in life. He states that acting uncritically before the hegemonic institutional power of school serves the interests of others, but not our own. He insists that attending school is an idea that needs to be revisited and recontextualized to generate personal validity and justification for its pursuit. He sustains that success is not related to being educated and that new forms of justification must be considered when evaluating education.

I argue that Breaks' discourse is an argumentative discourse type because (a) it presents statements in forms of premises and conclusions as rational activity aiming at persuading a predetermined audience to accept his claims, and (b) it involves a process of deliberation where considerations are balanced through various "interpretative frames" (Fairclough & Fairclough, 2012, p. 29). I further contend that Breaks presents an inductive argument because he speaks of probability by using personal experiences and tacit theories rather than validity and certainty to reach general conclusions (Fairclough & Fairclough, 2012).

Breaks' Proposal: Reflection

The following are some final excerpts of Breaks' discourse where he argues that there are more ways to become educated in a contemporary society. He introduces reflection as the claim premise.

> Now, I am not saying that school is evil and that there's nothing to gain, all I am saying is understand your motives and re-assess your aims . . .
>
> If you don't build your dream, someone else will hire you to help build theirs.
>
> Redefine how you view education; understand its true meaning. Education is not just about regurgitating a fraction of a book on someone else's opinion on a subject and to pass an exam . . .
>
> I once saw David Beckham take a free kick, I watched as the side of his Adidas sponsored boot hit the painted leather of the ball at an angle which caused it to travel towards the skies as though it was destined for the heavens, and then as it reached the peak of its momentum as though it changed its mind, it switched direction . . .
>
> As though reciting to himself the laws of physics, and as though his brain was negotiating with his eyes that was indeed witnessing the spectacle of the lever swung that was sweeping towards it and then reacted. But only a fraction of a millisecond too late and before it net of the goal embraced the FIFA sponsored ball as though it was of the prodigal son returning home . . .

Looking at David Beckham, there's more than one way in this world to be an educated man. Peace.

In these excerpts, Breaks exposes his ideology about contemporary education through critical language awareness in visual media. By using argumentation which is a "verbal, social *activity*, in which people attempt to criticize or justify claims" (Fairclough & Fairclough, 2012, p. 23), Breaks appears to support that school creates ideological indoctrination and recreates uncritical individuals that fit in a box who alienate to what they are told to do, told to be, and told to say. He attempts to explain why getting a degree is something people need to think about instead of following what others expect from them or simply because the word "school" is institutionalized in the society (goal premise). He finally calls for people to reflect and reevaluate the instances that motivate a professional academic pursuit.

As part of his solution, Breaks proposes a course of action through reflection (claim for action). He proposes that various routes to become educated should be entertained. His claims for action are noble. However, I argue that if we consider a macro-level discursive analysis, which helps unveil inequalities, conflict, and dominance among social groups, we need to elucidate solutions for people with different access levels to education. Breaks fails to mention the multiplicity of positive aspects that come with obtaining a higher education degree, such as being a productive citizen in a society, becoming an intentional agent of change, and being an advocate for democratic, just, and peaceful movements of emancipation—also acquiring a lifetime sense for learning, just to mention a few.

Seemingly inspired by Edward Herman and Noam Chomsky's propaganda model, which "can help activists understand where they might best deploy their efforts to influence mainstream media coverage of issues" (Herman, 2003, p. 4), Breaks attempts to call for public scepticism to investigate the truthfulness in propaganda service of the concept of school. He tries to shape the political discourse of a society by making reference to elitist-constructed information (heavily oriented in exceptional statistics) toward a public comprised by a specific audience (those interested or not in education) and with specific power resources (accessibility to media). He seems to merely drive on personal archives or "inherited consciousness" (Blommaert, 2005, pp. 126–127).

Interestingly put, media is a domain where "public is exposed to various ideologies which influence and blind-fold their mind as a certain ideology is enforced on them in their daily life" (Ramanathan & Hoon, 2015, p. 63). In his article "Political Conscientization and Media (IL) Literacy," Paul R. Carr (2009), an assistant professor in the Department of Educational Foundations of the Beeghly College of Education at Youngstown State University in Ohio, asks, "What can we learn from the interplay between the mainstream media and education?" (p. 3). Carr (2009) appoints youth as disseminators of "their own media through YouTube video clips, blogs and internet discussion-groups" (p. 6). Concurrently, the concern that implicit advertising and false misinterpretations in media could potentially deter critical understanding of the minorities is a task that all educators must consider important to help students understand the power of media in creating surrealities than inhibit emancipatory discourses.

According to Kaul (2012), the media enhances opportunities for public debate and exchange of information in "democratic environments" (p. 52). The more transparent information is made available in the media, the more informed decisions people will make regarding their lives and democratic possibilities. However, Breaks presented a one-sided story (Adichie, 2009), which is dangerous because it fossilizes unique interpretations of reality as normal and universal. Since democracy is "a factor of peace" (Kaul, 2012, p. 57), promoting spaces in media that is free, independent, pluralistic, and inclusive contributes to democratic developments (Kaul, 2012). Therefore, had Breaks presented both sides of the stories about *his* journey in school, he would have helped his audience make democratic and informed decisions about education and thereby would have promoted peaceful formations for social change.

Conclusion

Drawing from CDA and argumentation theory, this chapter intended to explore the potential of the media as a mechanism that venues emancipatory discourses to catapult democratic ideological transformation and social change. Participating in a society that values media as a medium of power requires of individuals to manufacture consent to ways of thinking, speaking, feeling, and doing toward differences in gender, race, language, values, and class. Specifically, the media is a mechanism where discourses of self-representation, group representation, and identity could be nested democratically. Therefore, it is the media users' job to be cognizant of the hidden agendas that try to control, manipulate, and reproduce mainstream ideologies. As Loehwing and Motter (2012) explain, the role of the media users is to find the emancipatory potential of self- and group representation. They caution that "the mere existence of discursive space presumably open to all may yet facilitate powerful normative exclusions that privilege some voices over others even when all voices are ostensibly heard" (Loehwing & Motter, 2012, p. 36).

Layers of historicity play an important role in the appropriation of discursive hegemony; hence, a critical momentum for democratizing media must take place in despaired contemporary times for social accountability. The goal is to counteract the recreation of institutional parameters and societal controversies that promote structured inequalities and social biases. My contention is that media could be much more than a colonizer's propaganda means that articulates assimilation practices. I position the media as a contemporary medium that could promote social change when being used, viewed, and interpreted critically. Finally, I urge educators to become aware of the power invested in their voices to dismantle hegemonic discursive practices in the social media and to focus more on the reflective exercise that Suli Breaks proposes to promote change and educational transformation in contemporary, digital-oriented, diverse global communities.

References

Adichie, C. (2009). The danger of a single story. *TEDGlobal*. Retrieved from http://www.ted.com/talks/chimamanda_adichie_the_danger_of_a_single_story.html

Altheide, D. L. (2011). Media logic and social power. *Empedocles: European Journal for the Philosophy of Communication, 3*(2), 119–136. doi: 10.1386/ejpc.3.2.119_1

Anderson, A., Aronson, B., Ellison, S., & Fairchild-Keyes, S. (2015). Pushing against the limit-horizon of educational change: A critical discourse analysis of popular education reform texts. *Journal for Critical Education Policy Studies (JCEPS), 12*(3), 338–370.

Azzouz, B. (2009). *A discourse analysis of grammatical cohesion in student's writing*. [Dissertation]. Mentouri University-Constantine. People's Democratic and Republic of Algeria. Ministry of Higher Education and Scientific Research. Faculty of Letters and Languages Department of Foreign Languages/ English. Retrieved from http://bu.umc.edu.dz/theses/anglais/AZZ1086.pdf

Bernhard, J. K., Freire, M., Pacini-Ketchabaw, V., & Villanueva, V. (1998). A Latin-American parents' group participates in their children's schooling: Parental involvement reconsidered. *The Free Library. Canadian Ethnic Studies Journal*. Retrieved from http://www.thefreelibrary.com/A+Latin-American+parents'+group+participates+in+their+children's . . . -a082883437

Biography Channel (n.d.). *Steve Jobs bio. True story*. Retrieved from http://www.biography.com/people/steve-jobs-9354805?page=1

Blommaert, J. (2005). *Discourse: A critical introduction*. New York: Cambridge University Press.

Breaks, S. (2012, December 2). *Why I Hate School but Love Education ‖ Spoken Word*. [Video File]. Retrieved from http://www.youtube.com/watch?feature=player_detailpage&v=y_ZmM7zPLyI

Breaks, S. (2014). *Suli Breaks website*. Retrieved from http://sulibreaks.com/

Carr, P. R. (Fall 2009). Political conscientization and media (IL) literacy. *Multicultural Education*. Retrieved from http://files.eric.ed.gov/fulltext/EJ871358.pdf

Coombs, N. (2010). *Making online teaching accessible: Inclusive course design for students with disabilities*. San Francisco, CA: Jossey-Bass.

Fairclough, I., & Fairclough, N. (2012). *Political discourse analysis: A method for advanced students*. New York: Routledge Taylor and Francis Group.

Fanon, F. (2008). *Black skin, white masks*. New York: Grove Press.

Freire, P. (1998). *Pedagogy of freedom: Ethics, democracy, and civic courage*. Lanhman, MD: Rowman & Littlefield Publishers, Inc.

Gramsci, A. (1971). *Selections from the prison notebooks of Antonio Gramsci*. New York: International Publishers.

Hall, P. M. (1987). Social theory and multiple realities: The social conditions of rule enforcement. *American Sociological Association, 6*(1), 33–35.

Herman, E. S. (2003). The propaganda model: A retrospective. *Against All Reason-Propaganda, Politics, Power, 1*, 1–14.

Herman, E. S., & Chomsky, N. (2002). *Manufacturing consent: The political economy of the mass media*. New York: Pantheon Books.

Jansen, I. (2008). Discourse analysis and Foucault's "archeology of knowledge". [Special Article]. *International Journal of Caring Sciences, 1*(3), 107–111.

Kaul, V. (2012). Interface between media, democracy and development. *China Media Research, 8*(3), 52–64.

Kincheloe, J. L. (2010). *Knowledge and critical pedagogy: An introduction*. Lexington, KY: Springer.

Loehwing, M., & Motter, J. (2012). Cultures of circulation: Utilizing co-cultures and counterpublics in intercultural new media research. *China Media Research, 8*(4), 29–38.

Maxwell, J. A. (2012). *A realist approach for qualitative research*. Thousand Oaks, CA: Sage.

Memmi, A. (1965). *The colonizer and the colonized*. Boston, MA: The Orion Press Inc.

Metz, R., Ortutay, B., & Robertson, J. (2011, October 20). Steve Jobs authorized biography: Author Walter Isaacson sheds new light on Apple co-founder's life. *HuffPost* [website]. Retrieved from http://www.huffingtonpost.com/2011/10/20/steve-jobs-authorized-biography_n_1022903.html

Popps, R. K. (2010). Visual culture, public space, and piety in focus on the family's citizen magazine. *Critical Studies in Media Communication, 27*(5), 498–518.

Quin, R. (2003). A genealogy of media studies. *The Australian Educational Researcher, 30*(1). 101–121. doi: 10.1007/BF03216783.

Ramanathan, R., & Hoon, T. B. (2015). Application of critical discourse analysis in media discourse studies. *The Southwest Asian Journal of English Language Studies, 21*(2), 57–68.

Ríos, S. [Susana Ríos]. (2012, July 30). *What is epistemological curiosity by Paulo Freire*. [Video File]. Retrieved from http://www.youtube.com/watch?v=9svFnyWFmvU

van Dijk, T. A. (2007). *Critical discourse analysis* [chapter 18]. Retrieved from http://www.discourses.org/OldArticles/Critical%20discourse%20analysis.pdf

4   Toward Emancipation

Critical Discourse at work in a Composition Classroom

Debasmita Roychowdhury

Introduction

For this chapter, I selected the YouTube video of the American celebrity and gun rights advocate Mr. Charlton Heston's 1998 National Rifle Association (NRA) speech that he delivered at a NRA Banquet in Philadelphia. This was Mr. Heston's first speech as the NRA president. Since 1998, Mr. Heston had become the face of the NRA. Earlier in his life, Mr. Heston was engaged in the Civil Rights Movement, and for a short while, he endorsed the Democrats in the U.S. Congress and Senate. However, he switched his party allegiance and became a registered Republican in 1987 (Raymond, 2006, pp. 1–3). Following that, he campaigned for Ronald Reagan, George H. W. Bush, and George W. Bush (Raymond, 2006, p. 276). Mr. Heston, perhaps inadvertently, became the proverbial poster boy for the neoconservative/neoliberal discourse that has affected U.S. domestic and foreign affairs. To understand and analyze Mr. Heston's discourse, we now shift focus to the neoconservative/neoliberal ideology.

The Rise of Neoliberal and Neoconservative Discourse: An Overview

Both neoliberal and neoconservative ideologies are parts of a conservative, right-wing social reconstruction effort. Michael Apple (2000) calls it the "conservative restoration" (p. 59). Neoliberalism, taking an oppositional stance against the American egalitarian liberalism, adopted the idea of individual freedom solely through the free market economy. The rise of the conservative restoration can be seen from a historical perspective. Apple (1989, 2000) analyzes how this phenomenon came to be. Apple argues that following the Second World War, American social and educational ideologies were somewhat focused on egalitarianism. While America was establishing its formidable imperial and economic might globally, it was also taking care of important domestic issues. Government took active initiatives to extend equal opportunities to the minority groups and to expand welfare to the needy and vulnerable, namely to the historically disadvantaged women and African Americans. For a brief period, this era offered what Apple defined as the "social democratic accord" (p. 39). But this accord was not devoid of hegemonic struggles of race, gender, and class.

A certain elite section of the American polity soon began an ideological campaign against the "traditional social democratic 'statist' solutions" (Apple, 1989, p. 40), which indeed provided much needed opportunities for minority groups. However, the neoconservative and the neoliberal elite intellectuals soon started a campaign against the democratizing efforts, defining them as the root causes of all social problems in America. "[T]he project," Apple (1989) explains, "was aimed at constructing a 'new majority' that would 'dismantle the welfare state, legislate a return to traditional morality, and stem the tide of political and cultural dislocation which the 1960's and 1970's represented'" (p. 40). This was the beginning of the New Right discourse that gave rise to neoliberalism and neconservatism.

This power struggle and its effects on disenfranchised Americans intensified in 1960s and 1970s. Since then, both these ideologies have been working in concert with the "conservative restoration" of American social and economic arena. According to Apple (2000), with the emergence of these ideologies, the idea of democracy shifted from being a political and social justice issue to an all-encompassing economic trend. Jodi Dean (2009) defines this phenomenon correctly as "a philosophy viewing market exchange as a guide for all human action." Expanding the claim, she states that by "[r]edefining social and ethical life in accordance with economic criteria and expectations, neoliberalism holds that human freedom is best achieved through the operation of markets" (p. 51). Rejecting the embedded liberalism, neoliberalism gained popularity in 1980s and 1990s and soon became hegemonic during the Reagan and Thatcher era. Entirely focused on privatizing and controlling the marketplace, this ideology served only a fraction of the population. Fully dedicated to the profit economics, eventually it became "the dominant ideological rationalization for globalization and contemporary state 'reform'" (Peck & Tickell, 2002, p. 1). The effect of this discourse has been devastating locally and globally.

Today, we are witnessing the erosion of humanity everywhere as the neoliberal greed economy is steadily encroaching into American society. Using the metaphor of a top-heavy wineglass, Chilean Economist Manfred Max-Neef (1998) describes how our world has become a rich man's world over the years. According to Max-Neef, only a small group of people is hoarding and controlling the entire world's economic wealth. Max-Neef (1998) states, "Today's world is like a wine glass, with the upper part representing the 20% richest people of the world, who appropriate 87% of the planet's wealth, while in the lower part the 20% poorest are left with 1.4% of the world's riches" (p. 66). This group of rich people practices neoliberalism as a religion and worships money as God. In fact, they blatantly manipulate dominant traditional religious doctrine in putting forth their economic agenda.

Stefan Halper and Jonathan Clarke (2004) identify and analyze the underpinnings of the neoconservative/neoliberal ideologies in their book

America Alone: The Neo-Conservatives and the Global Order. The first pillar of neconservatism, for example, is the religious deterministic belief that quality of life is determined only by good or bad choices people make. The correct political posture is to resist the "evil" with "good" doctrine. The second tenet, building upon the first one, asserts that evil can be defeated by the "good" (defined by certain social and/or religious doctrine), and the relationship between states can be maintained by the "good" with the use of military power. The third tenet, according to Halper and Clarke, portrays the Middle East as the frontier where the good encounters evil (Islam) (pp. 10–11). In short, neoliberals believe in the " 'unipolar' power of the United States, seeing the use of military force as the first, not the last, option of the foreign policy" (Halper & Clarke, 2004, p. 11). Whether the proponents of this discourse truly believe what they say or they promote it for financial gains is a matter of scholarly debate. However, when prominent neoconservatives like Robert Kagan and Bill Kristol unabashedly announce that America will "need foreign and defense policy that is unapologetic, idealistic, assertive, and funded well beyond existing appropriation. America must not only be the world's policeman or its sheriff, it must be its beacon and guide" (in Halper & Clarke, 2004, p. 18), we get a good glimpse of their political agenda. Unfortunately, the two attacks on Iraq, and the continuing war with Afghan and Pakistani insurgents, do not show America as the beacon of democracy; instead they confirm its role as the promoter of the "military-industrial complex." President Dwight D. Eisenhower's (1961) prophetic forewarning about the "unwarranted influence" of the "military-industrial complex," unfortunately, has become a harsh reality today (Ledbette, 2011, pp. 2–3).

Many contemporary scholars such as Noam Chomsky (2005), Naomi Klein (2007), and Andrew Feinstein (2013), point out that since its inception, neoconservative discourse had influenced public opinion about the war on global terrorism. Because of the recent wars, a lot of American and European arms-producing corporations have been able to amass great wealth. Journalist Amy Goodman, while interviewing Joseph Stiglitz, asked who is profiting from the Iraq war. The Nobel laureate economist answered, "Well, actually, there are two big gainers in this war and only two: the oil companies and the defense contractors" (Interview transcript, 2008, para. 77–78). Defense contractors like Halliburton, Lockheed Martin, Boeing, General Dynamics, Raytheon, and Northrop Grumman, which supplied weapons and other utilities needed for the wars America waged with Iraq and Afghanistan in recent times, fulfilled the neoliberal economic and ideological visions while fattening the wallets of those who promoted this discourse.

Discourse of War and Weapon: A Counter Perspective

After September 11, 2001, fear of terrorist attack intensified in America. To remedy this problem, the U.S. government proposed a new security policy in *National Security Strategy of the United States* (White House) in 2002. Noam Chomsky (2005), defining this policy, states

> unusually extreme doctrine on the issue of force in the world, and it's not accidental that the drumbeat for war in Iraq coincided with the report's release.
>
> The new doctrine was not one of *preemptive* war. . . . [It is] namely, *preventive* war. That is United States will rule the world by force, and if there is any challenge to its domination-whether it is perceived in distance, invented, imagined or whatever-then the United States will have the right to destroy that challenge before it becomes a threat.
>
> (pp. 1–2)

Capitalizing on the growing fear of terrorism, America waged a war against Iraq in March 2003 based on Saddam Hussein's presumed involvement in 9/11 attack. While American soldiers went to Iraq, the military-industrial complex boomed in America. According to Stockholm International Peace Research Institute (SIPRI), United States's military expenditure increased from $413 to $724 billion during the presidency of George W. Bush (SIPRI, 2012). The North American arms industry became rich and powerful by controlling the global market of arms and military services. SIPRI (2012) records show that "[a]rms-producing and military services companies headquartered in North America and Western Europe continued to dominate the Top 100 list" (para. 3) among arms-producing companies. Additionally, as noted by the SIPRI database, sales of the largest arms-producing companies in 2011 totaled $410 billion, and North American corporations such as Lockheed Martin, Boeing, General Dynamics, Raytheon, and Northrop Grumman remained the first five largest profit-making companies ("The SIPRI Top 100," 2013).

With their economic power, these corporations heavily influenced and infiltrated U.S. public and private institutions. In an interview with Amy Goodman, Andrew Feinstein (2012), author of *The Shadow World: Inside the Global Arms Trade*, explains how the leading arms-producing corporations, blurring the line between legal and illegal trade practice, are making profit and breeding corruption.

The global arms trade, led by American corporations, has intensely impacted U.S. domestic situations. Policies regarding guns are pretty lax in America, and many Americans have access to illegal, unregistered, and unregulated firearms. Since 2009 to 2013, 20 cases of mass shooting have made the news headlines in the United States (Wing, 2013, para.10). The most recent incidents of the Sandy Hook Elementary School shooting in 2012 and the Washington Navy Yard shooting in 2013 are evidence of growing gun-related violence in America.

So far, very little has been done to regulate the free flow of guns in the streets of America. The NRA, the largest and most active firearms rights organization in the world, invokes the second amendment to oppose any attempt of regulating weapons sales within and across the borders. According to Andrew Finestine (2012), the NRA's interest as the largest pro-gun establishment is intertwined with arms industry interests. In answering Amy Goodman's question how interlinked the NRA is with the weapons manufacturers, he says:

> I would extrapolate from how this trade works around the world that there would be fundamental links and that those links would be at a number of levels. They would include, for instance, dialogue about products. They would include dialogue about marketing. They would include dialogue about strategies. They would also include, I'm pretty sure, money. I would be extremely surprised if American weapons manufacturers were not providing the NRA with a significant portion of its funding.
>
> (Finestine, para. 31)

Finestine goes on to say that

> the NRA, the gun sellers, the gun users seem to be afforded an extraordinary level of protection by government, by law enforcement authorities, just as happens on the global level. And part of this is because of the revolving door of people between, for instance, the NRA and government. Recent figures suggest that 15 of 28 . . . lobbyists in the NRA came from important positions within government dealing with some of these same issues, so that the sorts of decisions being made by government are being informed disproportionately by those who want guns to be unregulated, by those who are making massive profits out the suffering of the victims of gun crime.
>
> (2012, para. 12)

The discourse of seizing power by the barrel of a gun has been proven to be dangerous for American citizens and for the world at large. Mr. Heston, as the president of the NRA, has played a pivotal role in promoting this discourse. In the section that follows, I critically analyze the ideology that Mr. Heston's speech represents and the power that drives it.

Jan Blommaert (2005), in defining CDA, says that "power, and especially institutionally reproduced power is central to CDA" (p. 24). CDA is an amalgamation of many different approaches that are used to examine different social domains. I believe that Heston's speech—underscored with neoconservative political ideology—stands for a hegemonic and coercive power. A critical analysis of his speech may reveal that he has shaped his ideas and argument around the notion of repressive power that he believes in. To Mr. Heston, American citizens can enjoy a true sense of freedom, protection, and security only by the power coming from the barrels of guns.

Noticeably, Heston's rhetoric in the speech resonates with that of Chairman Mao-Tse-Tung. In a different context, he also once said, "Political power grows out of the barrel of a gun" (1938, para. 6). It is rather ironic that the discourse of power is used by two very different people from different times who believed in two opposing political doctrines.

As CDA practitioners, we need to be cognizant of both corruptive as well as constructive power of institutionally reproduced discourses. Discourses do hold power to create both social harmony and/or discord. In light of this view, I set out to investigate Mr. Heston's speech to see if, in fact, it upholds neoconservative political ideology and how that ideology is reflected through the linguistic and rhetorical patterns.

Discourse Analysis: Theoretical Grounding for the Representative Artifact

Discourse could be described as any type of systematized or non-systematized sign (including verbal, nonverbal, written, unwritten, visual, nonvisual, physical, nonphysical etc.) that signals purposeful or casual communication within a group. It is a rhetorical dialogue people often have with others for personal, social, economic, political, and institutional purpose. Discourse and its critical analysis can be intricately connected to social, cultural, and economic politics that affect our lives directly and indirectly. In a society governed by politics, one group often maintains hegemonic power over other groups of people through a particular discourse. Living within a certain political environment, either people choose to accept its discourse and operate within it, or they can reject it. Yet others can decide to reject the notion of politics altogether. Regardless of the decisions we make, social and economic institutional politics influence our lives in many critical ways. Political ideologies entering our lives through active and passive discourse can be quite pervasive and powerful that way. Blommaert (2005) points out that when we think of ideology, we are, in fact, combining the two terms "discourse" and "power" together (p. 150). In recent American politics, power, ideology, and discourse, all three forces, are put into motion for maintaining social and economic dominance. Starting from this premise, perhaps any social discourse today could be analyzed from the perspective of critical political discourse.

My perspective was reinforced when I read *Political Discourse Analysis: A Method for Advanced Studies* written by Norman and Isabella Fairclough (2012). The authors are focused on political discourse analysis (PDA). To them, PDA is characterized by the "political actors—individuals (politicians, citizens), political institutions, and organizations, engaged in political *processes* and *events*" (Fairclough & Fairclough, 2012, p. 17).

Mr. Charlton Heston, a four-time president of NRA, clearly positions himself as a powerful figure to the American people. As a vocal gun rights advocate, Mr. Heston represents the neoconservative/neoliberal ideology of power that has been institutionalized and normalized today in its political discourse. Fairclough and Fairclough (2012) say, "Political contexts are *institutional* contexts" (p. 18). The context of Mr. Heston's speech is both institutional and political. As an agent of the neoconservative agenda—a powerful political ideology—he has influenced a large section of American society. Therefore, I would like to analyze his NRA speech (NRA News, 1998) as a political artifact. To that end, I would follow Norman Fairclough's three-dimensional framework for CDA. They are *discourse-as-text, discourse-as-discursive-practice, and discourse-as-social-practice* (Blommaert, 2005, pp. 29–31).

Transcript of the Charlton Heston NRA Speech

1 Thank you, (LOUD applause) thank you, thank you very much very much
2 Well this is where it all started isn't?
3 Right here in Philadelphia.
4 Two and a quarter centuries ago a bunch of amazing guys travelled here
5 They had freedom's business to attend to
6 Brave wise gallant man.
7 They knew their signatures on that declaration of independence
8 Told everybody that they were willing to die for it.
9 By daring to put on parchment what our founding fathers felt deep in their hearts.
10 A long silence soul of liberty rose up from a commoner's dream to become everyman's birthrights.
11 That is, as long as patriots like you kindles its flame.
12 Freedom has only one enemy
13 It cannot defeat and that is negligence
14 So, your presence here now today is an active reverence of all man's work beneath the heavens none shines better than our constitution
15 I think Jefferson and Payne, Adams, Madison, Mayson, Franklin
16 I think they are looking down right now
17 At us
18 I think they understand what we are trying to do
19 What we strive to do
20 I came here to make help them proud of us
21 Why have you come here?
22 You came here to celebrate our freedom or to divide this membership?
23 Have you come here to show the world our unity or to splinter it?
24 Because before we go any farther, I want to know who is with me who is again' me? (big applause) pause
25 Before (pause) wow, well, before, are you, you saw through me didn't you!
26 Before I take one more step on this march into the next century though, I really need to know

27 So, I want those who stand with me, please right now rise from your chairs, take your feet and show me show the world, stand with me (standing ovation, great applause)

28 Thank you, good, good, well

29 Let me tell you why I came here

30 First I came here to heal

31 We don't have to agree with each other on every point of every issue everyday

32 The second amendment has room for the first amendment

33 But after you had your free speech, your say, the votes are counted, dye is cast, get together or get out of the way (big applause)

34 Thank you, you reassure me

35 Next, I come here to take back what's ours

36 Too many gun-owners think we have wandered into some fringe of the American life and left them behind

37 I can tell you why they think that

38 Year after year, lie after lie of the press and the politicians who are hook line and sinker stupid about lock stock and barrel freedom (big applause)

39 I will promise you we will win back our rightful place in main stream of American political debate

40 Main stream doesn't mean giving up anything, it means getting back everything (big applause)

41 Everything shooting used to be, a wholesome sport, an American tradition, proudly practiced in clubs, and campuses, and country sides

42 A rite of passage treated with reverences and respect

43 The main stream is where NRA should be, speaking in one, one proud prudent voice and believe me

44 Your voice rumbles like thunder (uses his baritone voice, I have come here standing in the shadow of the founding fathers to elect pro-gun candidates

45 No more leaders who toy with the truths and get away with anything including our gun rights

46 If I am not being clear, let me spell it out

47 Mr. Clinton, sir, America didn't trust you with our health care

48 America didn't trust you with the gays in military

49 America doesn't trust you with our 21 year old daughters (big applause, laughs)

50 And we sure lord don't trust you with our guns (prolonged pronouncement, big applause)

51 I came here to educate America's children and their parents those who do not know us, we must reach out with open arms not clenched fists

52 Never again should you think twice before saying you're an NRA member or think twice about that NRA decal in your car

53 I can even believe me see a day when for heaven's sakes some Hollywood luminary beside me finds the courage to admit they own and enjoy guns (big applause)

54 There are more of them than you think (big applause)

55 And, finally I came here because I am proud

56 I believe the second amendment is America's first freedom among the entire of that magnificent bill of rights

57 It is the first among equals

58 It is the one freedom that makes all freedoms possible

59 The one right that protects all the others

60 I am proud of our guns, proud how we use them, and proud of what they stand for

61 No organization in the history of the world has done more to preserve personal freedom to insure personal security, to fight violent crime or taught more kids and adults about firearm safety than your National Rifle Association. (big applause)

62 I came here today because like you and those brave men who travelled here two and a quarter centuries ago

63 Because of them, we have freedom's business to attend to.

64 I thank you. (standing ovation and big applause)

Mr. Heston's Speech Analysis: Discourse-as-Text and Discourse-as-Discursive-Practice

As a popular cultural figure, Charlton Heston is highly successful in generating an uptake from his audience. Heston, in this 9.22-minute-long speech, was applauded 13 times, and he received two standing ovations from the audience (lines 27 and 64). Although his speech does not approach the issues of second amendment and freedom, critically contextualizing them in light of the current social issues, it efficiently sets the historical indexicality through repetitive references to "freedom" (lines 5, 12, 22, 38, 58, 61, and 63), "liberty" (line 10), "declaration of independence" (line 7), "founding fathers" (line 4, 6, 7, 9, 44, 62, and 63), "constitution" (line 14), "second amendment" (line 32), "first amendment" (line 32, 33), and "Jefferson and Payne, Adams, Madison, Mayson, Franklin" (line 15).

These disjointed, repetitive utterances in the text are used without having any logical cohesion. In certain context, they sound outright nonsensical. Yet, his references to history have been able to produce indexical meanings[1] for his audience. We witness the audience enthusiastically responding to him. Blommaert (2005) succinctly points out, "What people do with words . . . is to produce *conditions for uptake*, conditions for voices, but as soon as these conditions are produced, uptake is a fully social process, full of power" (p. 45). When this uptake is generated, the speaker can expect his/her audience to internalize it and carry it out to others. Heston has been able to do it quite successfully during his tenure as the president of NRA.

We are also able to recognize the intertextualizing[2] process at work when Heston makes numerous references to the U.S. constitution and its creators. He repeatedly "cite[s] and re-cite[s]" them (Blommaert, 2005, p. 46). In this brief speech (9:15), Heston frequently utters the words popular to the Americans in general. The word "freedom" was used eight times, "constitution" six times, and Heston refers to the Founding Fathers and the Bill of Rights altogether 14 times. Repeated utterance of these words and phrases in the speech has produced a semantic pattern, which in turn, created a social sphere where the discourse relating to guns, power, and freedom acquired its legitimacy.

Moreover, this speech is an excellent example of entextualization.[3] Creation of the Bill of Rights was a historically situated, unique event that happened 200 years ago. The Second Amendment, no doubt, is highly controversial and the most debated one among the other constitutional rights outlined in it. However, since its inception, a section of American population has embraced the Second Amendment unquestioningly. Historian Richard Hofstadter (1970) has defined this phenomenon as the onset of "gun culture" in America. According to him, this culture was essentially borne out of America's agrarian and frontier narratives. In his famous article "America as a Gun Culture", Hofstadter (1970) stated, "What began as a necessity of agriculture and the frontier took hold as a sport and as an ingredient in the American imagination" (para.11). He was critical about the gun culture as far back as in 1970s, when here wasn't as much gun-related social violence occurring in America.

Today, most gun rights enthusiasts tend to forget that in last 200-some years, America has progressed toward a different era of civilization from the time of western and southern frontier cultures. Private American citizens now do not necessarily need military-grade firearms or deadly arsenals to protect themselves. Yet, in America, the "cultural mythology" shaped around guns (Spitzer, 2004) keeps on thriving through modern times in the pro-gun rhetoric of Heston and others like him. This speech also continues with that mythology as the narrative of the Bill of Rights is "lifted out of [its] original context and transmitted . . . by inserting them into another discourse" (Blommaert, 2005, p. 47). The recurring reference of constitutional rights becomes a point in history from where the speech begins to structure a synchronic event.

Replete with historical intertextuality, Heston's speech also develops a pattern of synchronization. Synchronization, defined as a "point from which one speaks, a point in the history" (Blommaert, 2005, p. 134), can be powerful in political discourse. Talking from this point, a skilled speaker can create synchronicity by offering everyday rationality, surface-level clarity, and cohesion by diverting audiences' attention from the differences, contradictions, and multilayered reality that history offers. Heston is critical about government, politicians, policies, and the media but he—whether intentionally or not—doesn't provide a deep critical analysis of the claims he makes. Perhaps, to NRA audience, he doesn't need to. Instead, preaching to his choir through synchronization, Heston creates an imaginary American society where "we" are bound by the most simplistic and one-dimensional American interpretation of "freedom" that is only realized through gun power. Moreover, Heston's own pro-gun position reflected in his text generates an extremely divisive and aggressive image of the United States. The synchronicity in the speech forces the audience to take a side; Heston directly asks the audience, "Who is with me who is again[st] me?" (NRA transcript, line 24). And, then he squarely rejects the others who may not subscribe to his discourse, saying, "But after you had your free speech, your say, the votes are counted, dye is cast, get together or get out of the way" (NRA transcript, line 24). The speech thoroughly manipulates audience's emotions but does not offer any educated argument. Heston's "assemblage" of historical references are "evidently a reduction of enormously complex processes and events to a very simple scheme organized around oppositions between the "pro-gun US('us')" (Blommaert, 2005, p. 140) and the other U.S. citizens. He creates an image of a seemingly united United States regarding the gun issue using an illusory coherence and clarity in the speech by repeated utterance of history, and his audience responds enthusiastically to his charisma and his message.

Speech Analysis: Discourse-as-Social-Practice

This dimension is defined by Blommaert as the social power play. According to him, powerful individuals or institutions can create alliance by "integrating classes and groups through consent" (2005, p. 29), which they can mobilize to their advantage. Earlier in this chapter, I discussed how power as a dominant force creates ideologies, which in turn, control the politics in a society. Antonio Gramsci defines the process as the " 'cultural domination' of the bourgeoisie over the rest of the society" (cited in Blommaert, 2005, p. 166). The social, economic, and political dominations are sometimes openly forced upon people as state-mandated policies, and often the domination is achieved through consent by covert manipulation, that is, through discourse with hidden agenda. Gramsci calls it "power by consent" (cited in Blommaert, 2005, p. 167). In the NRA speech (NRA News, 1998), Heston uses the discourse of gun culture and glorifies NRA's, and his own, image as the all-powerful protectors of American freedom. Aligning himself with the Founding Fathers, he becomes their messenger and establishes himself as the NRA leader who will "win back the mainstream political debate" (NRA transcript, line 39). He promises to take back "what is ours" in the next century (NRA transcript, line 35). Using this rhetoric during his tenure, Mr. Heston was able to mobilize a large section of the American people under the banners of NRA and Republican Party. Indeed, history and current politics, fused rather crudely in the speech, worked favorably for the Republican Party. Positioning NRA against Bill Clinton's presidency, Heston rallied for the next "pro-gun candidate" (NRA transcript, line 44). In 2000, the NRA endorsed George W. Bush as the Republican Party candidate, and in 2001, Bush Junior became the 43rd president of the United States. This speech clearly shows how discourse can be "a sphere of cultural hegemony and the hegemony of a class or group over the society or over particular sections of it . . . is in part a matter of its capacity to shape discursive practices and orders of discourse" (Fairclough, 1995, p. 95). Of course, there were other issues involved in the 2001 Republican Party win. However, the speech, in its micro format, demonstrated the characteristics of a powerful and domineering macro social discourse that is capable of shaping public opinion.

There could be an argument that the connections among arms trade, war, corruption, and domestic and international gun violence is far-fetched, and it is absurd to hold the NRA responsible for gun-related ills in America. Perhaps it is true that one single institution is not responsible for everything. However, multiple public and private enterprises with vested economic and political interests can have additive effects. A close scrutiny will reveal that these issues are often intertwined. Powerful institutions and individuals influencing public policies shape these issues, and these issues ultimately diminish the quality of our life. To prevent this from happening, we need to be careful about subscribing to a discourse or in creating one that could be harmful to our society.

Notes

1 According to Blommaert (2005), "Indexical meaning is what anchors language usage firmly into social and cultural patterns" (p. 12).

2 Fairclough (1992) defines the term "manifest intertexuality" as the process of borrowing materials from the other sources to shape a particular text (pp. 104 and 118–123).

3 Entextualization process, according to Blommaert (2005), happens when "socially, culturally, and historically situated unique events—are lifted out of their original contexts and transmitted, by quoting or echoing them, by writing them down, by inserting them into another discourse" (p. 47).

References

Apple, M. W. (1989). The politics of common sense: Schooling, populism, and the new right. In H. A. Giroux and P. McLaren (Eds.), *Critical Pedagogy: The State, and Cultural Struggle*. Retrieved from Google Books database.

Apple, M. W. (2000). Between neoliberalism and neoconservatism: Education and conservatism in a global context. *Globalization and education: Critical perspectives*, 57, 77. Retrieved from http://www.southalabama.edu/coe/faculty/fregeau/615readings/BetweenNeoliberalismNewconservatism.pd

Blommaert, J. (2005). *Discourse*. New York: Cambridge University Press.

Chomsky, N. (2005). *Imperial ambitions: Conversation on the post-9/11 world*. New York: Henry Holt and Company, LLC.

Dean, J. (2009). *Democracy and other neoliberal fantasies: Communicative capitalism and left politics*. Durham and London: Duke University Press.

Fairclough, I., & Fairclough, N. (2012). *Political discourse analysis: A method for advanced studies*. New York: Routledge.

Fairclough, N. (1992). *Discourse and social change*. Cambridge, UK: Polity Press.

Fairclough, N. (1995). *Critical discourse analysis: The critical study of language*. London and New York: Longman.

Feinstein, A. (2012). *The shadow world: Inside the global arms trade*. Retrieved from Amazon Books database.

Goodman, A. (Interviewer) & Stiglitz, J. (Interviewee) (2008, February 29) [Interview transcript]. Retrieved from http://www.democracynow.org/2008/2/29/exclusive_the_three_trillion_dollar_war Gun Control vs. Gun Rights. Retrieved from http://www.opensecrets.org/news/issues/guns/index.php

Goodman, A. (Interviewer) & Feinstein, A. (Interviewee) (2013, February) [Interview transcript]. Retrieved from http://archive.democracynow.org

Goodman, A. (Interviewer) & Stiglitz, J. (Interviewee) (2008, February 29) [Interview transcript]. Retrieved from http://www.democracynow.org/2008/2/29/exclusive_the_three_trillion_dollar_war

Gun Control vs. Gun Rights. (2013). Retrieved from http://www.opensecrets.org/news/issues/guns/index.php

Halper, S., & Clarke, J. (2004). *America alone: The neo-conservatives and the global order* (pp. 10–13). Retrieved from Google Books database.

Hofstadter, R. (1970). *America as a gun culture*. Retrieved from http://guncontrolnowusa.wordpress.com/2013/01/26/america-as-a-gun-culture-by-richard-hofstadter/

Klein, N. (2007). *The shock doctrine: The rise of disaster capitalism*. New York: Picador.

Ledbetter, J. (2011). *Unwarranted influence: Dwight D. Eisenhower and the military industrial complex*. Retrieved from Google Books database.

Max-Neef, M. (1998). Economy, humanism, and neoliberalism. In O. Fals-Borda (Ed.), *Peoples participation: Challenges ahead* (pp. 63–80). New York: The Apex Press. Chapter 8.

NRA News (Producer). (1998). *NRA annual meetings: Charlton Heston*. Philadelphia, PA [DVD]. Retrieved from http://www.nranews.com/resources/video/charlton-heston-1998-meetings/list/heston-speeches

Peck, J., & Tickell, A. (2002). Neoliberalizing space. *Antipode, 34*, 380–404. doi: 10.1111/1467–8330.00247. Retrieved from http://onlinelibrary.wiley.com/doi/10.1111/1467–8330.00247/pdfsss

Raymond, E. (2006). *From my cold, dead hands: Charlton Heston and American politics*. Retrieved from http://www.amazon.com/dp/0813124085/ref=rdr_ext_tmb#reader_0813124085The SIPRI top 100. (2011). *The SIPRI top 100 arms-producing and military services companies in the world excluding China*. (SIPRI Report). Retrieved from http://www.sipri.org/research/armaments/production/Top100

Spitzer, R. J. (2004). *Gun cultures in the USA*. Retrieved from http://en.wikipedia.org/wiki/Gun_cultures_in_the_USA

Tagespost, D. (Interviewer) & Woods, T. E. (Interviewee) (2003). *The split on the right* [Interview transcript]. Retrieved from http://archive.lewrockwell.com/woods/woods20.html

Trends in arms industry 2011. (2013). Retrieved from http://www.sipri.org/research/armaments/production/researchissues/long-term_trends

Tung, M. T. (1938, November 6). *Problems of war and strategy.* Retrieved from http://www.marxists.org/reference/archive/mao/works/red-book/ch05.htm

Wing, N. (2013). *We've had so many mass shootings in the U.S., we've had to redefine the term.* Retrieved from http://www.huffingtonpost.com/2013/09/17/mass-shootings-us_n_3935978.html

5   Discourse as a Pilgrimage
The Past of My Memories and the Future of My Hopes

Paulo A. Oemig

"[E]very utterance has a history of (ab)use, interpretation, and evaluation, and this history sticks to the utterance."
—Blommaert (2009, p. 46)

Introduction

It is my intention to provide the temporality of my discourse as it unfolds in time from one place to another. Through spoken and unspoken communication, discourse enacts our identities and levels of emancipation and freedom. However, I contend that freedom and identity are value dependent and society driven. Whether I identify myself as free or not is contingent upon how society understands freedom and how others perceive me. In all pilgrimages, we begin by going back to our roots. For me, it begins in Argentina, where the formative years of my discourse were shaped. Speaking of discourse and recognizing language as an object of power and inequality, Blommaert (2009) asserts that an "analysis should not start . . . as soon as people open their mouths. It should have started long before that" (p. 67). I traveled my early journey during the midst of a military dictatorship, where schooling was used as a mechanism to shape the minds of the youth into accepting military domination. It is important for me to address this history that accounts for the development of my discourse. I endeavor to interpret and reinterpret the meaning of my discourse, entextualizing[1] it in a dialogical dialectic of becoming.

It is my belief that pilgrimages are channels to fulfill promises, to pay homage, and also to let go. Most of all, I believe pilgrimages for me are symbolic acts to express my faith, love, and ethical commitment. To arrive at a sacred place, an open heart is required. In the process solidarity may be found, as it is with my discourse. It was December 7, 1985, when I embarked upon my first titled pilgrimage. Three of my friends from childhood and I walked about 40 miles from the city of Flores to the city of Luján in the province of Buenos Aires to pay homage to La Virgen de Luján, the patron saint of Argentina. With rosaries in hand, we were determined to recite the litany of the Blessed Virgen Mary throughout our walk. We succeeded for about

15 miles, when one of my friends started to fall behind. I waited and asked him if he was all right; he replied that he needed to slow down. Carlos was not in good shape and was short of breath. I advised him to sit down at an empty fruit crate on the side of the road. I hurried to catch up with the others, and we returned. Carlos kept telling us to move on, that he would be fine and would find us in the town of Las Rejas, a resting spot about midway from Luján. We chose to stay with him as we were in this together; it was our belief in each other and our tacit commitment to each other that gave purpose to our pilgrimage, not our destination.

A Pilgrim in My Discourse

It is not uncommon to hear that our lives are a journey. There is the biological journey from birth to death, just as there is the spiritual journey of our relationship with the divine. The latter takes us through the tribulations of wilderness, and the valley of the shadow of death, but also through green pastures and still waters. As I retrace and narrate my journey, there are certain referents, road signs, and tropes, along the way, for which the entextualization[1] of my discourse opens up. I, thus, forge a new understanding, historicized in space and time. I decontextualize and recontextualize my thoughts and discourse in the new context from which I find myself today. These referents assume a unique meaning for me, framed by temporality, scale, and locality; it bespeaks of a subjective narrative. Braudel (1969/2012) studied the implications of focusing on the short term as it masks the effects of long-term processes and structures of history. In contrast, Luckmann (1991) analyzed how social actors themselves outlined their experiences in terms of discrete temporalities in personal narratives ranging from body time, temporality dealing with immediate time to biographical time, the temporality of life in phases, and stages gaged compared to socialized notions of normative or typical biographies to historicity, understanding of how our biographies fit within larger stretches such as eras, lineages, and so on.

As a pilgrim in my discourse, I need to draw upon distinct temporalities and an autobiographical inquiry linked to reflection and ethnography. In the process, I bring together my autobiography to connect it to the sociopolitical and cultural aspects of my lived experiences, (Ellis, 2004, p. 43), my *vivencia*. Gingrich, Ochs, and Swedlund (2002, p. S3) describe temporality as "how beings experience such processual qualities (of time) in different sociocultural contexts, for example, through memory or anticipation." As a pilgrim in my discourse, my personal experiences cannot be isolated; I recognize a political dimension that permeates, directly or indirectly, all aspects of my life (Holman Jones, 2005). Discourse comprises not only "language in action" and "power effects" but all "human activity seen in connection with social, cultural, and historical patterns and developments of use" (Blommaert, 2009, p. 3).

Blommaert (2003, 2010) contends that there is a constant shift between the here and now of local practices and the wider scale historicity of the world system. These practices are embedded within the historicity of the world system as well as the intermediate time scales that span the whole range. Holland and Lave (2001) interpret the complex relations among these latitudes of temporal scale in social practice, emphasizing "history in person," or how social agents' "intimate self-making" relate in complex ways to their participation in localized sites of practice (p. 6). This "conflicted local practice," in turn, reflects and produces the "enduring struggles" that constitute broader scale historical or social practices (Holland & Lave, 2001, p. 6). The concept of "history in person" points to the observation that distinct scales of temporality constitute a valid framework for understanding sociolinguistic practices but also to the understanding of the mediated relation of one's self to history and subjective experience. But, before I continue, let me be clear: As my father told me years ago, a pilgrimage is not so much about going to a particular sacred place to find God but about putting myself in a particular place for God to find me. Our pilgrimage must begin by returning to our roots and insightfully reflecting on where we have come from.

Discourse in Argentina

In Argentina, I grew up immersed in the Catholic faith and was taught that education is a means to make a decent living. I learned to understand the importance of family, enjoying life, and feeling closer to the divine. Growing up there, a strong sense of nationalism and patriotism was inculcated. For instance, I grew up with the iconic image of Che Guevara's face, the legend of his feats and the mystery of his narrative. I find a strange resemblance between Ernesto Guevara's early life and that of Siddhartha Gautama. Both came from privileged families, and both underwent a personal conversion after leaving the protection and confinement of their homes. However, that is the only resemblance; both took different paths toward social action. Siddhartha became Buddha, Ernesto became Che. Conversion, of course, means turning around, finding a new understanding, new direction, and acting on it. That conversion comes while engaging in an internalized self-pilgrimage.

For a long time, I thought of the construction of knowledge as a complex web with many agents and nodes of communication that eventually should arrive at verified statements about reality. Yet, when it comes to discourse, the understanding of reality is contested and contextual; a true grasp of discourse is an ever-evolving practice since it requires one to embark upon an ever-evolving journey. There is no room for the realism of science, but as my discourse represents the dialectic interplay among economic, historical, and social structures, and the everyday practices that both produce and reflect these structures in specific localities, reality becomes institutionally mediated and socially constructed.

My schooling and socialization in Argentina exposed me to an ideology and dreams of sovereignty, freedom, patriotism, soil, blood, and God. Discourse for me, back then, was not contested, but it was set against the backdrop of a military dictatorship legitimized through that ideology. I recognize ideology as a set of knowledge, beliefs, and values that provide validity to the social structure. For those in power-making rules, this level of understanding facilitates a façade of legitimacy. Such ideology was promoted in my country, at the time, by the oligarchy. However, "ideas themselves do not define ideologies; they need to be inserted in material practices of modulation and reproduction" (Blommaert, 2009, p. 164). Schooling afforded those "material practices" or "ideological state apparatuses" (Althusser, 1971) for us to become socially regulated citizens accepting our places in life and beyond in relationship to Catholicism. I believe that my schooling experience, both as an elementary school student and a first-year high school student, was regulated with the same intent by the educational experts and bureaucrats of my home country. During those years, my family and I experienced certainty and, at the same time, angst: certainty in the order and status quo of life and, paradoxically, the angst of not knowing if and when the military would come for us.

My older brother and sister shared with me stories of military men stepping into their classrooms in high school holding a list of names. Even though they wore civilian clothes, their polished shoes, haircuts, and holsters stowing nine-millimeter pistols gave them away as paramilitary agents pursuing and putting away subversive people. The *subversivos* were those identified as vocally opposed and organized against the military junta and labeled by the government as enemies of the nation. I personally remember seeing them in their green Falcon cars amidst the streets of the city. Those picked up by the military were sent to clandestine detention centers, tortured, killed and disposed of in undisclosed locations. Communal graves and throwing bodies from helicopters and planes to the Rio de la Plata was common practice during the 1976–1983 dictatorship.

My discourse experience in Argentina cannot be isolated, just as it cannot be isolated anywhere else; it obeyed a power elite who mediated a socioeconomic reality. It follows a history of military coup d'états with the pretext of stabilizing democratic institutions and civic life. In Latin America during the 1960s, support and hope for democracies were hesitant and latent at the same time. For authoritarian rulers, the development of national security was a priority, and for those who confronted those rulers, the only alternative was a revolution to bring about liberation. Cuba stood as a prime example of such an opportunity. Che Guevara's role in Bolivia demonstrated the possibilities and limits of a revolutionary awakening. However, Che's image around the world symbolizes struggle and resistance for independence and emancipation. Sprinkled throughout the region, various guerrilla groups were organized, most of them of a Marxist or populist bent. In Chile, the Marxist political party secured the presidency for Salvador

Allende. In Colombia, the death of Camilo Torres, a priest and guerrilla member, represented real outcomes for the followers of Liberation Theology (Romero, 1998).

In Argentina, the solidarity among the people came to be identified with Peronismo. In the early 1970s, Juan Domingo Perón arrived in Buenos Aires with his wife María Estela Martinez de Perón, for constitutional elections. The modus operandi of Perón-Perón won, ending another period of military dictatorship in Argentina. Soon after assuming the presidency, Domingo Perón died; his wife continued as president, and in 1976 she was over-thrown by a military junta. My father had been an army captain during the first presidency of Perón (1946–1955) and retired after Perón was toppled and forced into exile. My father informed our family that he decided to leave the army because those in the military who supported the ousting would have come after him and imprisoned him.

In 1976, when a military junta took over the government, it began the darkest period in Argentina history—the Dirty War; it was a period of guer-rilla warfare against left-wing guerrilla groups, a period of kidnappings, torture, and killings. Economic and social upheaval paved the way to a National Process of Reorganization for which the main instrument was the clandestine and overt repression of all dissidents. The state was governed by fear, synchronizing an official discourse. Purposely, the dissolution of all political parties and free speech was justified by the need to expedite national order and the security of the state. In combining simultaneity and synchronization, every discourse is *on* history and *from* history (Blommaert, 2009, p. 136). It is *on* history, as it is used as a point of reference to craft a coherent message, and *from* history to make a particular stand. Those being oppressed, during our Dirty War, exhibited hidden transcripts and/or in silence expressed a helpless solidarity.

The general strategy and tactical supervision of the Dirty War operation was performed at the highest levels of the military, and many high-ranking officers did not shy from performing executions themselves. This level of involvement characterized the institutional character of their actions and the collective commitment. Executions required a complex managing appa-ratus as it had to track the kidnapping process from the beginning to the disappearance stage of a great number of people. Each detainee, from the moment he or she was considered suspect of conspiring against the govern-ment, was assigned a personal file. Suspects were followed, assessed, and then a decision was made either to kidnap or murder them. That decision fell to the higher ranks of the military. The repression was systematically thought out and exercised through the estate. It was truly a terrorist activ-ity, divided into four stages: kidnapping, torture, detention, and execution. The groups in charge of carrying out the kidnappings operated at night, and the whole family, in many cases, was included. Many operations were also carried out in factories and schools and even in neighboring countries, with the collaboration of the local authorities.

The green Falcon was the vehicle used in these kidnappings, which combined with the manpower and weapons, increased the terrifying effect. The kidnapping was followed by the ransacking of the homes. At detention centers, torture took place—the *picana*, sustained electric shocks, *submarinos*, submerging the head of the kidnapped in water and rapes were the most common forms of torture. The purpose of the torture was to extract information, gather intelligence, and obtain the names of other suspects, but above all, its main purpose was to extinguish the detainees' dignity and break the resistance of subversives. Many died during torture; for those who survived in any of the more than 300 clandestine detention centers, an indefinite period of time laid ahead of them. The detention centers were located in military centers and police stations.

The amount of people involved in keeping these centers operational, and the coordination needed within this network of horror attest to the complexity of the operation. The babies of those who were kidnapped or born in the detention centers were taken by the kidnappers and adopted by families involved in the repression. The women shared the same fate as the others, which was the *traslado*, the execution. It is ironic that even though the military junta established the death penalty, it was never applied; instead all executions were performed underground. Sometimes, bodies found lying in the streets were presented as victims of police confrontations. In most cases, however, the bodies were concealed, buried, burned in common pits, or thrown out to the sea with weights after having been drugged. Thus, there were no deaths but disappearances, or *desaparecidos* (Romero, 1998). In Mar del Plata, the city where I grew up, I learned that people suspected the existence of clandestine detention centers in many police stations and at the local navy base. Not knowing who would accuse who of speaking against the government, there was a complicity in silence. This facilitated a self-regulated censorship as "the oppressor exists within their oppressed comrades" (Freire, 1970/1996, p. 44).

Argentina's repression continued even after leftist guerrilla groups were dealt with and disbanded. The state's incessant program of eliminating all activism, preventing social protests, and extinguishing all criticism aimed at securing a tunnel narrative went unchallenged by the people. There were thousands of victims through a *masacre administrada* (Vezzetti, 2002, p. 147), but the goal was to subjugate society and control it with fear. The state assumed two roles: one terrorist and clandestine group that carried out the repression, and the other, the public part, supported by the judicial system that silenced any voices of discord. Between the terrorism of the state and the corrupted judicial system, only the voice of the state survived. Terror and fear took hold of Argentine society, a culture of fear ensued; those who could flee to other countries left.

My mother sent my brother and sister to the United States to learn English. Most accepted the discourse of the state and justified what they could with sayings such as *por algo será* (there must be a reason for that) and *cosas dejadas a Dios son bien vengadas* (things left to God are well avenged). This fatalistic attitude seems to be common among those who have been oppressed for a long time. Interestingly, reminiscent of Memmi's (1991) and Fanon's (2008) accounts, where a colonized society is kept oppressed by a few, there was a sort of internalization of the official discourse and self-censure among people. The military junta, however, was never able to shore up the consent of the people.

My father was fond of saying, *Soy el dueño de mi silencio pero el esclavo de mis palabras* (I'm the owner of my silence but the slave of my words). I am not sure what he meant by that; he was a man of few words and always seemed to be grounded in wisdom. Every time he spoke, we all listened intuitively. I remember him reading often by the window, drinking *mate*, an Argentinean infusion tea, in the living room. He read the local and national newspapers, *Reader's Digest*, and books such as *Either/Or, One-Dimensional Man* and *Nausea*. I am sure he read works of authors such as Kierkegaard, Marcuse, and Sartre because he had an inquisitive mind but also because they came with the national newspaper on Sundays' special editions. His aphorism stemming from such readings is worth being acknowledged. From my mother, I learned that silence and telling as little as possible about my family affairs was a survival mechanism in the military-ruled country of ours.

Most people growing up in Argentina between 1976 and 1983 joined in a pilgrimage of muted understanding, the silenced discourse of the oppressed. When my father was struck with prostate cancer, I used to go with him to the chemotherapy sessions. I watched him become weaker and rebound for periods of time. My faith in God was shattered when I felt that he had ignored my prayers. I knelt at church and in my room. In my journey for the unattainable, I simply could not comprehend why God would not spare my father's life and take mine instead. "My soul for my father's" as I recalled referring in my prayers; out of love I prayed or perhaps out of selfishness in not wanting to see him go through the suffering. I did pray, and I did it with all of my heart. My father and I traveled together to the United States, where he eventually passed away with my mom, my sister, and I at his side. I remember thinking that God must have other plans for me; otherwise, why would he not take me instead? In the breath of my own son, I found the answer.

In 1982, I was a student in a Catholic high school in Argentina; that year our country was retaking our Islas Malvinas (known as Falkland Islands). I remember wanting to be there, to be part of the "invading" forces, fighting for my land, being part of a noble *reconquista*; after all, the British epitomized the imperialistic hunger of the lion. I was too young and too naïve to go to war—too young in the midst of arising chauvinistic sentiments and too young to be immersed in the propaganda-driven righteousness to know otherwise. Even my Jesuit science teacher, Father Borgia, with his caring and analytical attitude and his "in science and life question everything—don't leave rocks unturned" mantra supported the efforts of the military junta in reclaiming our islands. Paradoxically, in his conception of happiness as a consequence of acting right, he never told us to question authority. My science teacher enacted a curriculum that was engaging and heuristic.

My school, like all others in the nation, was busy pledging help drives to send support to our troops. We later learned that not much of the goods actually got to them. I too was not only in the "belly of the beast" (Smith, 2002); I was another limb of the beast. This was the military's attempt at holding onto power, to unite the people through a war that could not be won. I do not blame Father Borgia for his hypocrisy, for not pushing us to question all histories, even our own; we were one under our flag. We accepted the challenge to take back the islands; we approved the state discourse in this instance. It is not so much "which perspective is true and which is false. It is rather *whose* perspective we adopted and granted authority" (Blommaert, 2009, p. 156).

State apparatuses and institutions have a knack in perfecting their tunnel narratives; "human nature is manipulated and capitalized upon powerful interests. We categorize individuals and imagine they are all in it together— the government simply takes the opportunity to choose labels for us" (Smith, 2002, p. 348). It is almost a cathartic experience to lose a war; it halts you, and compels you to reflect on the whys, the reasons, and the myths and to mediate after the anger upon the injustices of war. God, perhaps, allowed this forlornness, this war, and the other, but I want to believe that God does not condone any injustice. In revisiting my experience, in following the steps of my discourse during this time, I am finding the complexities in my pilgrimage.

Our world of knowledge and experience constitutes a totality, a multiplicity of interconnected processes and inquiries that breaks asunder the totality into pieces and fails to reassemble it, distorting reality. If I take various components of discourse such as voice, nation, and identity as road signs along my pilgrimage and find their contextual places from which they were lifted and adopted, I can avert deceptive inferences and increase my phenomenological understanding. There is a certain ambiguity in those road signs, and ambiguity may well be an essential aspect of the human condition. This leads me to contemplate whether tolerating ambiguity is a virtue. I would certainly not argue that ambiguity is preferable to clarity, though it is preferable to false or easy answers. "I constantly end up framing thoughts in terms of black and white, left and right. . . . The best I can do is to try to point my attention toward the genuine complexity of reality" (Smith, 2002, p. 348). The implications for understanding discourse through reflection and autobiographical inquiry are clear: that of extracting the individual and having him/her confront the larger societal scheme. The endurance of these binaries reflects the practicality in differentiating and classifying; these serve as procedural thinking shortcuts and have helped identify friends from foes—us versus them—since humanity's tribal beginnings. In engaging in my autobiographical pilgrimage, there is hope for reconciling my own dichotomies and understanding my actions and inactions in light of my discourse. I believe that holding strong to false dichotomies evokes alienation and encourages delusion.

Discourse in the United States

When I left Argentina, it was with the conviction that I would return. I came to the United States to study English as a second language in Provo, Utah, at Brigham Young University (BYU). My parents thought that BYU would be a good place to learn English since it was where Mormon missionaries went to learn the languages of the world. Coming from the edges of the Pampa's plains and shores of the Atlantic Ocean, I felt suffocated as if the mountains were closing in on me. I felt torn between two countries; I began my treading between worlds, between insecurity and security. I felt insecure in a foreign country with a foreign language, and I felt insecure in having left the "security" of my homeland. Nevertheless, I was strong-minded in learning the English language and determined not to forget my *Castellano*. While pursuing anthropology studies at the University of Utah, I learned about language ideology as a set of beliefs about languages that link language, identity, and power relations (Heath, 1989; Woolard, 1998).

Language or linguistic ideology allows one not only to consider culture as a verb and group membership in terms of language in action but also to take a critical stance. The hierarchical position that a particular language enjoys is shaped by political factors. This can be understood as a "condition of language *markedness*, resulting from the relative political position of the target and native languages" (Edelsky, 2006, p. 28). In the United States, the English language has assumed a high-status position; it is the unmarked language of public schools and institutions. This is particularly relevant to my discourse and voice in the United States. I learned, firsthand, that there is a consensus regarding the alleged superiority of certain standardized languages. My spoken English exhibits an accent that defines me as the *other*; the Spanish language does not seem to be held as superior or equal to English. The connotation is that Spanish-speaking countries represent the periphery of the world system. In my early years in the United States, I was surprised that very few people knew where Argentina was located; many thought it was somewhere in Europe. I thought that represented an insular mentality unlikely for the greatest power in the world. In Argentina, we were victims, consciously and unconsciously, of cultural imperialism. All things "American" were coveted, yet at the same time in schizophrenic fashion, Americans were not welcome in Argentina. I also learned that many of the military dictatorships in South America, in countries such as Argentina, Brazil, Chile, Uruguay, Paraguay, Peru, and Bolivia were possible thanks to the involvement of the United States. The Dirty War in Argentina was orchestrated with support from the Central Intelligence Agency (CIA) in what is known as Operation Condor. France also provided lessons to the military junta from the Algerian days. The support, however, was withdrawn during President Jimmy Carter's administration (Vezzetti, 2002).

After learning English and studying anthropology, while working full time as a chemist in an environmental laboratory, my fiancée and I moved to New Mexico, where I pursued graduate studies in anthropology, and Sherrie taught at a high school. Having completed the master's program, I substitute taught in Spanish, science, and math classes in the local high schools until I was hired to teach eighth-grade dual-language science. That was going to be my first experience as a teacher in the U.S. public school system. The week before classes began, I was very apprehensive. The principal handed over the keys to my classroom saying, "This is it [the classroom]. Welcome again to Zia; you can arrange the desks any way you want to"; there was a pile of desks in the middle of the room. My assigned mentor teacher provided me with the standards and benchmarks, which became a crucial guide for me. However, I do not believe I would have survived my first year of teaching without my wife's support. As an experienced teacher herself, she was able to guide and encourage me through the early period of my teaching career.

I held high expectations for all my students, yet I was ingenuous about the politics of grades, assessments, helicopter parents, and cultural tendency for instant gratification. I took those standards and benchmarks and built my curriculum from scratch. I chose not to use the textbook for two reasons—first, the textbook was not portraying the content in depth, and second, my teachers in Argentina, for the most part, and the ones I remember the most, did not use them. Another reason that steered me away from the textbook was that it did not represent the demographics of my students well. In most textbooks, white European Americans are disproportionally represented more than any other ethnic groups. This is part of a silencing curriculum. The invisibility of ethnic diversity, or visible token appearances, from many educational materials does not promote cultural inclusiveness. Textbooks also validate only a particular knowledge for the sake of standardizing students and maintaining dominant ideologies current (Freire, 1970/1996; Giroux, 1981; Grant & Sleeter, 2009). I provided my students with published journal articles and taught them how to read rich informational texts. Teaching science in Spanish, two out of five classes, was invigorating and kept me motivated as well. I believed that Spanish was recognized as an important language and felt a special connection with those students. My belief that Spanish was as important or equal to English, however, was short-lived; the effects of language ideology were felt here, too. Most teachers presumed that content area instruction for English learners (ELs) should wait until English language skills are fully developed. This type of discourse encourages subtracting schooling; it is not surprising that EL students often fall behind their English-speaking school mates in content area learning. This is rationalized by another discourse that adheres to deficit thinking—William

Ryan's (1971) *Blaming the Victim* exposes the ideological base of this discourse. Essentially, those in a position of privilege set the norms and get to blame the less privileged for their lots in life. The steps in providing credence to this discourse are seemingly straightforward: Those in power identify social problems, studies are conducted to see how the advantaged and disadvantaged are different, the differences are described as the causes of the social problem, and the government enacts policies to fix those differences or deficiencies. Ryan (1971) states that "all of this happens so smoothly that it seems downright rational" (p. 8).

During my first year of teaching, I found myself applying the scientific method to achieve clear objectives from the standards and benchmarks to address content knowledge "deficiencies" in my students and to get them ready to achieve content proficiency. Today, I realize, it is a proficiency and deficiency misplaced at the service of an economic and political system that does not foster inclusiveness and the best interests of all students. To understand this as the basis of the dominant discourse that guarantees inequalities requires what Lilia Bartolomé (1994) describes as *political clarity*:

> Political clarity refers to the process by which individuals achieve a deepening awareness of the sociopolitical and economic realities that shape their lives and their capacity to recreate them. In addition, it refers to the process by which individuals come to better understand possible linkages between the macro-level political economic and social variables and subordinate groups' academic performances at the micro-level classroom. It requires links between sociocultural structures and schooling.
>
> (p. 43)

In the studies and lived experiences that shaped my discourse along my journey, there are no epiphanies, only realizations within my journey. The temporality of knowledge, experiences, and emotions are contextual and situational, long-lasting but never the same, always evolving into something else. At times, I wish I could go back, speak with my father at our home, transcend pain, and feel the ocean breeze on my face. It is an intimate, ineffable sensation in which "all meaningful knowledge is contextual knowledge, and much of it is tacit and experiential" (Capra, 1996, p. 70). The scientific method, or more precisely the scientific cycle, as Albert Einstein drew attention to it (Kemeny, 1959), strongly influences my everyday life—inductive reasoning, inferences, and emotions. I realize, however, that induction and science have to be complemented with self-reflection. Only through self-reflection do I become someone in the world able to achieve awareness of my relationship with the world, the dialogical dialectic of becoming. My belief in science is not incongruous with my religiosity; there is a latent actualization with me knowing that "there are wider truths and finer perspectives within which a reconciliation of a deeper religion and a more subtle science will be found" (Whitehead, 1967, p. 185).

I believe when I started teaching, educational theorists would have considered me a traditionalist or essentialist—organizing the learning environment around myself, the teacher, following my educational experience from Argentina. I tried to instill the rigid discipline needed to carry out scientific investigations, and my students' work developed into inquiry-based practices and projects. My survival mode, especially during my first semester, gave way to revival. I was especially proud of using not only my technical content knowledge but, even more so, of teaching in Spanish. I was able to relate and connect to my students. I saw in their eyes that twinkle of awe and enthusiasm that only parents, teachers, and people in love recognize. That love or *agape* effaces strangeness, gives way to shear enjoyment, and commits me to the teaching profession. For a short time, I was sort of frozen within my journey. I saw a disparity between this place and my other classrooms as a student in Argentina. The commitment and demeanor of many of my students were not as I hoped it to be. Was I too harsh? Were my expectations too high? Did my emphasis on achieving objectives obscure the bigger picture? Was my accent too thick?

It is ironic that the United States professes a culture of student success driven by the discourse that everybody can make it if they try hard enough, but this reflects values as blinders that assist in maintaining inequalities. These values and supporting beliefs paint a unique picture of reality. There is a general consensus over values in what makes people in United States uniquely "American." Robin Murphy Williams (1970) highlights values such as achievement (doing well), freedom (feeling there are many options to pursue our goals), activism (trying to master and change situations), progress (improving ourselves and the world around us), efficiency (performing things in a rational and practical way), and materialism (acquiring material objects).[2] These values, overall, are shared by most people to varying degrees. Interestingly, what counts at the end of the day are tangible results in terms of students doing well in standardized tests; the sense of achievement by students in these tests is taken by society as an absolute measure of performance. I might never know for certain the answers to my questions, but like John Dewey (1906) said, "I believe the ultimate solution will be found, not along the line of mechanical devices as to election or non-election, but rather through the more continued and serious study of the individual in both his psychological make-up and his social interactions" (p. 113). I do not believe in a psychological makeup in a deterministic or reductionist sense but in how different factors, in the interplay between individuals and society, mediate certain actions or affect reactions. These factors affect agency, voice and the ability to effect change. The bigger picture requires projecting myself onto the world in which I create and enjoy within the context of my life's pilgrimage. In my discourse, I realize that the process is as relevant as the destination. The destination for me is plural and ideal; it is toward what I wish to be, to become, to reach that authentic self. Authenticity demands living honestly and courageously without relying on excuses and without recurring to groups or institutions for meaning and purpose; the authentic self is possible through the choices we make independent of the values of others. I believe Alfred North Whitehead would sympathize with my pilgrimage, with everyone's pilgrimages, when "all actualities are in a constant process of becoming, their substance can only be known as a function of that process" (Gaztambide-Fernández, 2010, p. 88).

Conclusion

In my mind, I will always return back to memories of that pilgrimage in Argentina. For the four of us friends, it was a symbolic act, a promise fulfilled, and it represented the celebration of our families' ethical commitment. Carlos was 10 years old when his family was kidnapped. The night that it happened, he was sleeping over at Fede's house, my other friend in the pilgrimage. Early that morning we received a call from a neighbor of Carlos's; my dad called Fede's family. That same day, we brought Carlos to our house, and he spent a couple of nights with us. I vividly remember my mom and dad telling us that Carlos's family had to make an emergency out-of-town trip and that he would be spending some time with us and the other two friends' families. Carlos rotated among the three homes for about four months; eventually, he was picked up by his great uncle and moved to another province. There was solidarity in silence, in the secrecy that our families shared. At the time, I did not know what really had happened, and my parents did not tell me until after the democratic elections of 1983. My parents and the other families had the courage to act on a very risky choice—that choice was not easily taken; it was followed in defiance of the military dictatorship discourse. There should be "no areas in which one must be silent. We can talk about everything, and we can give testimony about everything" (Freire, 2005, p. 103). This recount is my testimony; I resuscitate the needed dialogic spirit to reach a new understanding. My father's decision and action to shelter my friend Carlos, his silence, silenced all words.

Sartre (1947) will emphatically propose that "there is no reality except in action" (p. 37). Love in action, then, is my work toward freedom, that elusive freedom—whatever path I choose, that road becomes my reality. In my ethical commitment, I seek fulfillment in realizing wisdom, the wisdom to step outside myself in an act of liberation. But, wisdom takes time, patience, and the refinement of my lived experiences. My ethical commitment finds me today in a "conscientization" effort to show great care and carry out my role—half realized, half submerged. The self-determination I built during my youthful days in Argentina may not be enough to achieve a more just state of affairs in my immediate and global environment. It seems to me that love must be conceptualized in action to reach out to all pilgrims along the way. I must go back to my faith, not necessarily in a religious sense, but faith in trusting myself and allowing my existence to become love in action. Love endures all temporality and pervades all localities.

I am the past of my memories
The future of my hopes
The breath of my son

I am
Ever striving
Ever evolving
Ever gazing to past and new horizons

I am
My father's
My mother's
My own

I am
Me in everyone
And everyone in me
Humanity's past, future and present

I am the past of my memories
The future of my hopes
The breath of my son

Paulo Oemig

Notes

1 Entextualization refers to "the process by mean of which discourses are successively or simultaneously decontextualized and metadiscoursively recontextualized" (Blommaert, 2009, p. 47). Remnants of earlier discourses are translocated onto new contexts. Understanding discourse requires a synchronic and diachronic stance; the field of view projects into the future and reaches into the past.
2 See Baker (2013) for a discussion of core values which supports the currency of Williams's classic work.

References

Althusser, L. (1971). Ideology and ideological state apparatuses. In L. Althusser (Ed.), *Lenin and philosophy and other essays* (pp. 127–188). New York: Monthly Review Press.

Baker, W. E. (2013). *United America: The surprising truth about American values, American identity and the 10 beliefs that a large majority of Americans hold dear.* Canton, MI: David Crumm Media.

Bartolomé, L. (1994). Beyond the methods fetish: Toward a humanizing pedagogy. In G. C. Noya, K. Geismar & G. Nicoleau (Eds.), *Shifting histories: Transforming education for social change* (pp. 39–60). Cambridge, MA: Harvard Educational Review.

Blommaert, J. (2003). Commentary: A sociolinguistics of globalization. *Journal of Sociolinguistics, 7*, 607–623.

Blommaert, J. (2009). *Discourse: A critical introduction.* Cambridge, UK: Cambridge University Press.

Blommaert, J. (2010). *The sociolinguistics of globalization.* Cambridge, UK: Cambridge University Press.

Braudel, F. (2012). Histoires et sciences sociales: La longue durée [History and the social sciences: The long duration]. In F. Braudel (Ed.), *Ecrits sur l'histoire* (pp. 41–83). Paris, France: Flammarion.

Capra, F. (1996). *The web of life: A new scientific understanding of living systems.* New York: Anchor Books.

Dewey, J. (1906). The educational situation. *Journal of Curriculum and Supervision, 17*(2), 104–118.

Edelsky, C. (2006). *With literacy and justice for all: Rethinking the social in language and education* (3rd edition). Mahwah, NJ: Lawrence Erlbaum Associates.

Ellis, C. (2004). *The ethnographic I: A methodological novel about ethnography.* Walnut Creek, CA: AltaMira Press.

Fanon, F. (2008). *Black skin, white masks.* New York: Grove Press.

Freire, P. (1970/1996). *Pedagogy of the oppressed.* New York: Continuum.

Freire, P. (1996). *Pedagogy of the oppressed.* New York: Continuum.

Freire, P. (2005). *Teachers as cultural workers: Letters to those who dare teach.* Boulder, CO: Westview Press.

Gaztambide-Fernández, R. A. (2010). Toward creative solidarity in the "next" moment of curriculum work. In E. Malewski (Ed.), *Curriculum studies handbook—the next moment* (pp. 78–94). New York: Routledge.

Gingrich, A., Ochs, E., & Swedlund, A. (2002). Repertories of timekeeping in anthropology. *Current Anthropology, 43*(Suppl. 4), S3–S4.

Giroux, H. (1981). *Ideology, culture and the process of schooling.* Philadelphia, PA: Temple University Press.

Grant, C. A., & Sleeter, C. E. (2009). *Turning on learning: Five approaches for multicultural teaching plans for race, class, gender and disability* (5th edition). Hoboken, NJ: Wiley & Sons.

Heath, S. B. (1989). Language ideology. In E. Barnouw (Ed.), *International encyclopedia of communications* (pp. 2393–2395). New York: Oxford University Press.

Holland, D., & Lave, J. (2001). *History in person.* Santa Fe, NM: School of the American Research.

Holman Jones, S. (2005). Autoethnography: Making the personal political. In N. Denzin & Y. Lincoln (Eds.), *The Sage handbook of qualitative research* (5th edition) (pp. 441–442). Thousand Oaks, CA: Sage Publications.

Kemeny, J. G. (1959). *A philosopher looks at science.* New York: Van Nostrand.

Luckmann, T. (1991). The constitution of human life in time. In J. Bender & D. E. Wellbery (Eds.), *Chronotypes: The construction of time* (pp. 151–166). Palo Alto, CA: Stanford University Press.

Memmi, A. (1991). *The colonizer and the colonized.* Boston, MA: Beacon Press.

Romero, L. A. (1998). *Breve historia contemporánea de la Argentina.* Buenos Aires, Argentina: Fondo de Cultura Económica.

Ryan, W. M. (1971). *Blaming the victim.* New York: Random House.

Sartre, P. (1947). *Existentialism.* New York: Philosophical Library.

Smith, N. (2002). In the belly of the beast. *Anthropology and Education, 33*(3), 338–349.

Vezzetti, H. (2002). *Pasado y presente: Guerra, dictadura y sociedad en la Argentina.* Buenos Aires, Argentina: Siglo Veintiuno Editores.

Whitehead, A. N. (1967). *Science and the modern world.* New York: The Free Press.

Williams, R. M. (1970). *American society: A sociological interpretation.* New York: Alfred A. Knopf.

Woolard, K. (1998). Introduction: Language ideology as a field of inquiry. In B. B. Schiefflin, K. A. Woolard, & P. V. Kroskrity (Eds.), *Language ideologies: Practice and theory* (pp. 3–47). New York: Palgrave Macmillan.

6 Teaching and Learning in the Diaspora

A Transformative Pedagogy

Donna-Marie Cole-Malott

Port Antonio, Jamaica is considered by many to be one of the most beautiful cities in the world. The high mountains overlooking the ocean are both breathtaking and stunning, the landscape so lush and the land so fertile that it seems, perhaps, that it is a place only found in dreams. However, Port Antonio, like many other beautiful cities around the world has an unfortunate past, a history shrouded under the veil of colonialism, imperialism, and slavery. It seems that not even such an awe-inspiring city could escape the wrath of capitalism and its insatiable thirst for wealth. As a resident of this city I was compelled through education, propaganda, and naivety to believe that there lies a country beyond our shores where the streets were literally paved in gold and anything you wanted was at your disposal. It is for this reason that in 1989 when my mother departed for America, many in our community envied her. She had hit the proverbial lottery, and it seemed the world reminded me of this during those many years that I longed for her. You see, reader, I was a child who lacked the understanding that small cities such as the one I resided in were so completely exploited during slavery and beyond that all that was left was for us was to make our escapes to our imperial motherland. The following summer after my mother's departure, my brother and I, along with some friends, went mango picking. It was a bountiful season, and we took advantage of every opportunity to venture out into the woods for our prize. We considered ourselves expert climbers, so it was to everyone's surprise when I came tumbling two stories out of a tree. I was unconscious. I could hear my brother and our friends beckoning me to awake, but I could not respond. All I could think about at that moment was that I would die and that I would never be able to see America. I hadn't thought of my mother and the fact that I wouldn't see her again; I only thought of America and all her glory. Presenting this memory to you may portray me in a particularly vulnerable light; however, it's important to understand that the mind of a young colonized child is an impressionable landscape and fertile ground where the seeds of inferiority had long since been planted, and for that reason I was compelled to believe the unbelievable and accept the most unreasonable ideas as truths. You see, the wheels in my head had begun turning long before I had an understanding of myself or even the familiar world around me. In his text, *Wheels in the Head* Joel Spring (2008) argues that

> [t]he wheel convinces people that they should willingly submit to the rule of the few who claim to have knowledge of *true goodness* or the *good*. Embedded in this wheel is the acceptance of the idea that some people are better than others as a result of education.
>
> (p. 22)

I present these ideas in order that you can fully understand the challenges that educators face when confronted with young people in the urban context.

At seven years old my education in Jamaica had prepared me to support the authoritarian state. It had conditioned me through religion to accept that society much like the church had a hierarchical structure. America in this sense was God, and my goal even in youth was to worship, respect, and not question her authority. In his text, *We Can't Teach What We Don't Know*, Gary Howard (1999) tells us, "The use of the Bible and Christianity as a tool of oppression has been a particularly sad chapter in the establishment of white dominance." He states that furthermore, "In most countries invaded by Europeans, missionaries became the advanced guard for the 'civilizing' process. Good Christians made compliant subjects" (pp. 40–41). Because religion plays such a central role in the lives of individuals and Jamaicans alike, it's quite difficult for loyal worshipers to separate their devotion to God from the reality that their religion is used as a tool to condition them to be loyal worshipers of the state, slavery being a prime example of religion as a tool of oppression. In this chapter we will explore the many factors that stand in the ways of educators being able to create critical thinkers among the young people they encounter. We will examine the legacy of colonialism and its transformation due to the current needs of capital and how present-day neoliberal policies are essentially a new type if imperialism. We will explore the impact such policies has on poor communities such as the one I worked in, in Brooklyn, New York, and we will try to understand why individuals continue to support the ideologies of the authoritarian state even when the evidence reveals that their interest is in direct contrast with the that of the state. What educators are faced with in schools such as Boys & Girls High School in Bedford Stuyvesant, Brooklyn, where I worked for many years, are young people, much like the example I provided of myself, who have bought into a particular story about themselves and their positions in society. These students struggle with formal education because they realize early on that the American dream does not include them. They resist schooling because they find that schools are not providing them with the tools they need to face the *real world*. Educators tell them that they should be good students, that they must graduate; their only goal should be to get into college. However, when these students look around them, all they see are the staggering unemployment numbers among blacks in their communities and the socioeconomic factors preventing them from accessing a dream that they are told is readily available to them. I will provide concrete examples in this chapter of how I was able to challenge these ideas and create the conditions that transformed these students from passive learners to passionate activists. Educators, I will argue, have one of the toughest jobs in our society, but black educators face an even greater challenge. Throughout our lives we are told that blacks are inadequate, that because of genetic predispositions, we are incapable of being successful; if we are a success, then somehow it's because of some stroke of luck. Not only are we faced with the task of creating thinkers who will change the world, but we are also compelled to confront those ideas about ourselves that are roadblocks in our journey to ideological freedom or change. What we must ask ourselves is this: what will we have to offer our students if we in fact are unable to offer ourselves the truth?

In August of 2012 Jamaica celebrated her 50th year of independence, 50 years, we're told, of freedom from her imperial ties to Great Britain and the queen. There is a tremendous amount of joy among Jamaicans, a sense of pride, that their destinies are in their own hands; however, there are those among us that recognize that her independence is in vane. We know without question that Jamaica and her neighbor Trinidad and the Bahamas, who also celebrated independence this year, could never be free from their ideological, philosophical, and economical ties with the West; the relationship between labor and capital would never allow this. We recognize that a transformation has occurred in the needs of capital. Although there is a clear recognition that on paper they are free, we know with all certainty that they are still at the mercy of the authoritarian state, specifically, the International Monetary Fund and the World Bank. These countries and many like them are forever indebted to the West, with land and property in these former colonies owned by Westerners. The minds of individuals born in these nations are also owned by the West; individuals from the third world such as the aforementioned countries are not even free to travel to the countries that once controlled them for centuries, and yet the celebration continues. What this reveals to the reader is that if people can believe that they are free in spite of the overwhelming evidence that reveals otherwise, then they are compelled to believe anything. Joel Spring (2008) says of the authoritarian state, that history

> [i]s written so that the historical images causes citizens to believe in the past glory and rightness of the state and its rulers. Furthermore historical, instruction aids in the development of patriotism and a willingness to sacrifice for the common good. . . . The authoritarian state uses the educational system to place people in specific vocations and social roles. Through the myth of the metals, students are taught to accept their assigned social positions and that any difference between social classes are good and just.
>
> (p. 23)

Education once again plays a central role in hegemonizing the natives to believe that all that is wrong in their world, with their countries, and their lives are a direct result of their actions. It convinces them that if they work just a little harder, then maybe somehow, someday, they will be able to change their socioeconomic conditions. Dear reader, Boys and Girls High School in Brooklyn, New York, is on the front lines of an ideological war. Within this edifice are students from such countries. These students come to us, with a diabolical belief that they are free in every sense of the word. However, it is the job of the educator to show these young people that freedom of the mind means freedom to construct your own thoughts and ideas. The challenge, therefore, is getting them to see for themselves that the dominant paradigm is quite powerful and persuasive and that their young minds present the perfect bed of soil for irrational and unreasonable ideas to grow into fully accepted ideologies.

Consequently as Jamaica celebrates her 50th year of *freedom*, I am apt to think of my youth and the young people I have encountered as an educator who have internalized the idea that their one role in this life is to serve the capitalist state. When they reflect on their existence, all they think of is "How will I serve the powers that be?" rather than "How can I change this system in order that my needs and the needs of my community and the world are also represented?" As Jamaicans proudly display flags and come together to celebrate, educators once again pass up a significant teachable moment. Drawing from the histories of people who have resisted a relationship with capital countries, such as Haiti at the end of the 19th-century and present-day Cuba, it is clear that true freedom comes with consequences and repercussions. Aime Cesaire (1972) in his text, *Discourse on Colonialism*, contends that

> no one colonizes innocently, that no one colonizes with impunity either; that a nation which colonizes, that a civilization which justifies colonization—and therefore force—is already a sick civilization, a civilization which is morally diseased, which irresistibly, progressing from one consequence to another, one denial to another, calls for its Hitler, I mean its punishment.
>
> (p. 39)

Accordingly, as my fellow countrymen and women raise their flags in celebration, I bring my flag to half-staff to mourn the lives of my ancestors and to lament over the current conditions of despair all brought on by colonialism and a dangerous relationship with capitalism. What makes Cesaire's statement such an important part of the dialogue is the recognition that due to the volatile nature of colonialism, everyone involved in this relationship suffers consequences. For example, if we were to visit the third world, we would be able to see firsthand the immediate destruction brought on by hundreds of years of this unsettling relationship with the West. Schools are in disrepair, the infrastructure hasn't been updated since the early days of colonialism, natives are living in small shantytowns, and food is in short supply; we accept this because it's the third world, and yet when we look at communities across America, in neighborhoods such as Bedford Stuyvesant, we are faced with a similar reality. The lesson is immediate, the teachable moment upon us. We must recognize that our role as educators is to teach for a more just society and to equip learners with the tools necessary to confront, tackle, and create change.

My first year as a teacher was filled with both passion and defeat. I wasn't sure what to expect, and yet by the time my first year had come to an end, I knew that if I intended to continue down this career path that something drastic needed to change. Although I was teaching at the high school level, my students seemed highly unprepared and disinterested in what they were learning. It appeared that for most of the year, they were either indifferent or distracted by the simplest things. I reflected quite a bit that year and questioned my position as an educator. I thought certainly that if I intended to have a better second year, then I must take the necessary actions to make this possible. The summer following the end of the school year, I participated in a literacy workshop designed to aide teachers in improving their skills and also provide them with literature that students would be able to relate to. Consequently, the university that created the curriculum included stories about gangs, drugs, broken homes, and young promiscuous teenagers living on the margins of society. Reader, I was compelled to accept this packet presented to me just as I had accepted and internalized the many lies concerning my race and my position in society. It is for this reason that when I began sharing these stories with my students, I continued to complain that it seemed nothing could get through to them. I was unable to see that I was a contributor. I was what Franz Fanon (1963) called the "Native Intellectual," a tool of the state used to ensure that natives are fed the ideologies of the elite few, by a familiar face, someone from their community and possibly even their home country. In his book, *Wretched of the Earth*, Franz Fanon (1963) writes,

> Colonialism is not satisfied merely with holding a people in its grips and emptying the natives brains of all form and content. By a kind of perverted logic, it turns to the past of the oppressed people, and distorts, disfigures and destroys it.

(p. 210)

Mid semester after months of reading and analyzing, one of my students raised his hand and posed a question to me. He asked, although I can't remember verbatim, "Ms., why do all the stories we read have to be about such negative stuff concerning blacks?" I was ashamed. I had for the first time in my career realized that each week in my classes, I was reinforcing those very stereotypes that I had vowed to challenge when I became a teacher. The unfortunate thing was that I didn't realize it. Hidden within the curriculum were all the ingredients necessary to cripple, alienate, marginalize, and destroy. There it was right in front of me, and I didn't even see it. How could I then challenge these young people to be thinkers, activists, and leaders if I struggled with these concepts and ideas myself?

In his essay "The Negro Artist and the Racial Mountain," Langston Hughes (Hughes, 1926) says of the youth in America, that

> [s]tanding in the way of any true Negro art in America is this urge within the race toward whiteness, the desire to pour racial individuality into the mold of American standardization, and to be as little Negro and as much American as possible.
>
> (p. 1282)

Although written in 1926, this essay is still as relevant today as it was then. It still rings true particularly because the education urban students of color receive in classrooms toady, in spite of who is teaching it to them, is an education that is not representative of who they are. The task therefore is for blacks and other minority groups to present a representation of themselves and their social reality to students that is more revealing than what comes in a prepackaged curriculum. It is to expose them to the reality of other groups of disadvantaged peoples in their country and in the world and to show them that when they ignore injustices committed against others, they inevitably leave the door open for injustices to be committed against themselves. It is our job not just to look at today and the immediate problems ahead of us but to reflect on the past and fight the demons of inferiority that are metaphoric mountains standing in the way of us making progress. We must ask ourselves as we educate: Is this education even relevant, and what is it that I want to teach for and teach against? What follows will be concrete examples for the reader to see how such teachings are possible and what this might look like in practice.

Let us for a moment address the power of hegemony. In 2010 a debate erupted in neighborhoods across New York City as to whether or not it would be appropriate for a mosque to be constructed in close proximity to ground zero. Once again, across the city, on the train ride to work, on a bus, within the school building, there arose a tension and feelings of mistrust, and much like the months and early years after 9/11, there was great anti-Muslim sentiment. My Muslim students expressed fear and contempt for those who believed that all Muslims were terrorists. Indeed, what I was faced with was a significant teachable moment. As an English teacher and the head of the Film and Documentary Club in the school, I stepped beyond the confines of the curriculum to address this important issue. When I extended my film campaign to the classroom setting, students were initially resistant, but it became an integral part of us being able to reflect on our ideas and misunderstandings concerning issues we didn't understand. We began by reading articles; we looked at the perspectives presented by the media and juxtaposed them with student perspective, and often what was found was a direct correlation between the reporting of the media and student beliefs. We debated, discussed, and addressed the roots of our ideologies. You see, reader, my students believed that Islam is a religion centered on terrorism. They believed that Muslims hated America (with some exceptions of course), and they believed that Islam is a religion of oppression and violence. My role, as I saw it, wasn't to tell them that these ideas weren't true but rather to equip them to with the skill necessary to decide what in fact constituted truth. In his book, *Education for a Critical Consciousness*, Paulo Freire (2010) points out, "The important thing is to help men (and nations) help themselves, to place them in consciously critical confrontation with their problems, to make them agents of their own recuperation." He goes on to say that for once-subjugated individuals to create change in the societies they live in, there has to be

> a form of education enabling the people to reflect on themselves, their responsibilities, and their role in the new cultural climate—indeed to reflect on their very power of reflection. The resulting development of this power would mean an increased capacity for choice.
>
> (p. 12)

What Freire discusses here rang true for my students and the reality we were confronting. Once students were able to see for themselves the danger of silence, many among them began to find their voices.

The curriculum is confining, and to escape the confine of the status quo, you must be willing to take a risk, to make learning real and relevant. So as we continued the debate concerning the construction of the mosque, opportunities presented themselves for students to visit mosques across New York City and even within their communities. Within the school the tension continued to mount, the rhetoric became dangerous, and it became even more important for students to break up in different groups, each tasked with either filming, interviewing, or discussing but all equipped with journals for the important task of reflecting. There were many firsts as we worked on this project, and visiting a mosque was one of them. Religious leaders opened their doors to students to answer any inquiries they had. They were for the first time face-to-face with some of the same people they feared or lived in suspicion of. Ladies and gentlemen, we had embarked on quite an important mission—a mission centered on truth. Reader, in my first and second years as a teacher, I wasn't equipped to lead my students out of Plato's metaphoric cave, for I was in that cave myself. However, with a new sense of urgency upon me, I intended to provide them with the skills to think critically, to develop their own ideologies, and to uncover truths. It is for that reason that on 9/11 of 2010, armed with our cameras, we attended the rallies in lower Manhattan as observers, interviewers, and researchers. We interviewed both people who supported the mosque and those who loathed the idea of it being constructed. The tension was palpable, the debates heated, the racial rhetoric intimidating and even scary. Face-to-face with this active learning experience, students were moved, many at a loss for words. There were only a few who were able to see these rallies firsthand, but the others were able to examine the data we collected. The educator's job is filled with much complexity, for as we teach we also learn. It would've been easy to stay in my classroom and talk about a situation that was happening in the community, but I recognized that the classroom extends beyond the confines of the school building. I recognized that learning and engaging learners meant that I had to challenge them to break free of their hegemonic shackles.

This ever-changing relationship between labor and capital places the educator in one of the most important roles of her life. She has to decide (if she is at all aware that such a relationship exists) if she will educate students to serve the current needs of the capitalist state or if she will educate them to change the world. All eyes are on her, the state visits her school regularly to hold her principal accountable, and her supervisors provide her with workshops to emphasize the importance of the Common Core Standards. She is told that she cannot deviate from the curriculum; she is reminded often that her job is on the line. Her colleagues keep a watchful eye on her because they recognize that supporting the state is a group effort; they cannot do it alone. They need her; however, she is conflicted. Does she comply, or does she break free? Such is the challenge of the conscious educator. Peter McLaren (1998), in his text, *Life in Schools: An Introduction to Critical Pedagogy in the Foundations of Education*, tells us,

> Absent from the discourse is any recognition of the importance of viewing schools as sites for social transformation and emancipation, as places where students are educated not only to be critical thinkers, but also to view the world as a place where their actions might make a difference.
>
> (p. 6)

The mountain stands before the educator. The dominant paradigm is ubiquitous and the rhetoric compelling. I confront these ideas here, for it's important to understand the peculiar situation standing in the way of educators such as myself being able to teach for critical consciousness. When I was willing to present condescending ideas to my African American, black and minority students, I was praised for my ability to construct lessons that centered on the lives of students. However, when I presented Edwidge Danticat's and Langston Hughes's work to my students, I was scolded for deviating from the recommended readings listed within the curriculum. My initial response was an overwhelming sense of disappointment. I was disappointed that this administrator was so blinded by her devotion to the dominant paradigm that not only was she willing to remain in Plato's metaphoric cave, but she was compelled to keep the students in there with her. McLaren (1998) argues, "Without a critical pedagogy, (students and I would argue educators as well) they lack the analytical skills both to analyze their location within the social order and to alter the conditions of their oppression" (p. 205).

A critical perspective is necessary if we intend on transforming and challenging dominant ideologies. Based on the current economic and political climate, it seems that such perspective is urgently needed.

Realizing that race is a contributing element which affects the position of the black man and other marginalized groups in America, we continually challenge this racist system, hoping to convince those who support racism that they should view us as "equals," an ideological battle we are not apt to win. As we put all of our efforts and focus into confronting racial issues, we prevent ourselves from seeing the real issue at hand—the issue of class. In his book, *Critical Race Theory and Education*, Mike Cole (2009) states,

> In the United States while it is the case that the number of black people living below the poverty line is some three times that of whites, this still leaves over 16 million 'white but not hispanic' people living in poverty in the United States. This is indicative of a society predicated on racialized capitalism, rather than indicative of a white supremacist society.
>
> (p. 27)

The challenge therefore, is not so much inspiring students to focus on race as the only reason for the socioeconomic conditions they face in their communities but rather getting them to see that the capitalist state is nondiscriminatory; it destroys white communities as much as it does any other poor community in this country. It divides us, on the merit of race, by convincing poor whites that they are better off, and in spite of how bad things are for them, it's much better than the conditions faced by people of color. We do not allow ourselves to mobilize, or to connect, because we are unable to see that our interests are one in the same. All whites see is our color, and all that we see is their privilege. In their book *The Destructive Path of Neoliberalism: An International Examination of Urban Education*, Bradley Porfilio and Curry Malott (2008) argue that neoliberal policies and practices in the United States

> have undermined the ability of workers to unionize, reduce worker benefits, butted social programs and entitlements for the impoverished and elderly, intensified the work day, and fueled mass incarceration of minoritized population, while concomitantly aiding and abetting the country's richest families in their quest to concentrate their wealth and power.
>
> (xiiv)

Understanding what neoliberalism is and how it affects all people puts us in a position of strength. It gives new meaning to an old issue. What it essentially does is put the responsibility of change on the individual (collectively) rather than on the system. It makes it more about the relationship between race and capitalism rather that treating these things as if they are separate entities. Cole (2009) says of capitalism,

> Capitalism from a Marxist perspective by definition, a system in which a majority (the capitalist class) exploits the minority (the working class) by extracting surplus value from their labor power. It is a system without morality and without shame. It is a system of intense and relentless exploitation.
>
> (p. 95)

It's essential to recognize that class is the real culprit; the challenge is getting others to recognize this as well.

McLaren (1998) reminds us, "We must always problematize the term 'race' and see it as an ideological or social construction produced within the historical and geopolitical specificity of its explanatory deployment and as an artifact of the social science literature itself" (p. 238). Indeed, in acknowledging his argument, we also know that in our present neoliberal societies, blackness is not only a representation of skin color but a determining factor of social, economic, and political conditions. Those born white immediately have an advantage; they are not born burdened with the reality of racism. When they open their history books, they feel a (false) sense of pride and patriotism for all their ancestors have accomplished. They can trace their ancestry back to the early days of America's emancipation from Britain (although their very ancestors could possibly have been indentured servants, or for new immigrants, and their history may be rooted in the ugly legacy of European Imperialism). They unfortunately see their history as different and unrelated to the history of the marginalized groups of our society. Juxtapose that with their black counterparts, who when faced with the reality of their history, are left in a constant state of melancholy. Although we fight to reject it, deep within our consciousness is that voice, that reminder that tells us that we could never be like them, we could never have what they have, and they are better than us. We fight to reject these ideas, but yet as we examine the world, we see that societies are structured to serve their needs, to benefit them, and to keep us on the margins. Daily we are confronted with the reality of whiteness, the ideological and physical reality. We struggle to accept the things about ourselves that are inherently African. When we look at the representation of what society deems culturally acceptable, nowhere in that picture do we find ourselves. Our dialect, our ability to code switch, our broken forms of the European languages we now own are constant reminders of our imperfections. Dear reader, this is the reality that black educators face, that minority students in the urban context face.

They are thirsty for self-acceptance, they are hungry for justice, and yet their education pacifies them; it reassures them that they could one day, be as white as they want if they are compliant and passive. It assures them that they can have access to the white world if they study hard enough, work hard enough, and if they strengthen their belief in God. For they are told that anything is possible in America! In his text, *Black Skin White Mask* (1967), Frantz Fanon holds that

> [t]here is a fact: White men consider themselves superior to Black men. There is another fact: Black men want to prove to white men, at all cost, the richness of their thought, the equal value of intellect. How do we extricate ourselves? . . . However painful it may be for me to accept this conclusion, I am obliged to state it: For the Black man there is only one destiny. And it is white.
>
> (p. 10)

As an ideology, whiteness is powerful. It convinces whites to accept society as is, and it convinces blacks that they are much better off today than they ever were at any other time in American history. In encourages complacency and perhaps worse than that—apathy.

Teaching in a predominantly African American and Caribbean black school puts an additional set of responsibilities on the educator. The cultural differences among students are so unique and prominent that students have a tendency to segregate into cultural subgroups. Such groups entertain stereotypes about each other that come from a highly racialized society. American students are believed to be lazy, unambitious people who survive on the welfare system, while the aforementioned Muslim students are accused of having some affiliation with terrorism. The misunderstandings are vast; however, no other group suffers more from the ignorance of others than our Haitian students. They carry the weight of an entire nation on their shoulders; for them stereotypes are their reality, and they live under constant suspicion that other students might discover their nationality. But on January 11, 2010, they could no longer hide. Their tears gave them away; the long hugs they shared with one another told their peers that they were from the first truly independent black nation. When they cried out in Creole, we didn't understand them but didn't need to. The language of pain spoke to us, and our empathy was overwhelming. What the earthquake of 2010 did was bring a divided school and people together. A horrible tragedy had destroyed lives, families, and nearly an entire country. There was scarcely a Haitian student or staff member who didn't suffer a loss. However, the greatest tragedy of the 2010 earthquake was the belief students held that this had happened to Haitians because they made a pact with the devil to ensure their freedom. They cursed God for their constant struggles. They wondered and asked constantly, "Why us? What have we done to deserve all that has happened to us?" Reader, understand when I tell you that there was scarcely a day that I wasn't brought to tears by the heartbreak suffered by my students. For weeks some of them waited for word concerning whether or not a father, a mother, an uncle, or a friend, had survived. In a few cases, entire families were lost, and yet students blamed themselves. Once again I was faced with the challenge of decolonizing the minds of these young people. However, this time the challenge was even more overwhelming, for how was I to convince them that it was their responsibility to challenge the system of globalization and exploitation in order that their fellow countrymen and women would have a chance in this world? What I was telling them seemed quite uncertain, for the only certainty they knew was that fighting the system of oppression caused them to be cursed by God. They believed that because their fellow countrymen and women embraced Voodou as a religious practice, they further deserved all that had befallen them. The system of colonization had taught these young people to hate everything African, and for a nation so much more African than any other country outside of the continent, it meant hating themselves. They were conditioned to accept the notion that fighting oppression and injustices left them cursed. Reader, they resented the efforts of their national heroes; they like other peoples from colonized nations believed that white people had come to civilize them, and because they rejected it, they would be forever damned. Once again, I was ready to challenge their ideologies and did so successfully with the help of Haitian artists, musicians, historians, photographers, respected Voodou leaders, and their peers. The educator in the urban context is always confronted with obstacles, and it is our responsibility to take on those challenges head-on, especially when those challenges threaten to create apathy among our students.

In his text *The Black Jacobins: Toussaint L'Ouverture and the San Domingo Revolution*, C.L.R. James (1989) says of the revolution in San Domingo (Haiti) that

> [t]he slaves destroyed tirelessly. . . . [T]hey were seeking their salvation in the most obvious way, the destruction of what they knew was the cause of their sufferings; and if they destroyed much it was because they had suffered much. They knew that as long as these plantations stood their lot would be to labour on them until they dropped. The only thing left was to destroy them. From their masters they had known rape, torture, degradation, and, at the slightest provocation, death. They returned in kind. For two centuries the higher civilization had shown them that power was used for wrecking your will on those whom you controlled. Now that they held power they did as they had been taught. . . . The cruelties of property and privilege are always more ferocious than the revenges of poverty and oppression. For the one aims at perpetuating resented injustices, the other is merely a momentary passion appeased.

> (pp. 88–89)

With such an inspiring history of fighting oppression, I was sad that my students weren't aware of this history. They were not aware that of all nations that held slaves, those in Haiti would not be deterred. Every opportunity they were afforded was an opportunity to plot against oppression. Their efforts were relentless. When they tried and failed, they merely tried again, this time with lessons learned from past revolts. But colonization like Fanon told us earlier in this chapter is not merely satisfied with destroying the people but also their history. Haiti, because of her brave people and their courage, was used as an example throughout history to show other black nations that revolting against the worst kinds of oppression would lead to the worst kinds of consequences. Unable to sustain herself after her emancipation, Haiti has become one of the poorest countries in the Western hemisphere. So powerful were the consequences that it took more than a century for other countries once ruled by imperial powers to gain their "independence." Let us for a moment consider the facts presented. Throughout schools, even when I first came to America in the early 1990s, one of the first things you learned about Haiti was that her people were evil devil worshipers who would use their powers on you if you interfered with them. You learned that they had AIDS, and somehow befriending a Haitian would also give you the disease. You learned to fear Haitians and to scorn them because of their abject poverty. You never once learned of the courageous Africans who were punished for standing up against the evils of colonialism and the nefarious efforts to capitalize on the their labor power. Although students were never told this, I had intended to present this information to them. I felt a sense of responsibility to my students who were not only mourning for their families but a nation.

Together with local organizations we worked tirelessly to create a significant amount of resources for teachers who wanted to incorporate the story of the Haitian people in their curriculums. We created resources for nearly every subject area, for there should be no excuse for why this information wasn't taught. We recruited the most informed and conscious individuals from the community to work with our students. Many of them brought with them a representation of Haiti that we were completely unfamiliar with. Photographer Regine Romaine was one such individual. She brought to students a visual representation of Haiti that appealed to a sense of familiarity within all of us: a place of love, beauty, and resilience. Her photography was profound; students were moved. What she aimed to challenge were those images we became so familiar with: kids in the streets with no parents, naked children, starving children, the sick and dying. She confronted those images thrown at us by the mass media and was able to show us a people much like the people within our own communities who were facing injustices and dealing with them in the ways that they knew best. With my guidance, students created a documentary film that included a perspective about Haiti that they had never heard. It included student voices and voices from those within the community who had lived in New York City during the

1980s and early 1990s, when stereotypes perpetuated against Haitians had a tendency to create deeper wounds. Students were able to reflect and speak openly for the first time about what was happening within their families, their lives, and their hearts. Drawing from the very history of the people who liberated Haiti and inspired revolts around the world, I reminded students of their strength, of the resilience of their people, and we spoke of the millions who had died in Haiti during her fight for freedom. We talked about the millions who were killed in the name of Christianity long before Africans were brought to the island as a source of labor power. I reminded them that the earthquake was a natural disaster that with the right infrastructure, hundreds and thousands of lives could've been saved. But more importantly I reminded them that present-day Haiti is no accident, and drawing from the revolutionary spirit of their ancestors, it is their responsibility to help Haiti finds her new destiny. C.L.R. James (1989) presents an account written by Hilliard d'Auberteuil, which was banned shortly after it was written in 1784, relating to his interactions with the early Africans brought to Haiti. James (1989) notes,

> One has to hear with what warmth and what volubility, and at the same time with what precision of ideas and accuracy of judgment, this creature, heavy with taciturn all day, now squatting before his fire, tells stories, talks, gesticulates, argues, passes opinions, approves or condemns both his mater and everyone who surrounds him. *It was this intelligence that refused to be crushed, these latent possibilities, that frightened the colonist, as it frightens the whites in Africa to-day.* No species of men has more intelligence.
>
> (p. 19)

Such is the history I needed my students and colleagues to be familiar with— a history, fit to inspire, not to scorn, condemn, or manipulate in an effort to convince young people that their history is only relevant if they somehow it has to do with white liberation.

The urban school is a place of possibilities. It is a place where if given the chance, it would create the Toussaint L' Ouvertures, Che Guevaras, and Huey P. Newtons of our day. But the consciousness for such possibilities does not exist. If we teach, it is to support the current status quo. The urban school does not aim to create visionaries. They do not teach a history to inspire; they merely teach us a distorted history of ourselves. The urban school does not encourage comradery with the rural or suburban schools. The urban school of today is arguably as segregated as it was prior to *Brown v. Board of Education* (1954). The question arises: How can we teach critical-thinking skills to students who have internalized their very oppression? The answer is that we push, challenge, present ideas, and encourage student to be researchers rather than passive learners. We must make them responsible for their learning. If we are unable to penetrate their minds, then perhaps we should try another approach. We should recognize that we have many different types of learners within our classrooms and try to appeal to them in ways that they would understand. For what we will find, as I have found working at Boys and Girls High School in Brooklyn, New York, is that once they know just a little, they want to know so much more. Once awakened to the possibilities that exist, they no longer want to play around in the classroom; they are somehow more serious and pensive than they had ever been. Frerie (2010) tell us in his text,

> As a people emerge into a state of awareness, they discover that the elite regard them with contempt; in reaction they tend whenever possible to respond aggressively. The elite in turn, frightened at the threat to the legitimacy of their power, attempt by force or by paternalism to silence and domesticate the masses; they try to impede the process of popular emergence.
>
> (p. 29)

Nevertheless, in spite of the obstacles that they will face as they challenge dominant ideologies and paradigms, these students must take on these challenges. They must consider that throughout history, if change was desired, then it had to be fought for.

After falling out of that tree over 20 years ago, I did finally make it to America. Reader, I had arrived, but to what? I was taken away from all that made sense to me, and I decided that if I wanted to become an American, I had to assimilate. I had to reject everything about me and become like everyone else. I would walk through those Brooklyn neighborhoods, trying tirelessly to change my accent, to reject my culture, and to accept my new fate as an American. Such is the reality for so many immigrant students within urban classrooms across America. These young people are afraid of the possibilities of self-acceptance; they are afraid of their skin color, their hair texture, their language, and their cultural history. It is the responsibility of both black and white educators to educate themselves and their students concerning the true causes of such complexes—capitalism. Inspired by the billionaires and millionaires of the world or the "one percent," students dream that one day they too can accumulate such wealth. Driven by delusions of grandeur, these young people don't realize that the wealth of the people they idolize comes at the expense of people like themselves. Within classrooms across America, we are faced with such misunderstanding. If the educator is informed, then he or she can teach for a more rational understanding of society; if perhaps the educator is also passive and uniformed, then we run the risk of further perpetuating these false ideologies among young people.

Indeed, the would-be educator faces a mountain of obstacles as they aim to create critical thinkers among the young people they encounter daily. However, the greatest challenge they may actually face is themselves. We can argue that great leaders are born, but for those among us who are placed in leadership roles, we must assert ourselves and consider that we have one of the most important jobs in society. We can teach to perpetuate the current injustices within our society, or we can educate students to create change and challenge injustices wherever they encounter them. Neoliberalism, or the commodification of everything in society, has also placed a price on a new generation of young people. What they and also those who educate them have to decide is if they will support a system that does not support them, or if they, like the many inspiring revolutionaries of our time, will fight to create a more just system.

References

Bartilow, H. A. (1997). *The debt dilemma: IMF negotiations in Jamaica, Grenada and Guyana*. Caribbean.

Césaire, A. (1972). *Discourse on colonialism*. New York: Monthly Review Press, Inc.

Césaire, A. (2001). *Discourse on colonialism*. (J. Pinkham, Trans.). New York: Monthly Review Press.

Cole, M. (2009). *Critical race theory and education: A Marxist response*. New York: Palgrave Macmillan, Inc.

Cole, M. (2012). Critical race theory in education, Marxism and abstract racial domination. *British Journal of Sociology of Education, 33*(2), 167–183.

Fanon, F. (1963). *Wretched of the Earth*. New York: Grove Press, Inc.

Fanon, F. (1967). *Black skin white masks*. New York: Grove Press, Inc.

Freire, P. (2010). *Education for critical consciousness*. New York: Continuum, Inc.

Gates, Mckay. (1997). *The Norton anthology African American litera*ture. New York: W.W. Norton & Company, Inc.

Howard, G. (1999). *We can't teach what we don't know*. New York: Teachers College Press, Inc.

Howard, G. R. (2006). *We can't teach what we don't know: White teachers, multiracial schools*. Teachers College Press.

Hughes, L. (1926). "The Negro Artist and the Racial Mountain." *The collected works of Langston Hughes, 9*, 31–36.

James, C. L. R. (1989). *The black Jacobins: Toussaint L'Ouverture and the San Domingo revolution*. New York: Vintage Books, Inc.

McLaren, P. (2015). *Life in schools: An introduction to critical pedagogy in the foundations of education*. Routledge.

Porfilio, B. (Ed.). (2008). *The destructive path of neoliberalism: an international examination of education*. Rotterdam: Sense Publ.

Porfilio, B., & Malott, C. (2008). *The destructive path of neoliberalism: An international examination of urban education*. Rotterdam, The Netherlands: Sense Publishing.

Spring, J. H. (2008). *Wheels in the head: Educational philosophies of authority, freedom, and culture from Confucianism to human rights*. Routledge.

7 The Learner, the Teacher, and the Classroom Community

Building Safe Spaces for Emotional Sharing

Karen R. Trujillo

Introduction

During 2008 my husband and I had numerous decisions to make with regard to our future. As owners of a residential real estate brokerage, the bulk of our conversations centered on financial decisions that would not only affect me as the qualifying broker but also the associate brokers working in our office. My husband's position as a lieutenant for our city fire department provided our family with the consistent financial support needed to cover household overhead, but little was left to supplement a second income when commissions ceased. Needless to say, I worked hard to avoid business discussions with my husband during that time as I knew that we would eventually need to consider merging our boutique brokerage with another larger brokerage or entertain closing our doors.

During a weekend drive my husband approached me with the request that I return to school during the lull in real estate activity. College was no longer an experience I considered for myself as our oldest son was nearing his senior year of high school. "I can't compete," I said, as if my declaration would end the conversation. One of my least fond memories of college from my teenage years was the nontraditional student who discounted the knowledge of younger undergraduates based on their years of life experience and workplace know-how. I also noticed that many of the older students I encountered as a teen did not participate in conversations or interact with fellow students until near the end of the semester unless forced to do so during activities. The last thing I wanted was to be the nontraditional student who would feel out of touch with her peers and removed from the classroom community.

After a long discussion, my husband and I acknowledged that our future depended upon earning degrees. Thus, we agreed to register for the spring semester that would begin weeks from our decision. Begrudgingly, I was willing to give college a try many years after having last been enrolled, but feared that I would never "fit in" as I assumed I would be much older than most of the students in my classes.

Background

The global economic downturn has resulted in an increased number of nontraditional students entering or reentering the university, changing the face of the undergraduate population. This change has called for the necessity of instructors to revisit the ways in which discussions are facilitated as diverse classroom communities engage in both face-to-face and online settings. Upon entry into the academy, this change has also altered the need for the student to "invent the university," in Donald Bartholomae's terms, as the students inventing the university are doing so from variety of levels of life experience as well as cognitive and ethical development (1986, p. 4). Pressure is placed upon the teacher and classroom community to manage the diverse dynamics of the age groups represented in classes in addition to the numerous intersectionalities important to each classroom community member. While I recognize that this chapter does not begin the discussion of the regulation of emotion for nontraditional students, I align this discussion with CDA, considering the social injustices suffered by the nontraditional student as a result of power dynamics necessitating negotiation by the professor. This chapter calls attention to the nontraditional student's monitoring emotional responses to classroom content and the ways in which the learners within the class and the teacher can work toward removing the need for this monitoring.

Donald Bartholomae's (1986) seminal essay "Inventing the University" served as a stepping-off point into my considerations of the ways in which I reinvented the university for myself. As a woman in her early 30s initially reenrolled in courses across the disciplines, I eventually found my home in the Departments of English and Women's Studies where "writing pedagogy is as much bound to emotional literacy as it is to critical literacy" (Wenger, 2011, p. 45). Within such learning communities, emotion is often the product of discussion and close readings as many of the teachers work against the theoretical framework being resisted is that which views "emotion as individualized, internally located, and privately experienced" as discussed by Shari Stenberg (2011 in "Teaching and (Re) Learning the Rhetoric of Emotion."

In "Teaching and (Re) Learning the Rhetoric of Emotion," Shari Stenberg (2011) refers to Gloria Anzaldua, Audre Lorde, and Hillary Clinton as women who have resisted the need to regulate public emotion and have been taken to task for doing so. As a way of avoiding this situation in the classroom, Stenberg asks that when students attend to these sort of texts, they be given a vocabulary to define the rhetoric of emotion. These emotions spoken of by Stenberg are called *outlaw emotions* and are listed as feelings such as anger and resentment. When expressed publicly, these emotions are said to "challenge cultural hegemony and open avenues for social change" (p. 350, 2011), thus making it more important to bring emotion from the private into the public. Further, I recognize that "to claim that a group such as workers, women, or students is oppressed and in need of liberation is to assume a collective experience among members within the group" (Sather, 2007). I speak only in this instance of my own feelings of limitation on emotional oppression based on assumed feminized roles. It is important at this point that I recognize that "to claim that a group such as workers, women, or students is oppressed and in need of liberation is to assume a collective experience among members within the group" (Cook-Sather, 2007). Thus, this chapter includes a reflection of my own feelings of limitation and emotional oppression as I cannot ignore my personal narrative or positionality or the difficulties I encountered as a student in need of assistance to be retained in the university system.

Student Retention

Retention & Resistance: Writing Instruction and Students Who Leave by Pegeen Reichert Powell identifies varying issues centered on student retention. Within her text, Powell recognizes that there is not one single thing that universities can do to reduce attrition rates, as I noted in this chapter; there are numerous issues faced by students, in particular those centered on the ability to express one's self emotionally. Powell notes that the discourse on retention has put the student at the forefront of successes and failures based on the prior work by Vincent Tinto (2014, p. 22). Attending to Tinto's prior approach to student retention, Powell asks that the administration and faculty focus on the students who are enrolled at present rather than working to try to assure that they do not leave. In addition, the author presents the knowledge that the first-year composition course is likely one of the only factors all students will have in common regardless of whether or not they obtain a degree. The first-year composition course is oftentimes attended largely by traditional students, thus creating a space of discomfort for the nontraditional student. A potential resource for lessening this discomfort, Powell suggests, is that the first-year composition classroom become a space in which students are taught to write to present interests and relevant topics rather than preparing them to transfer learning to the next courses leading to graduation.

In this chapter, I posit that the classroom community is shaped by the ways in which the teacher and peers respond to emotional expression in the classroom as well as by the ways in which the teacher works toward making the course content pertinent to "real-world" issues, as is suggested by Powell. After experiencing retention efforts at her home university, Powell (2014, p. 140) noted that collecting data, modifying faculty and staff behaviors, and creating social activities for students were not the answer to retaining students. Powell recognized that outside circumstances, which extend beyond the student's life within the academy, caused them to either drop out of school, transfer, or leave and then return to school. This led her to acknowledge that the curriculum in the first-year composition class should not be geared toward the students' futures once having obtained a degree but to the student that sits in the seat, fully knowing that the student may or may not remain in college and, if leaving, may or may not return. Important to these issues also are the needs that nontraditional students face when response to course content is imperative to finding their place among the classroom community, a place in which they are oftentimes on the margins of the dominant voices being shared in the classroom space.

Similar to the student with the "Clay Model," as described by Donald Bartholomae, "the problem of audience becomes enormously complicated" (1986, p. 407). The relationship between the classroom community and the reentering student becomes problematic as age serves as a separator between the student who is "inventing the university" for the first time and the student who is "reinventing," or "inventing" from a nontraditional experience. The teacher as audience also contributes to the situation as oftentimes faculty are of similar age to the nontraditional student, and complicating this issue is also the role of the female nontraditional student and ascribed expectations that this student is likely to express emotions differently or more often than her nontraditional male counterparts.

Emotion and the Female

For the sake of this chapter, I will draw on the definition of emotion from Lyn Worsham's, "Going Postal: Pedagogic Violence and the Schooling of Emotion," as "the tight braid of affect and judgment socially and historically constructed and bodily lived, through which the symbolic takes hold of and binds the individual in complex and contradictory ways, to the social order and its structure of meanings" (1998, p. 216). An additional definition is provided by Christy Wenger (2011) in her essay, " 'Feeling Lore': The Problem of Emotion of Practice and Teaching," during which Wenger calls upon Patricia Harkin's (1991) reference to "emotion as reason's inferior (female mate)." The academy oftentimes does not know how to quantify, honor, or discuss the emotional contributions that come from reflection and personal experiences. Thus, the need for a classroom community in which the teacher and learners value emotion becomes even more important, leading to the necessity to offer the nontraditional student a space in which emotional contributions can be safely shared and they can receive feedback. This safe space must be created for both the female and male students as the risk exists of "identifying emotion primarily with irrationality, subjectivity, the chaotic and other negative characteristics, and in subsequently labeling women as the emotional gender, cultural belief reinforces the ideological subordination of women" (Lutz, 1986, p. 288). This does not minimize however, the gendered expectation placed upon the male student to behave as the unemotional contributor to classroom conversation. As a result, participation is affected, thus compromising the formation of community.

I call on Robert R. Weaver and Jiang Qi's article, "Classroom Organization and Participation: College Students' Perceptions," to reiterate that "[s]tudents' perceptions of and experiences within the social organization of the classroom play a crucial role in shaping their participation in class" (2005, p. 571). For most students, classroom participation is more than showing up and turning in assigned work and becomes a socially constructed discourse community with shared goals and interests. Within dialogical classrooms, emotional sharing is a necessity in that knowledge is largely drawn from shared personal experience, thus reinforcing the knowledge that experiences are rarely unique. The sharing of personal experience presents vulnerability for the student in that the teacher and classroom community, as receivers of the emotion, impact student sharing as a result of their responses. The give-and-take of emotional expression points to Ronald Barnett's statement that by sharing, a student is "gifting not just 'her' work but also 'she is always offering herself'" (2007, p. 182), and "both the teacher and the taught put themselves forward, offer themselves, give themselves. They even, to some extent, exchange themselves" (p. 183). It is this exchange that strengthens the trust within the classroom community in that the community learns to express the value of peer emotional experiences.

The teacher, like the student, is under the microscope when sharing emotion in that socially constructed behavioral expectations exist for learners and teacher alike. Shari Stenberg (2011) discusses emotion in terms of the way that for female teachers, has meant "self regulation by removing or controlling . . . emotion." Per Stenberg, restraint is taught as a method of harnessing and controlling emotion in various public spaces. Teachers and learners must cling to the debate of the "*doxa* itself—that emotions are things internal, irrational, and natural" (Lutz & Abu-Lughod, 1990, p. 2). Undoing the doxa necessitates introduction of rules with the classroom as a practice in attentive listening by the classroom community and, finally, enactment of trust through consistent sharing.

Aside from the nontraditional student and the teacher, the classroom community is a focus as the community will contribute to the discourse that will create the space in which fellow students and the teacher are safe to share. It is not uncommon for syllabi to denote the rules of engagement for student discussion. However, because rules for communication are written, the teacher is not always trained in facilitating discussions that maintain respect among peers. The classroom community must be built prior to students feeling the trust necessary to believe that if personal emotion is shared, the teacher and/or peers will not react negatively. Laura Micciche in her 2005 piece, "Emotion, Ethics, and Rhetorical Action," draws attention to Gary Olson and his 1999 essay, "Encountering the Other." Olson implicitly underscores the gap between theory and practice in identity-based pedagogies, "the gap between what we *say* we do and what we *actually* do" (Micciche, 2005).

The Nontraditional Student/Learner, the Teacher, and the Classroom Community

Defining what it means to be a nontraditional student is difficult due to popular considerations of the nontraditional student as anyone who did not start college the fall after graduating high school with continuous attendance toward a terminal degree. The National Center for Education Statistics (NCES, 2011–2012) acknowledges the difficulty in defining the nontraditional student but in a 1996 study included anyone who satisfies at least one of the following:

- Delays enrollment (does not enter postsecondary education in the same calendar year that he or she finished high school)
- Attends part time for at least part of the academic year
- Works full time (35 hours or more per week) while enrolled
- Is considered financially independent for purposes of determining eligibility for financial aid
- Has dependents other than a spouse (usually children but may also be caregivers of sick or elderly family members)
- Is a single parent (either not married or married but separated and has dependents)
- Does not have a high school diploma (completed high school with a GED or other high school completion certificate or did not finish high school)

Critical to these definitions is that they apply to the majority of students. A modification of the label "nontraditional" could serve as a valuable starting point for welcoming student voices in that the student's social situation is not important to his or her ability to perform academically. In his article, "Definition of Non-Traditional Students: A Paradigm Change," (2014) Frank Palatnick suggests, "A non-traditional student is an individual who attends post secondary school either by distance, through life experience portfolios, by taking either course created tests or standardized tests, by life experiences itself (i.e. apprenticeship or by any other modality outside of the classroom experience)." This revisitation of the definition of nontraditional students pays regard to life experience, thus honoring the learning that the mature adult student has done outside of the classroom setting. I posit that all students be referred to as learners in the image of pupils guided by teachers rather than as students based on the image of the student as pupil educated by the sage.

According to the U.S. Department of Education, *National Study of Postsecondary Faculty* (2004), the characteristics of 56% of a total sample of full-time faculty reveals that 59% are male with an average age of 48. Of these teachers, 12% are single and have never been married, and 51% have dependent children. For 67% of these teachers, a PhD or first professional degree is held, and for 46% of these teachers, they are teaching in their first postsecondary job. Eighty-one percent of the teachers identify as white or non-Hispanic (Tab, 2005).[1]

This data supports the knowledge that the female teacher is underrepresented and that the majority of teachers are contemporaries of the adult returning student. This also means that nearly half of the teachers are teaching postsecondary courses for the first time, thus in need of continuing education with reference to creation and maintenance of the classroom community. Pertinent to the building of a university classroom community is the expectation that the teacher "nurture students' engagement through authentic activities and opportunities to work with classmates" (Education. com). It should be noted however, that it is not enough to nurture students in the classroom space but also to retain the student for future semesters.

An Opportunity

As a result of administrative response to student attrition rate, Pegeen Reichert Powell began a grant-funded program called Student Faculty Partnership for Success. Within her text, Powell (2014) shares the stories of Helen, Cesar, and Nathan, who demonstrate that retention is not a solvable problem, and these are not a "problem to be solved." While these students would not be considered nontraditional with regard to age, all three students are nontraditional in the sense that they need to hold full-time jobs or do not benefit from the familial support systems oftentimes enjoyed by the student who has entered the university setting immediately after graduation and with the emotional or financial assistance of friends and/or family. These student stories support Powell's position that whether students stay in college is oftentimes dependent on factors that take place outside of the campus, like those experienced by the nontraditional student who oftentimes holds the responsibilities of caring for a spouse, children, or both. It is for this reason Powell posits that faculty should focus on making class time relevant and transferable to the outside world rather than focusing on trying to keep the student. Within this section, Powell considers the role of faculty and the extent to which they can help students to remain in school, acknowledging that the best faculty can do is make the student's time in school meaningful. It is also noted that students do not "leave college" but simply do not register for another term. Further, Powell confronts Vincent Tinto's assertion that students will remain in college if they are encouraged to participate in the culture of the campus. This model, as stated by Powell, puts the onus of success back on students rather than on faculty.

Chapter 2 of her book *The Seduction and Betrayal of the Discourse of Retention*, presents Powell utilizing the politicized methodology of CDA. Applying this method the author considers how, rather than which, oppressive structures lead to high attrition rates in a corporatized university structure. Honoring the voice of the oppressed student, Powell introduces the story of Cesar, who exemplifies why some students leave college and some students stay under the corporatized organization that the academy has become. By considering "how" to integrate safe expression of emotion for the nontraditional student, rather than why the expressions of emotion differ from fellow classmates, it is more likely that all students in the classroom community will benefit from the provision of a space in which all can convey both comforts and discomforts with classroom material, responses to readings, or sharing stories of life experience that have socially constructed the student's perceptions of classroom content.

Reflections

Student

As a nonnative academic writer, I found it difficult to formulate responses to class conversations and discussion board postings, which were free of personal experience, and feared that these experiences and the emotions from those experiences were to be kept private. With these experiences came the need to adopt a new language as provided by the university in which to express emotional responses to discussion as a means of providing me with comfort for sharing. This transition from the workplace to the university can oftentimes draw emotional confusion as the communicative traditions of workplace writing to creative and academic writing are distinctly different. Engaging group work and writing of personal narratives, however, served as a meaningful bridge between experience and sharing.

Graduate Assistant

As a graduate instructor, it is oftentimes only through storytelling that I am able to understand how a learner is "oriented" in the academic setting and within the classroom. I have become sensitive to the position of my classroom community in that I clearly remember the apprehension I felt when deciding to reenter the academy.

Teaching Philosophy

A successful teaching day is one in which all or the majority of the classroom community has spoken or interjected an idea, one in which the learners move from their typical seating arrangement, one in which a learner meets or works with a person with whom they are not familiar, and one in which I have only presented an idea or activity, drawn responses to the reading, answered questions, and have set peer learners out to teach each other with time to return to share findings.

It is my expectation that each learner value peer contributions as exhibited by listening and being sensitive to each learner's positionalities. I encourage daily dialogue in my classroom, particularly when the knowledge comes from past experience or is newfound and still raw enough for the listeners to share in the emotions of this newfound knowledge. Lived experiences bring about connections, pathos, and construct the ethos of the speaker.

As members of a learning community develop and utilize their voices, their participation increases. It is also my belief that it is the responsibility of all learners within the community to support and encourage an authentic space for learning, where relationships are formed and ideas are grown and challenged. I believe that when the learning community cares about their own learning and the learning of their peers, they contribute and participate in formal discussion circles as well as in the more casual topics posted within the online space with an authentic voice and with a strengthened ability to "scratch the surface" of the original discussion questions. When voices are thoughtfully engaged in collective conversations, community is created.[2]

Classrooms across the curriculum serve as spaces for this exchange and open a space for emotional response, however, still with some restraint. I do recognize that the creative writing classroom is only one space in which there are emotional exchanges and use it as only one example of a successful space in which I felt that it was not a burden to carry private experiences into the classroom. This creative writing classroom was the first place in which I felt that I did not need to restrain the instinct to comfort a peer post workshop. I am left however, with the question as to whether or not success is based on the individual, the culture, both, or if it isn't until the learner becomes part of the classroom community through successful instructor facilitation that he or she can trust enough to allow themselves entrance into the classroom community.

Recommendations

There is still much work to do in terms of researching the rhetoric of emotion and the exploration of the ways in which instructors can assist nontraditional students who have yet to trust the classroom space or to contribute to dialogical settings in emotionally reflexive manners. It is not enough to attend diversity workshops and create syllabi demanding respect of interaction within the classroom community. As teachers, learners, and members of a discourse community, we must practice the negotiation of the sharing of emotion in the public and safe community that the classroom ideally represents. Training in creation of safe spaces for sharing and learning, although common in some departments, is still lacking in others. It is within this brief chapter that I see the beginnings of a study. Discovery of terminology attributed to particular emotions, and the process of becoming comfortable with using that terminology, is highly dependent on being able to draw on emotion and past experience.

Similar to experiences shared by many students, Powell's book returns to the stories of Helen, Cesar, and Nathan but resists closure. These student's stories do not end neatly. There is not a definitive answer to the issues of retention, which is supported by the structure of this book. These "unfinished, and perpetually written," (2014, p. 30) student stories are a direct reflection of issues of retention, which do not contain definite boundaries or definite answers. Negotiating student emotions in the classroom also does not have a definitive answer, or heuristic, that can be applied for successful integration of shared experiences by students who feel marginalized by circumstances created outside the university.

I will continue to read and research, with hopes that I will be able to eloquently present further research and know that I speak to an issue that nontraditional students and instructors will find valuable. As a starting point, my recommendations for the learners, teacher, and classroom community are to enact the following:

Learners

● Reconcile negative ideologies about nontraditional students.
● Recognize the workplace experience as valuable contributable knowledge.
● Respond to peer expression of public emotion in a sensitive manner.

Teachers

● Encourage and use the vocabulary of emotion.
● Enforce rules of respectful engagement in the class syllabus or class contact.
● Create opportunities for students to share personal experiences through writing, exercises, or discussion board posting.

Classroom Community

● Maintain a safe space in which all can share based on classroom etiquette.
● Resist sexist ideals of who should and should not share emotionally.
● Recognize that insensitive reactions to emotion can shut down peer responses.

Conclusions

Upon reentering postsecondary education, I found words for the policing I felt in business but did not know that there was research and scholarship on such comparisons. I related to the ways in which emotion and femininity seemed to consistently be tied together as I inhabited the positionality of a business owner by day and nontraditional student by night.

I see the potential for future study with the beginnings in this chapter. Discovery of terminology attributed to particular emotions, and the process of becoming comfortable with using that terminology are highly dependent on being able to draw on emotion and past experience from the co-learners with which I have contact. I will continue to read, research, and reflect with hopes that I will be able to eloquently present further recommendations for encouraging the expression of emotion in the classroom by both males and females, free from the doxa that the emotions have gendered parameters for expression. My energy for this research will be drawn from the knowledge gained as spoken by learners, teachers, and classroom communities. It is my intent to find meaningful and useful ways to encourage the building of safe spaces for emotional sharing.

Notes

1 Full sample includes 1,211,849 faculty members, 681,826 of whom are full time and 530,023 of whom are part time.
2 An excerpt from *My Teaching Philosophy*, by Karen R. Trujillo

Works Cited

Barnett, R. (2007). *A will to learn: Being a student in an age of uncertainty.*
Bartholomae, D. (1986). Inventing the university. *Journal of Basic Writing, 5*(1), 4 23.
Cook-Sather, A. (2007). Resisting the impositional potential of student voice work: Lessons for liberatory educational research from poststructuralist feminist critiques of critical pedagogy. *Discourse: Studies in the Cultural Politics of Education, 28*(3), 389–403.
Harkin, P. (1991). The postdisciplinary politics of lore. In P. Harkin & J. Schilb (Eds.), *Contending with words: Composition and rhetoric in a postmodern age* (pp. 124–138). New York, NY: Modern Language Association of America.
Lutz, C. (1986). Emotion, thought, and estrangement: Emotion as a cultural category. *Cultural Anthropology, 1*(3), 287–309.
Lutz, C., & Lughod, L. (1990). *Language and the politics of emotion.* Cambridge: Cambridge University Press.
Micciche, L. "Emotion, ethics, and rhetorical action." *JAC* (2005): 161–184.
Micciche, L. R. (2007). *Doing emotion: Rhetoric, writing, teaching.* Portsmouth, NH: Boynton/Cook, 163.
National Center for Education Statistics. (2011–2012). *Nontraditional undergraduates* (p. 2). Institute of Education Sciences, U.S. Department of Education. Accessed 13 April 2014.
Palatnick, F. Definition of non-traditional students: A paradigm change. *Nontraditional Undergraduates / Definitions and Data.* N.p., Accessed 14 April 2014. Web. 13 April. 2014.
Powell, P. R. (2014). *Retention and resistance: Writing instruction and students who leave.* University Press of Colorado, 140.
Stenberg, S. (2011). Teaching and (re-learning the rhetoric of emotion. *Pedagogy: Critical Approaches to Teaching Literature, Language, Composition, and Culture, 11*(2), 349–369.

Tab, E. D. (2005, May). *National Study of Postsecondary Faculty. 2004 National Study of Postsecondary Faculty (NSOPF:04) Report on Faculty and Instructional Staff in Fall 2003*: 1–41. National Center for Education Statistics. Retrieved 12 April 2014 from *Nces.ed.gov.*

Tinto, V. (1987). *Leaving college: Rethinking the causes and cures of student attrition.* Chicago: University of Chicago Press.

Tompkins, G., et al. (2014). *Literacy for the 21st century.* Pearson Australia.

Weaver, R. R., & Qi, J. (2005, September–October). Classroom organization and participation: College students' perceptions. *The Journal of Higher Education, 76*(5), 570–601.

Wenger, C. I. (2011). "Feeling Lore": The "problem" of emotion in the practice of teaching. *English Teaching: Practice and Critique, 10*(3), 45–59.

Worsham, L. (1998). Going postal: Pedagogic violence and the schooling of emotion. *JAC: A Journal of Composition Theory, 18*(2), 213–245.

8 Teacher, Learner, and Cultural Crosser

A Critical Reflection on the Construction of My Identity

Giselle Martinez Negrette

In Luis Aguilé's famous song, "Cuando salí de Cuba" (When I Left Cuba), the Argentinian-Spanish singer and writer captures the feelings of Cubans who have left their island home in search of a better future. As a Latino girl from Colombia, I grew up listening to this song. Its rendition by Celia Cruz, the Cuban salsa and bolero singer, reveals the secret sentiment of her heart's connection to her home as the lyrics resonate with her voice and her identity. As I write about my own identity, this song is playing in my mind. It reminds me of who I was when I left Colombia and of the complexity of my journey as a cultural crosser traversing different lands. I am aware that my identity is intricately linked to my language because as Gloria Anzaldúa (1987) said, "I am my language" (p. 2951).

This chapter reflects my need to retell the story of my identity in my own words (Bakhtin, 1981). It reveals my longing to "put order in the world, give it a handle so I can grasp it" (Anzaldúa, 1983, p. 169). Most importantly, it shows that individual identity is not immutable—it changes and shifts along with one's life experiences and is constructed as much by others as by oneself. Identity is unceasingly intersubjectively co-constituted. The concept of identity is complex. Despite attempts by social researchers, psychologists, philosophers, and historians to clarify it, the concept defies easy summary. Indeed, the various definitions and models exhibit remarkable variation (Brubaker & Cooper, 2000). According to James D. Fearon (1999), "in part, the differences reflect the multiple lineages that 'identity' has within the academy . . . even though everyone knows how to use the word properly in everyday discourse, it proves quite difficult to give a short and adequate summary statement that captures the range of its present meanings" (p. 2). Fearon (1999) argues that the current idea of identity is a "fairly recent social construct" (p. 2). He offers a dual definition:

> "identity" is presently used in two linked senses, which may be termed "social" and "personal." In the former sense, an "identity" refers simply to a social category, a set of persons marked by a label and distinguished by rules deciding membership and (alleged) characteristic features or attributes. In the second sense of personal identity, an identity is some

distinguishing characteristic (or characteristics) that a person takes a special pride in or views as socially consequential but more-or-less unchangeable.

(p. 2)

For the purposes of this chapter, I shall explore the term "identity" in both senses. I shall refer to it in some cases as personal identity: "people's concepts of who they are, of what sort of people they are, and how they relate to others" (Hogg & Abrams, 1988, p. 2). I shall also consider its social aspects as "the ways in which individuals and collectivities are distinguished in their social relations with other individuals and collectivities" (Jenkins, 1996, p. 4). In addition, I will incorporate notions advanced by James Gee (2011) in his CDA to examine identity as "different ways of being in the world at different times and places for different purposes" (p. 3). These concepts inform my continuing inquiry into the idea of identity, leading me to agree with Katzenstein's definition as "mutually constructed and evolving images of self and other" (Katzenstein, 1996, p. 59). I can say that my identity, as a significant part of my human nature, has been constructed, shaped, and reformulated within varying social, cultural, emotional, and psychological realms over the years.

My earliest sense of identity formed in my home country, Colombia, and the small town near the Atlantic Coast where I was raised in a very traditional home. As the only girl in my family, I was subjected to demanding standards of decorum, language, and behavior. Living with three brothers, however, brought out a boisterous side of my nature that developed through a special bond with them. In my brothers' company, I was not the girl of the family that the rules defined; I was one of them, as wild and free as they were. My mother consequently found it difficult to force me into the mold of that society. As a middle-class girl and a teacher's daughter, my status made it inappropriate to run with the boys or to speak without measuring my words. Constant reminders made me aware, from a very young age, of the differences between boys and girls and how these formed the bases of sexism and sexist restrictions in our society. I also understood that "how you use language (and more generally how you say, do and be) and how people respond to you are deeply consequential to you and for you" (Gee, 2011, p. 6). In short, my social identity as a female bound me to certain forms of social oppression and to the disadvantages of my gender role (Adams, Bell, & Griffin, 2007). Sexism was common and accepted in our society. It was legitimated institutionally, through schools and churches, and culturally, through music, art, literature, norms, and values.

Colombia's population is quite mixed, comprising many ethnic groups. Mestizos account for 58% of the population, whites 20%, mulattos 14%, black 4%, mixed Black-Amerindian 3% and Amerindian 1% (Colombia Demographics Profile, 2014). This diversity is particularly marked in the Atlantic Coast region of the country, where Africans were brought in as slaves, indigenous tribes inhabited many territories, and white Spaniards came as colonizers. Living in that region helped me to grow up with a certain "color blindness," unaware of racial issues. In the Atlantic Coast region of Colombia, most of the population is mestizo (a mixture of white Spaniards, indigenous peoples, and the descendants of African slaves—also known as Afro-Colombians). In my own family, we all have different skin colors (several shades of brown), so I always considered skin as nothing more than a simple physical trait. We had maids who came in all skin colors and personal dispositions. We were always taught to regard them as part of our extended family and to be grateful for their help. As I look back and think about my upbringing, I now realize that I grew up in a very sheltered environment. To be sure, I was raised in a loving and nurturing home full of positive affirmation, which produced a healthy self-esteem. Nevertheless, this environment also inculcated what many people would call naiveté about social issues.

Despite the varying roles of males and females in our society, my father always told me to believe in myself and to remember that I was as capable as anyone else; those words have always stayed with me. I believe that my father, a philologist and language teacher, was always aware that "language allows us to be things, it allows us to take on different socially significant identities . . . to take on any identity at a given time and place we have to 'talk the talk,' not just 'walk the walk' " (Gee, 2011, p. 2). In this light, my parents exposed me from an early age to a wide range of books, as well as to social and cultural experiences, which opened my mind to a wider world of possibilities for women. Despite the role gap between males and females, my father's position as a public school teacher brought monetary and status rewards that gave us our comfortable middle-class life and afforded my parents the possibility to instill in me a certain type of "habitus" (Bourdieu, 1984) that empowered me to navigate the social structures of our world.

As I matured and moved to a bigger city on the Atlantic Coast, I continued to experience a strong sense of self. I went to college and graduated with honors in the teaching of modern languages, after which I immediately began working as an ESL teacher. After teaching for a few years in Colombia, I seized an opportunity to work in the United Kingdom teaching English to immigrant children. This was the beginning of my journey in the larger world. I was ready to see that world and to let it see me for who I was and everything that I could offer. I never expected what I found once I left my comfort zone.

From the moment when I went to apply for my visa at the British embassy in Colombia, I felt rejected. When my interviewers looked at me, I was surprised to see doubt in their eyes; their questions revealed a sense of mistrust that I had never before encountered. Now, years later and with more maturity and intellectual tools at my disposal, I can place these events in perspective. As Gee (2011) explains, "[I]n using language, social goods are always at stake. . . . Social goods are the stuff of politics. Politics is not just about contending political parties. At a much deeper level it is about how to distribute social goods in a society: who gets what in terms of money, status, power, and acceptance on a variety of different terms" (p. 7). My credibility and acceptance as someone worthy of a visa was the "social good" at stake in that situation. After spending many hours at the embassy, I was finally granted a visa to the United Kingdom for one year. I was in my early 20s and had never even traveled beyond the Atlantic Coast of Colombia. It felt like a dream.

I spent a year in Birmingham, England working as a nursery teacher. From the moment I met my new boss, I noticed the cultural and social differences between this new environment and what I was used to. My outgoing Caribbean personality was seen as a disturbance in the comparatively reserved British society. My manager told me immediately to keep my distance because I was not in Colombia anymore. In that setting, it was clear to me that there were "social goods potentially at stake" (Gee, 2011) every time I spoke or communicated. Apparently, my social and linguistic interactions, my intimate personal expression, were without my consent to be repurposed as a measuring stick of whether I was "adequate" or "acceptable" in this society (Gee, 2011, p. 19).

Although most of the people I worked with in England were caring and solicitous, ensuring that I had everything I needed, they were also quick to point out everything they thought I lacked. On one occasion, I was told that my English was bad because I had learned American English, and that it was rubbish; this person said that I should feel privileged to be in England where I had the opportunity to learn the true "Queen's English." Comments like these sharpened my awareness of the "differential access to different identities and practices, connected to different sorts of status and social goods" (Gee, 2011, p. 30). British people often assumed a paternalistic stance to reinforce their assumed superior position as Europeans and inhabitants of the first world over what they may have seen as a poor Colombian girl from a third world country (Macedo, 2006). This attitude manifested itself in conversations about my origins and how different life was in Europe compared to my homeland.

That year in England transformed my life and perceptions of personal identity. I started to feel, for the first time, less fortunate because I was Colombian. Gee (2011) affirms that "we use language to build things in the world and to engage in world building" (p. 16). In my case, my social and linguistic interactions left me trapped in a wretched world. The process of resocialization I underwent during that period led me to start questioning my own identity. My ideas about life began to seem distorted even to me, compared to what I now saw as the enlightened British people.

After one year in England, I accepted a job offer from an international kindergarten in Qingdao, China. There I taught English to children of more than 20 different nationalities and confronted the reality of Chinese racism and discrimination. In China, fair skin is highly valued, and dark skin is associated with low-status hard work in the fields. My brown skin, dark eyes, and dark hair did not serve me well; they failed to meet the Chinese standards of beauty and expected foreign physical traits. In an editorial article in the *Asian Scientist* magazine (September, 2012) David Tan explains that "in dark-skinned South Asia, a fair complexion is considered the epitome of beauty while in already pale-skinned North and East Asia, pearly translucent white skin is a sign of affluence and glamour" (para 5). This deep-rooted cultural notion of beauty permeates all spheres of Chinese society and has boosted the beauty business in the Asia-Pacific region. For me, it was shocking to witness the obsession of this population with light-colored skin and to learn about the skin-lightening market, which is valued at over US$13 billion.

In my particular case, as an English teacher in China, I was expected to look and fit the white female mold. To be considered qualified as a woman, I needed to appear Western or Northern European, with blonde hair and green or blue eyes. Unfortunately, that was not the case. Almost no one cared about my credentials certifying that I was a capable professional or my excellent recommendations from previous jobs in England and Colombia. All that the Chinese community noticed was that I did not fit their visual template for a foreigner. The intersections of race and gender thus converged to further subordinate my sense of social position (Crenshaw, 1993). My line manager, an American, was the only person who stood by me when my students' parents and even my Chinese colleagues rejected me as a teacher. His Chinese wife actually said that my being a good teacher was irrelevant: What mattered most was my appearance. She asked her husband many times about my accent and sent the academic director to observe every single one of my classes. Now, of course, with time and distance, I can see my experiences as a woman of color in China as an example of how intersecting patterns of racism and sexism contribute to the heightened oppression of racial minorities in our contemporary world (Crenshaw, 1993).

To his credit, despite all the difficulties in that school, my manager kept me on as a teacher because he believed in me as a professional. For me, it was not an easy year, either personally or professionally. The Chinese teachers often refused to speak to me, and the expressions on parents' faces when they saw me teaching their children were deeply hurtful. Under the pressure of this social devaluation, I began to doubt my own concept of personal identity and even questioned my self-worth. At times, I began to imagine that white skin carried with it some unmeasurable quality of superiority that left me feeling inadequate. On one occasion, during a collective school celebration, one of my colleagues told me that I was lucky to be seated at the same table with everyone else. He said that if I had been just a shade darker, I would have had to sit at a different table because black people were considered inferior in China. Apparently, race is seen in China as a biological category; it has historically assumed the significance of white supremacy

(Adams, Bell, & Griffin, 2007). In the light of these experiences, I find it less and less surprising that such attitudes can permeate society.

For a long time, I wrestled with this "new" idea of race and discrimination. At times I would feel nauseated just to think that people cared about my physical appearance and nothing else. I witnessed the reality of many of my African friends being denied jobs because of their skin color, and I felt in my own skin the disgust of my fellow teachers who rejected me. My time in China was one of the most difficult periods of my life. I tried to leave, but my manager convinced me to stay and show through my actions that my worth was more than skin deep. It took all the strength I had in me to wake up every morning and teach children who were not aware of what I was experiencing.

The situation finally began to improve when, after a year of hard work and good results, the attitudes of the parents began to change:/they started to concede that perhaps I was not "too black," after all. The changing perception of race in this case validates Omi & Winant's (1994) explanation of race as a concept that "although . . . invokes biologically based human characteristics (so-called 'pheno-types'), selection of these particular human features for purposes of racial signification is always and necessarily a social and historical process" (p. 55). In my case, the fact that I had demonstrated my competence in this school compelled my Chinese colleagues and school parents to rethink their understanding of my "race." This "whitening" process made the rest of my stay in China easier.

In the end, however, after a year and a half, I realized that the thoughts and ideas I was developing had no place in that country at that time. By the end of my stay in China, I had managed to cultivate good relationships with the parents and teachers who had previously despised me. I will never forget the day I was getting ready to leave. One of the teachers who had openly expressed dislike towards me looked at me and said: "Giselle, you are beautiful and it took me this long to see it." The very same teachers and parents who had called me names because of my physical appearance were crying at the airport as I left. In the face of such experiences, I can only seek perspective in Omi & Winant's (1994) conclusions about the categories used in attempts to distinguish human groups along racial lines; these categories "reveal themselves, upon serious examination, to be at best imprecise, and at worst completely arbitrary" (p. 55).

After a few years, I decided it was time to go back to school to pursue my master's degree. I came to the United States in 2007 not as the naive girl who had left Colombia full of dreams and hope but feeling myself to be a more mature woman who had been exposed to life from different angles. Little did I know that I was to experience many more awakenings. When I arrived in the United States, I was not aware of the country's racial divide. I was living in New Mexico, and as a Latino woman I fit right in. My friends were typically white or Latinos, not because I was consciously selecting them but because those were the people I came in contact with in that part of the country. After a while, I decided to take time off and travel around the United States, visiting friends and family. I spent time in Florida, Texas, California, Pennsylvania, Alabama, Louisiana, Washington, DC, and Virginia. I enjoyed the diversity I found everywhere, but I also realized that diversity is often inseparable from divisiveness. As Daryl Cumber Dance (1978) says, "If you're white, you're right, if you're yellow, you're mellow, if you're brown, stick around, if you're black, step back" (as cited in Kennedy, 2003, p. 46).

As a Colombian woman, I was aware that my nationality came with many strings attached, mainly negative ones due to the media-encouraged perception of a connection between my country and drugs. In Asia, people did not seem to be aware of that perception, but as soon as I came to the United States, the stigma seemed to follow me everywhere I went. To make matters worse, not only was I Colombian, but I was therefore also ethnically Latina. I had, without warning, inherited a whole package of negative stereotypes, with the star feature being illegal immigration. My student visa to pursue my master's degree was denied at the U.S. embassy in Colombia because, according to the consular officer who reviewed my documents, as a young female, I was certainly going to the United States only to get married and stay in the country. She did not consider my international student scholarship from a respected U.S. university, my academic records, or the letters of support from professors and sponsors.

This encounter with first world attitudes of superiority humiliated me and left me feeling powerless. At that moment, I experienced personally how what should have been irrelevant social perceptions of my identity (young, brown, middle-class, Colombian woman) could interfere with my opportunities for education. As Gee (2011) mentions, "[W]e often enact our identities by speaking or writing in such a way as to attribute a certain identity to others, an identity that we explicitly or implicitly compare or contrast to our own. We build identities for others as a way to build ones for ourselves" (p. 18). The identity that the consular officer had built for me as a Colombian single female with "ill intentions" explicitly contrasted with her own identity as a married, American woman with the power to deny me entry to the United States. Looking back now, my circumstances at that point remind me of the experiences of the Navajo youth in Donna Deyhle's, 1995 study. Deyhle (1995) points out that "regardless of school success or failure, after high school, all of these youth face the same structural barriers in the community because they are Navajo" (p. 435). In my case, my academic achievements were not permitted to count, absurdly overridden by my origin, social class, gender, age, and ethnicity.

After some time, I returned to the United States on my tourist visa. I spent a few months in Washington, DC and came into close contact for the first time with African Americans. These new relationships exposed me to a whole new universe. I was introduced to the reality of racism and oppression in the United States, the struggles of black people, and the reality of imbalanced power relations. I vividly remember when a white friend informed me that the church I had chosen to attend on Sundays was a black church. I was speechless: Even places of worship could be divided by human social constructions. I mentioned this comment to one African American friend; he told me that if I wanted to see how truly segregated America still was, I needed to visit the different churches on Sunday. I was then introduced to the work of the Rev. Dr. Martin Luther King, Jr., and the famous sermon in which he declared at the National Cathedral in Washington, DC, (1968), that Americans "must face the sad fact that at 11 o'clock on Sunday morning when we stand to sing 'In Christ there is no East or West,' we stand in the most segregated hour of America" (Beckells & Marshall, 2012, para 1). I started learning about black activists such as Malcom X and W. E. B. Du Bois, and I began to better understand the struggles of Black America. As soon as my white friends realized that I was spending time with African Americans, they started to make racial comments about what they termed my new "infatuation" with black people. Within those interactions, I could see how *"language has meaning only in and through social practice*, practices which often leave us morally complicit with harm and injustice unless we attempt to transform them" (Gee, 2011, p. 12). It was shocking for me to see that despite the widely heard rhetoric about the United States as a melting pot, a democratic country, and the leader of the free world, the reality was totally different. Communities were often, or usually, divided by ethnicity; the illusion that in the United States, "all men were created equal under God" (Armitage, 2007) was shattered as I realized that the color of the skin often determined people's value in U.S. society.

Furthermore, spending time with my African American friends showed me yet another kind of discrimination, this time between minorities. In the African American community, I learned that prejudice is connected to notions of self and other, and that the other implies fear of the unknown and fear of people who look different from the self (Hall, 1997). I became the target of many negative comments. I was always seen as the Latina girl who was probably illegal and good for little but cleaning. It was hard for me to understand how members of a minority group that had experienced so much discrimination could themselves perpetrate the same kind of oppression. In Washington, DC, I felt the power of the white community, the struggles of the African American community, and the oppression of the Latinos. Several times, I was indeed mistaken for a cleaner. When I went to restaurants, the service was poor, and black and white men alike often treated me as an inferior exotic female, sexually available but not intellectually adept. Again, as a minority woman, I experienced for myself how the intersecting forces of gender and racial discrimination made me suffer from the "effects of multiple subordination" (Crenshaw, 1993, p. 1251).

Once again, my personal identity was strongly impacted, and social mirroring was taking cumulative and prolonged tolls on my senses of identity, group identification, and achievement (Suarez-Orozco, 2005). I started to feel that no matter how hard I tried, I was always going to be considered second-class in American society. In Colombia, I enjoyed many privileges as part of what I saw as my middle-class identity. I was also part of the racial majority, and as I mentioned earlier, the "color-blind" and racially mixed environment in which I had been raised had prevented me from facing issues of racial discrimination. As a female, I had, to be sure, experienced the oppression of sexism in Colombia, but class status and intellectual accomplishments had for the most part compensated for my gender. Leaving home had allowed me to witness the reality of humanity living under different social constructs, which in turn had determined how I perceived myself and accepted others. I can vouch for the reality of the intersubjective co-constitution of my identity and its clear and tangible connection to my own experiences (Katzenstein, 1996).

Five years passed before I was granted a student visa to pursue my master's degree in the United States. In 2012, I finally entered graduate school; there, I found that my thoughts were not only sharpened, but they were also valued. I was encouraged to become more critical about the reality of power and social inequalities. As a result, my time as a graduate student has accelerated my liberation process (Harro, 2000) as a Latina female. I am aware that, as Taylor (1989) says, "[M]y identity is defined by the commitments and identifications which provide the frame or horizon within which I can try to determine from case to case what is good, or valuable, or what ought to be done, or what I endorse or oppose" (p. 27). Empowered and emboldened by knowledge acting on my personal experience, I consciously choose my identity. I am not defined by a distorted belief in eugenics or racial superiority. I am engaged in a constant mental fight against cultural domination and the hegemony of racial and linguistic supremacy.

I have found in analytical research approaches such as CDA ways to speak to and perhaps, as James Gee (2011) asserts, "intervene in, social and political issues, problems, and controversies in the world" (p. 9). It is in the intricate and complex connections to language where I have found a "key way we humans make and break our world, our institutions, and our relationships" (Gee, 2011, p. 9). An African American friend who had grown up in the Southeast of the United States told me that as a child, he often wondered if there was really something wrong with black people. He mentioned, in a defeated tone, that maybe it was true that minorities were not as smart as white people. When I heard this, I could discern in his voice the misconstruction of a fabricated idea of personal and social identity. It was clear that the language and social practices had colluded in a type of ideological manipulation that had convinced him of his lesser value. Sadly, he had accepted the truth maintained by his oppressors and made it his own.

The history of the United States reveals processes of socialization that legitimize unbalanced power relations and systems of oppression with devastating effects on its population. According to Macedo (2006), schools in the United States promote a " 'poisonous pedagogy' designed to impart . . .

from the beginning false information and beliefs that have been passed on from generation to generation and dutifully accepted by the young even though they are not only unproved but are demonstrably false" (p. 66). I could perceive, in my Afro American friend's voice, the result of this kind of pedagogy at work in his mind. As a foreigner currently living in the United States, I have felt many times that I am fighting an uphill battle, stubbornly denying my own exhausted acceptance of an immersive system of negative beliefs about my own self and my socially situated identity—the "kind of person" I am seeking to be and "enact here and now" (Gee, 2011, p. 30).

I refuse to let American or any other society dictate my path or the political value of my human consciousness. I know that my personal identity goes beyond my skin color; my social identity is not a heavy burden in my life but one of the multiple aspects of my human nature, and language is powerfully connected to both of them. As a critical thinker, I have developed the ability to see the complexities of language, power, and racial domination, particularly as they relate to cultural and linguistic minorities and education. And it is within this context that I have found my strength to intervene in social matters as my own contribution to social justice (Gee, 2011). I will not accept as a fact the myth that the thickness of my accent determines the depth of my understanding. I have resolved to believe that the color of my skin does not establish the value of my thoughts.

As I reflect on who I have become after many experiences as a cultural crosser in different countries, I am more aware of the need to challenge certain socially accepted norms around race, ethnicity, gender and how these forces intersect to affect people (Crenshaw, 1989). As John Stuart Mill (1869) said, "[W]e must confront the arguments against our positions if we are to keep our ideas alive" (p. 67). Societal structures and cultural beliefs have not only influenced my thoughts and perceptions, but they have also informed my discourse—"language-in-use" (Gee, 2011, p. 34) and the Discourses—"language *plus* 'other stuff'" (Gee, 2011, p. 34) that I subscribe to as part of my collective awareness. As Gee (2011) expresses it:

> [I]n the end, a Discourse is a "dance" that exists in the abstract as a coordinated pattern of words, deeds, values, beliefs, symbols, tools, objects, times, and places and in the here and now as a performance that is recognizable as just such a coordination. Like a dance, the performance here and now is never exactly the same. It all comes down, often, to what the "masters of the dance" (the people who inhabit the Discourse) will allow to be recognized or will be forced to recognize as a possible instantiation of the dance.
>
> (p. 36)

I am aware that members of society still construct other people's identities based on their own ideas, some of which are objective and some subjective. I insist on defining myself without regard for those categories and assigned roles. I now know that the critical connection between language and my identity is integrally linked to questions of justice, equity, and power (Chomsky, 1979). To this end, I subscribe to what bell hooks (1997) calls "a practical model for social change that includes an understanding of ways to transform consciousness that are linked to efforts to transform structures" (p. 7). One type of transformation to pursue is the dissection of the poorly understood crosscutting social currents that affect minorities. I firmly believe that it is through this pursuit and by considering the differences that my difference makes (Crenshaw, 1993) that I can support long-lasting social change that starts within the person and bursts forth to transform the outside world.

In summary, I have developed a new consciousness about world building through language and the beauty of heterogeneity in humankind; this is one of the reasons why I find writing so powerful. I have also learned that a healthy concept of personal and social identity involves a cognizant effort to value myself and others beyond the physical reality. It requires being inclusive and appreciating individuals, not as products of a system but as significant elements of our shared world. The ongoing construction and reformulation of my identity demands constant soul searching on issues of race, class, gender, language, and religion but, above all, on power. My life is in constant change, but my worth need no longer be questioned. The set of attributes that form my identity have an intrinsic value because they are part of my place in this world. I am not simply a middle-class, Latina woman from Colombia who lives in the United States. I am all that and much more.

References

Adams, M., Bell, L. A., & Griffin, P. (2007). *Teaching for diversity and social justice.* New York: Routledge.

Anzaldúa, G. (1983). *This brigade called my back: Writings by radical women of color* (C. Moraga & G. Anzaldúa, Eds.). New York: Kitchen Table: Women of Color Press.

Anzaldúa, G. (1987). *Borderlands/La Frontera: The new mestiza.* San Francisco, CA: Spinsters/Aunt Lute.

Armitage, D. (2007). *The declaration of independence: A global history.* Cambridge, MA: Harvard University Press.

Bakhtin, M. M. (1981). *The dialogical imagination.* (M. Holquist, Ed., C. Emerson & M. Holquist, Trans.). Austin, TX: University of Texas Press.

Beckells, Y., & Marshall, J. (2012, February 15). Sunday morning, our country's "most segregated hour" unites people in Oakland. *Oakland-North.* Retrieved July 12, 2013, from http://oaklandnorth.net/2012/02/15/sunday-morning-our-countrys-most-segregated-hour-unites-people-in-oakland/

Bourdieu, P. (1984). *Distinction: A social critique of the judgment of taste.* Cambridge, MA: Harvard University Press.

Brubaker, R., & Cooper, F. (2000). Beyond "Identity". *Theory and Society, 29,* 1–47.

Chomsky, N. (1979). *Language and responsibility.* Sussex: Harvester Press.

Crenshaw, K. (1989). Demarginalizing the intersection of race and sex: A black feminist critique of antidiscrimination doctrine, feminist theory and antiracist politics. *University of Chicago Legal Forum*, 1989, 139–167.

Crenshaw, K. (1993). Mapping the margins: Intersectionality, identity politics, and the violence against women of Color. *Stanford Law Review*, 43, 1241–1299.

Cumber Dance, D. (1978). *Shuckin' and Jivin': Folklore from Contemporary Black Americans*. Bloomington, IN: Indiana University Press.

Deyhle, D. (1995). Navajo youth and Anglo racism: Cultural integrity and resistance. *Harvard Educational Review*, 65, 403–444.

Fearon, J. D. (1999). *What is identity (as we now use the word)?* Stanford, CA: Stanford University.

Gee, J. P. (2011). *An introduction to discourse analysis: Theory and method*. New York: Routledge.

Hall, S. (1997). *Representation: Cultural representations and signifying practices*. Thousand Oaks, CA: Sage in association with the Open University.

Harro, B. (2000). The cycle of liberation. In M. Adams, W. J. Blumenfeld, R. Castañeda, H. W. Hackman, M. L. Peters, & X. Zúñiga (Eds.), *Readings for diversity and social justice: An anthology on racism, antisemitism, sexism, heterosexism, ableism, and classism* (pp. 463–469). New York: Routledge.

Hogg, M., & Abrams, D. (1988). *Social identifications: A social psychology of intergroup relations and group processes*. London: Routledge.

hooks, b. (1997). *Killing rage, ending racism*. New York: Holt Paperbacks.

Index Mundi—Colombia Demographics Profile 2014. (2014, July). Retrieved from http://www.indexmundi.com/colombia/demographics_profile.html

Jenkins, R. (1996). *Social identity*. London: Routledge.

Katzenstein, P. (1996). *The culture of national security: Norms and identity in world politics*. New York: Columbia University Press.

Kennedy, R. (2003). *Nigger: The strange career of a troublesome word*. New York: Vintage.

Macedo, D. (2006). *Literacies of power: What Americans are not allowed to know*. Boulder, CO: Westview Press.

Mill, J. S. (1869). *On liberty*. London: Roberts & Green.

Omi, M., & Winant, H. (1994). *Racial formation in the United States: From the 1960s to the 1990s* (2nd edition). New York: Routledge.

Suarez-Orozco, C. (2005). Identities Under Siege: Immigration Stress and Social Mirroring among the Children of Immigrants. In M. Suarez-Orozco, D. Baolian Qin, & C. Suarez-Orozco (Eds.), *The New Immigration: An Interdisciplinary Reader* (pp. 135–156). New York, NY: Taylor & Francis Group.

Tan, D. (2012, September 18). Who's the fairest of them all? *Asian Scientist*. Retrieved July 12, 2013, from http://www.asianscientist.com/features/skin-whitening-products-asia-2012/

Taylor, C. (1989). *Sources of the self*. Cambridge: Cambridge University Press.

9 CDA

Lenses Concerning English Ownership for Africans

Loretta H. Wideman

Varying positions have been articulated about the usefulness of English. However, educators and people in general need to make educated decisions about their own views of the question of English ownership. An analysis that focuses on discourses as representations for action will provide reasons for that action (Fairclough & Fairclough, 2012). In this article I draw on Fairclough's (2003) version of CDA as being "based upon the assumption that language is an irreducible part of social life, dialectically interconnected with other elements of social life, so that social analysis and research always has to take an account of language" (p. 2).

Adichie's (2009) differing views from those of Wa Thiong'o (2013) concerning how English is seen from the African perspective prompted me to realize we need to hear even more from the Africans themselves. As the English language gains more speakers, the number of people concerned with hegemonic relations attached to the language also grows (Cooper, 1989). Ignoring the historical onset of English as a colonial language on Africa's continent puts teachers at a risk of also ignoring the larger picture of how language fits into a country's politics and culture (May, 2012).

While teaching English in various countries in Africa for the past 28 years, I developed the assumption that most people in Africa have positive attitudes toward the English language. After becoming a doctoral student at New Mexico State University (NMSU), I now more fully see another side to the story. I have come to realize how power in many forms, including economically, politically, and socially, influences the attitudes toward a language (Adegbija, 1994; Adichie, 2009; Chesire, 1991; Cooper, 1989; Indabawa & Mpofu, 2006; May, 2012; Phillipson, 1992; Schmied, 1991; Wa Thiong'o, 1986; Wolfson, 1989). To continue teaching English in Africa, I must believe in what I am doing. If people from Africa have deep-rooted positions related to the language, I must teach with the awareness of their views concerning English.

I became aware of some of the existing negative perceptions concerning this language through reading works by authors such as Phillipson (1992) and Wa Thiong'o (1986), while I was working on my master's degree in teaching English to speakers of other languages (TESOL). At that time, however, I used their work sparingly, citing passages that would support my position as an English teacher in Africa. Not having experienced any of the oppositions they discuss in their works, I ignored their positions. Because my lenses were based on the outward influx of students desiring to learn, I avoided directly addressing the idea that English has negative influence. I felt that English could be owned by Africans or whoever wished to appropriate the language. In fact, I still believe that Africans or people from any part of the world can own English. English is simply a language. It cannot be ordered online or through the mail. It cannot be bought at the market. It is a language that can serve our purposes. I have seen people from many countries in Africa learn English and then use it to go to Korea or Australia or India or the United States—taking the language as their own to allow them to be who and where they want to be. I do not want to simply look at my experiences to make a decision about English ownership, however. I have a responsibility to myself and to the people I teach to dig deeper, to find true meaning to the English language experiences in the African context.

One way to find out how people from Africa actually feel about the English language is through a comparative discourse analysis of African authors, listening to more than one view. In this chapter I have chosen to write a CDA concerning lenses of English ownership for Africans based on texts and oral discourses of two prominent authors from the continent of Africa: Chimamanda Ngozi Adichie from Nigeria and Ngugi Wa Thiong'o from Kenya. I had not previously read Adichie's works before starting doctoral course work at NMSU. In one of my first classes at the university, we viewed Adichie's (2009) presentation, *The Danger of a Single Story*, which made an impression on me in terms of one who has taken the language with all its past and then appropriated it to serve her purpose. Her work spurred me on to look at why others did not have the same lenses in regard to English. After exploring more of the work and interviews of Wa Thiong'o, who is vocal about English not being an African language and who also encourages Africans to use their native languages for writing, I decided to analyze their contrasting lenses.

Analysis

Fairclough and Fairclough (2012) emphasize how discourse needs to be analyzed in reference to its effect on society. Their further identification of explanatory critique shows us a way to explain the social phenomena of the discourse, describing the ideologies and belief systems associated with it. What one person or group says or does affects not just that person or group. It also touches everyone around them.

At times discourses by individuals can be recontextualized, creating an imposition of discourse upon other people, which according to Fairclough and Fairclough (2012), becomes a kind of colonization. The strength of this appropriation affects many people's lives, including mine. When I listen to strong opinions about English ownership, I make life decisions based on ide-ologies I am formulating. Whether or not they know what they are doing, people can represent their discourses singularly from their own views, thus eliminating another representation, the missing element that causes a misrepresentation.

In a deliberation process, Fairclough and Fairclough (2012) explain the importance of representing both sides of the argument. With representation in mind, I will attempt to give fair attention to the discourse analysis. As public figures in African literature, Adichie's and Wa Thiong'o's words carry weight in the social realm. What they say about English affects others' decisions. Looking briefly at their histories and the ideologies that have arisen from their experiences can help us understand the stands they take in regard to language.

Historical Lenses of Ngugi Wa Thiong'o and Chimamande Ngozi Adichie: An Overview

History means everything in terms of our lenses. How we see historical and political events, languages, and cultures, among other factors, depends upon the lenses through which we look at them. Adichie (2013) and Wa Thiong'o (2013) were born generations apart and had vastly different life-styles and upbringing. While Adichie grew up in an affluent Nigerian fam-ily and had a happy childhood as an avid reader of American and British books, Wa Thiong'o was born into a peasant's family under the scrutiny of a British colonized settlement. Both witnessed the suffering that goes along with war-torn countries albeit on different levels of experiences. Although Adichie and Wa Thiong'o both have high degrees of education, Adichie left Africa when she was 19 years old to go to study in the United States, while Wa Thiong'o was exiled from Kenya after two events caused a dramatic change in his life: writing his book, *Petals of Blood*, and the performance of his controversial play, which was presented in Limuru, Kenya. The two writers currently reside in the United States. Because their history cannot be separated from the way they see the English language, one must refer to various aspects of their experiences throughout the process of analyzing their discourse.

Lenses About Writing in African Languages

Both Adichie and Wa Thiong'o express the ills of colonialism in various writings and interviews. They both love their native languages—Igbo for Adichie and Gikuyu for Wa Thiong'o. However, they have different views concerning writing in the African languages. Adichie (as cited in Azodo, 2008) says,

> [T]he interesting thing, of course, is that if I did write in Igbo (which I sometimes think of doing, but only for impractical, emotional reasons),

many Igbo people would not be able to read it. Many educated Igbo people I know can barely read Igbo and they mostly write it atrociously.

(Azodo Interview, 2008)

On the other hand, while he was in prison, Wa Thiong'o (2013) decided to use his mother tongue of Gikuyu instead of English as his language of literary work (Wa Thiong'o, 1986). He urges all other African writers to also write in their mother tongue. Wa Thiong'o made a point of consideration on the BBC interview (2013) where he asked the viewers to imagine literature from one country being written in another language, for example, French literature being written in Zulu. To some extent, the question about audience becomes the consideration. Who is the audience of the writer? What languages are people from the audience reading? For Adichie, even if she wrote in Igbo, her work would not be read by a large population of people. She wants her message to be heard by many. Here again, however, Wa Thiong'o (1986) asks why "should an African writer, or any writer, become so obsessed by taking from his mother-tongue to enrich other tongues? Why should he see it as his particular mission?" (p. 8).

I have taken a selection of Adichie's and Wa Thiong'o's writings to compare their ideas concerning their views about which language should be used for writing. I could have chosen other writings or interviews of the authors because both Adichie and Wa Thiong'o are vocal about their views of language use. I chose the following excerpts because they were explicit in their descriptions of showing why the authors have made their language choices regarding English. I have numbered the lines for easy reference.

Decolonising the Mind, by Ngugi Wa Thiong'o (1986)

1   The English language opened the door to a wide range of fiction and it was this that eventually led me to the English Department at Makerere in 1959 and hence to the kind of writing which climaxed in *Petals of Blood* which was published in July 1977.
2   But I was becoming increasingly uneasy about the English language.
3   After I had written *A Grain of Wheat* I underwent a crisis.
4   I knew whom I was writing about but whom was I writing for?
5   The peasants whose struggles fed the novel would never read it.
6   In an interview in 1967 with *Union News*, a student newspaper in Leeds University, I said: 'I have reached a point of crisis.
7   I don't know whether it is worth any longer writing in English.' (p. 72)

The Danger of a Single Story, by Chimamanda Ngozi Adichie (2009)

1   I've always felt that it is impossible to engage properly with a place or a person without engaging with all of the stories of that place and that person.

2   The consequence of the single story is this: It robs people of dignity.

3   It makes our recognition of our equal humanity difficult.

4   It emphasizes how we are different rather than how we are similar.

5   So what if before my Mexican trip I had followed the immigration debate from both sides, the U.S. and the Mexican?

6   What if my mother had told us that Fide's family was poor and [emphasis added on *and*] hardworking?

7   What if we had an African television network that broadcast diverse African stories all over the world?

8   What the Nigerian writer Chinua Achebe calls "a balance of stories."

9   What if my roommate knew about my Nigerian publisher, Mukta Bakaray, a remarkable man who left his job in a bank to follow his dream and start a publishing house?

10   Now, the conventional wisdom was that Nigerians don't read literature.

11   He disagreed.

12   He felt that people who could read, would read, if you made literature affordable and available to them.

First of all, these passages show that Wa Thiong'o and Adichie have different audiences in mind. Wa Thiong'o's lines 4 and 5 show his struggles about who his audience would be. The people being written about would never even read the words. In contrast, Adichie's lines 7 through 9 show her audience to be the world. She wants the stories of Africans to be heard by the world so that people will not have such a shallow perception of Africa and its people. Both are sympathetic towards their countrymen and women but with different results.

Wa Thiong'o's lines 2, 3, 6, and 7 show his struggle and crisis in whether or not to continue writing literature in English. In his preliminary statement at the beginning of the book, he publicly announces that this book would be his last to be written in the English language, which shows how he solved his problem addressed in these lines. Adichie's lines 7 through 9 stress the need to get the stories out to others. Since her mother tongue, Igbo, would not allow this type of broadcast, she is not promoting only using African languages. Her argument is instead to reach many people through available languages.

My position regarding which language should be used when writing African literature stems from having taught many years in Africa and seeing multiple lenses in regard to language use. My primary concern is for people not to abandon their mother tongues. Guarding one's language and not letting it be taken away is important for everyone. Wa Thiong'o saw oppressive colonizers try to take away his language, thus contributing to his current view of preferring people from Africa refrain from using colonial languages for African literature.

While I respect Wa Thiong'o's position and do not argue his stand concerning his desire to use his mother tongue when writing, I also see another side for other individuals. When I taught writing in English in Ethiopia, I encouraged students to take what they learned in English and apply the concepts to their own languages as well. I recommended that they make their own choices about the language in which they would write. First, they needed to consider their audiences. Some students wanted to write in Oromo, while others wanted to write in Amharic, two of the many languages in Ethiopia. The decision was not one in which I imposed. It was theirs. If I tried to dictate to others what languages they should use for writing, would I not be, as Fairclough and Fairclough (2012) address, using my own lens, a recontextualization which can also be oppressive to others?

Lenses of English Ownership

Adichie (2009), in *The Danger of a Single Story*, expressed her feelings about the single story that people see, another way to say they are only looking through their own lenses. When she was in school, she read books that came from the United States and the United Kingdom. The characters in her books ate apples and talked about snow. These characters had white skin and blue eyes, and they talked about the weather with the sun coming out. All the literature was from a Western perspective. When she went to the United States, people saw her as African, as if she were from the state of Africa, not the country of Nigeria. She wanted to be identified as who she was. Later in life, however, she discovered that she also tended to view others through her own lens. Her voice is now heard globally, either through the Internet, her books, or her speaking engagements as she challenges others to see the world not only through a single lens with a single story but with eyes wide open and with many sets of lenses.

The importance I see in the relation to Adichie appropriating English is that she has evaluated the single story, but she has decided that English is her own. Adichie (as cited in Azodo, 2008) said,

> I'd like to say something about English as well, which is simply that English is mine. Sometimes we talk about English in Africa as if Africans have no agency, as if there is not a distinct form of English spoken in Anglophone African countries. I was educated in it; I spoke it at the same time as I spoke Igbo. My English-speaking is rooted in a Nigerian experience and not in a British or American or Australian one. I have taken ownership of English.
>
> (Interview)

Her position about English appropriation is clear. She owns English. Her situation is different from Wa Thiong'o's because she grew up with two languages that seemed a norm for her. Wa Thiong'o (1986) grew up experiencing the change from hearing and telling stories in Gikuyu at home, at work, and at school to seeing the colonizer come in, change the language to English at school, and degrade students when they continued to speak in their mother tongues. While he experienced hardships and oppression through English, Adichie experienced laughter and the longing to live through the lives of the people in the stories she read. Attitudes toward the language change drastically because of the lived experiences of the two authors

In Wa Thiong'o's (2013) interview on BBC, he had much to say about languages in general, but his main message was that "English is not an African language, full stop." He believes that if Africans continue to write in English, they are contributing to the power and oppression that colonialism started. Wa Thiong'o disagrees with Adichie in appropriation of English. Wa Thiong'o said, "[W]e should not deceive ourselves" (BBC Interview, 2013). He expressed that when Adichie uses English to write, she is contributing to oppression. He continues to write in Gikuyu and translate his works into English. Wa Thiong'o (1986) poses the question, "How did we arrive at this acceptance of the 'fatalistic logic of the unassailable position of English in our literature', in our culture and in our politics?" (p. 9). He cannot understand how Africans have become so feeble about their own languages and so aggressive in accepting the colonized languages.

I support Adichie's position of believing she has appropriated and owns the English language. My standpoint comes from the changes that have taken place since Wa Thiong'o first made the decision to abandon English in his writings. People are becoming more and more global. Students in classes I taught in Africa are now represented in countries all over the world. Their appropriation of English in addition to their native languages has contributed to their decisions to live wherever in the world they decide to go. I emphasize "decide." For some, they may have had to leave their homes because of war. For others, they want to join family who are already residing in other parts of the world. Still others make conscious decisions to travel or study in other countries. *They* decide. Students I have taught have been free to make these moves because of their abilities in the English language.

English Communication Lenses

The English communication level varies between Adichie and Wa Thiong'o. For Adichie, English is a mode of communication, especially when she goes past the single story. She has a message to give the world, and she wants to use English. For Wa Thiong'o, however, English has a negative meaning, which closes up the communication line. The concept of being forced to conform has been an oppressive tool in relation to people's identities.

No matter which language is used, we have a purpose in using that particular language—to communicate our message. No one can take ownership of a language unless she/he can use the language on a social level. Mere words cannot be appropriated. When I first started teaching English in Africa, I thought English was English. It was simply another language. Linguistically understanding what someone is saying in English, however, does not mean one understands the message. Real communication can only take place when it is practiced through known concepts that can make the message understood. Hymes's (1971) communicative competence exemplifies the understanding of a message through adding meaning to communication through a social environment. Over the years of teaching in various countries in Africa (Senegal, Gambia, Kenya, Ethiopia, Malawi, Djibouti, Rwanda, Sudan, Madagascar, Togo, and Tanzania), I have seen many occasions where people have struggled to communicate through Western textbook examples. For English appropriation to take place, speakers must be able to communicate on a level where they can create ownership.

Discussion: Making Meaning

Positions about English ownership vary from individual to individual. I now understand some of the layers of meaning that a language choice expresses. To some, perhaps when they hear the English language, they think of oppression; others think of identity; while still others may think of voice or emancipation. Examination of the lenses must involve making meaning to invest in forward thinking.

Oppression Through Language

We do not have to look far to see oppression being displayed through language, whether it be language choice that has been forced on others or language that is used as a tool of oppression through its meaning. Memmi (1965) shows oppression in its worst state in Africa through his descriptions of colonialism. How can I relate oppression to my position in Africa . . . to where I work . . . to what I do and say? How do I respond to students in my class when they declare varying beliefs different from my own? I believe the least oppressive way of responding is to respect others' beliefs, not denying, hiding, or elevating my own. I become an oppressor when I tell others that they have no right to believe the way they do. They are wrong. I utilize my authority to oppress them. A respect for others is a combatting tool for oppression. I will use this tool to help my students express themselves communicatively to build their English language, a language they should have a freedom to learn.

Identity Through Language

In African culture, it is not so much as what one says but in the way it is said. An Ethiopian proverb that I heard many times while I was living in Addis Ababa can be interpreted as follows: "If I could see your face, I would not need food." One meaning could be implied that having dignity is more important than having food. How one is perceived is more important than life itself.

Both Adichie and Wa Thiong'o have found identity through language. When establishing a position about English ownership, one can look at the identity aspect. Wa Thiong'o expresses his identity as a Kenyan by his refusal to use English in his writing, by declaring that English is not an African language. He says all languages are wonderful (BBC Interview, 2013), but they are not African. His identity as a Kenyan and an African is partially displayed through his language. Adichie, on the other hand, finds identity in her freedom as a Nigerian, an African, to use whatever language is available to her to suit her purposes. She can write in Igbo, or she can write in English. She owns both languages, so her identity as a free Nigerian is established.

Voice Through Language

Adichie and Wa Thiong'o both use English to exhibit voice about their ideologies. Blommaert (2005) recognizes the necessity of analyzing voice: what is said, the way it is voiced, and why it is spoken or not even verbalized. Voice is not just linguistics. Hymes (as cited in Blommaert, 2005) notes, "[T]here is a fundamental difference . . . between what is not said because there is no occasion to say it, and what is not said because one has not and does not find a way to say it" (p. 61). Too many times people are misunderstood because they cannot get their messages across in another language. I agree with Hymes's (as cited in Blommaert, 2005) arguments about helping people to understand and "establish desired functions in language" (p. 68) for them to have an understood *voice*. I have chosen and will continue to choose to do what I can to seek opportunities of *voice* for anyone I teach. I will also attempt to instill within others the need to give opportunities of *voice* to those they teach.

All people, if they so choose, should have the opportunities to learn languages to have . . . well, anything they want . . . including *voice*. If people start learning a language based on their own cultural functions, they will have context and value for the language and will learn it well. The shift to another cultural context will then be much simpler because they have already established good language skills based on their own context. Thus, English can be used for people from various countries in Africa to create their own voices. During the process, individuals can also establish voice as to the relevancy of English ownership.

Emancipation Through Language

Freedom comes in many different forms. People can be emancipated politically, socially, and even personally through thoughts or other personal rights. Emancipation is not a declaration, something given from one person to another. It must come from within. No matter that one person proclaims someone else to be free from some sort of oppression, there will be a significant amount of leftover emotions and memories that will be difficult to erase. Only when one is free from within will that person truly be emancipated. Emancipation should also include the right to speak and be understood as well as to speak through various forms of communication without being downgraded in the process. Language emancipation for Adichie is the freedom to own English. For Wa Thiong'o it is the right to use Gikuyu for his writing. The rest of us can develop our own emancipation, partially by making our own choices about languages we use.

Conclusion

Reflecting on Adichie's and Wa Thiong'o's views concerning English ownership has increased my grounding concerning my own position of the topic. Adichie has made a personal decision to use English in her writing and to claim ownership of it. Wa Thiong'o, because of the oppressive background he has experienced in English, denounces it as an African language. My position in this chapter is in respect to lenses. Adichie said that she saw jam leave her table when she was a child in Nigeria. While I was living in Kenya, I rarely saw jam on my table, but it was for different reasons than Adichie. Should I use my lens and say Adichie did not need the jam? That it was not necessary for her? She has her lens. I have mine. The point of oppression is again introduced when I tell her to see life the way I see it, to respond to her situation through my lens.

Appropriating English is a choice each individual should consider in terms of how the language can best suit one's purpose. While the mother tongue is the language of identity and should not be taken from individuals to be replaced with any another language, including English, people should also be free to appropriate other languages, as well.

References

Adegbija, E. (1994). *Language attitudes in sub-Saharan Africa: A sociolinguistic overview.* Clevendon, UK: Multilingual Matters, LTD.

Adichie, C. (2009). The danger of a single story. *TEDGlobal.* Retrieved from http://www.ted.com/talks/chimamanda_adichie_the_danger_of_a_single_story.html

Adichie, C. (2013). *Chimamanda Ngozi Adichie official website.* Retrieved from http://www.l3.ulg.ac.be/adichie/

Azodo, A. U. (2008). *Interview with Chimamanda Ngozi Adichie: Creative writing and literary activism.* Macomb, IL. Retrieved from http://www.iun.edu/~minaua/interviews/interview_chimamanda_ngozi_adichie.pdf

BBC World News HardTalk. (July 22, 2013). *Ngugi Wa Thiong'o: English is no a African language.* Interview. London, UK: BBC. Retrieved from http://www.bbc.co.uk/news/world-radio-and-tv-23367692

Blommaert, J. (2005). *Discourse.* New York: Cambridge University Press.

Cheshire, J. (Ed.). (1991). *English around the world: Sociolinguistic perspectives.* New York: Cambridge University Press.

Cooper, R. (1989). *Language planning and social change.* New York: Cambridge University Press.

Fairclough, I., & Fairclough, N. (2012). *Political discourse analysis: A method for advanced students.* New York: Routledge.

Fairclough, N. (2003). *Analysing discourse: Textual analysis for social research.* New York: Routledge.

Hymes, D. H. (1971). On communicative competence. In J. Pride and J. Holmes (Eds.), *Sociolinguistics.* Penguin, 1972. (Excerpt from the paper published 1971, Philadelphia, University of Pennsylvania Press.)

Indabawa, S., & Mpofu, S. (2006). *The social context of adult learning in Africa.* Capetown, South Africa: UNESCO Institute for Education. Bristol, UK: Longdunn Press.

May, S. (2012). *Language and minority rights: Ethnicity, nationalism and the politics of language.* New York: Routledge.

Memmi, A. (1965). *The colonizer and the colonized.* Boston, MA: Beacon Press. (Original work published 1957)

Phillipson, R. (1992). *Linguistic imperialism.* Oxford, UK: Oxford University Press.

Schmied, J. (1991). *English in Africa.* New York: Longman Group UK Limited.

Wa Thiong'o, N. (1986). *Decolonising the mind: The politics of language in African literature.* Nairobi, Kenya: East Africa Educational Publications.

Wa Thiong'o, N. (2013). *Ngugi wa Thiong'o official website.* Retrieved from http://www.ngugiwathiongo.com/

Wolfson, N. (1989). *Perspectives: Sociolinguistics and TESOL.* Boston, MA: Heinle & Heinle Publishers.

10 Accentism Exposed

An Anticolonial Analysis of Accent Discrimination With Some Implications for Minority Languages

Pierre W. Orelus

Drawing on the work of sociolinguistic and postcolonial theorists (Gee, 2012; Skutnabb-Kangas, 2000; Thiong'o, 1986), this chapter explores accentism and intersecting forms of linguistic discrimination. By accentism, it is meant accent-based discrimination often connected to one's nonstandard accent along with one's linguistic and social class background, nationality, and country of origin. Accent-based discrimination has affected many people, particularly bilingual and multilingual students speaking dominant languages with a distinct accent (Phillipson, 2010; Skutnabb-Kangas, 2000). What is accent? What does it mean to speak with an accent?

Linguistically speaking, an accent is a way of pronouncing words informed by one's region, country of origin, geographical location, caste, social class, racial and cultural backgrounds, and one's first language (Lippi-Green, 2012). Influenced by these factors, while speaking many people often put certain emphasis on, and use certain types of inflection and rhythm of, a word. When an individual or a group utters words in ways deviating from the so-called standard pronunciation, constructed by those in power, this individual or group is labeled as speaking with an accent often resulting in discrimination against them.

Acquiring a native-like accent in a language, however, does not necessarily guarantee that an individual or a group will be exempt from accent-based discrimination. It is contingent upon what language (i.e., dominant vs. dominate language) one acquires the native-like accent in. For example, a Nigerian or Ghanaian native speaker of English might be discriminated against based on his/her native-like English accent, whereas a white middle-class American, British, or Australian might not be subject to accent-based discrimination because white middle-class American, British, or Australian English accents have been represented as standard English accents (Phillipson, 2010).

As will be demonstrated throughout the chapter, accent-based discrimination is not a simple matter; it is inextricably linked to unequal power relations between dominant languages and groups. Stated another way, accentism is not a form of discrimination that is merely based on the language factor, although it is an important one. Many interwoven factors, such as asymmetrical power relations among speakers, their countries of origin and first languages, are connected to accentism.

To illuminate how this form of accent-based discrimination has occurred, this chapter provides a historical overview of the way many varieties of accents labeled as nonstandard or "foreign" were emerged and have been looked down upon, discriminating against those who spoke and continue to speak with these accents. Further, it demonstrates the way and the extent to which such actions have affected the cultural life, the learning process, the identity, and the subjective and material conditions of linguistically and historically marginalized groups, including linguistically and culturally diverse students. Finally, this chapter proposes alternative ways to challenge and counter accentism that minority groups, including linguistically and culturally diverse students, have faced in schools and in society at large.

To understand how accents are acquired and at the same time unravel the root causes of accentism, one must first know the history of human migration and Western colonization because such history might help us explain how people acquire accents and the origin of accentism. Equally important, one must understand the politics behind the globalization of U.S. and British English and its effects on many languages around the world (Canagarajah, 1999; Macedo et al., 2003; Pennycook, 1994; Phillipson, 2003, 2010; Skutnabb-Kangas, 2000). In short, issues of accents and accentism need to be situated and critically examined from a historical, postcolonial, and sociolinguistic perspective, which informs this chapter. Based on this premise, in the sections that follow, I explore the root causes of human migration. I then analyze Western colonization of non-Western countries and the large-scale linguistic, cultural, and socioeconomic effects of this form of colonization on these countries.

Human Migration and the Acquisition of Accented Languages

Before talking about accentism, it is important to understand how people have acquired accents, which is the factor linguistically insensitive individuals often base on to discriminate against those who do not speak, for example, English or French with the socially constructed standard English or French accent. The acquisition of accents does not happen in a vacuum. Such an acquisition takes place through human interaction occurring through migration, among other sociohistorical phenomena.

Human migration is not a new phenomenon. It has been happening since the dawn of humanity (Bessel & Haake, 2011; Chomsky, 2007; Goldin et al., 2012; Harziq & Hoerder, 2009). Throughout history people have migrated from place to place in search of a better life and sometimes for adventure purposes. Some people have voluntarily migrated from one region or a country to another, while others have been forced to do so, as a result of slavery, war, genocide, racism, poverty, political persecution, and ethnic, cultural, and religious conflicts, often politically motivated, resulting in people's dislocation and oppression (Cetinish, 2003; Cunningham, 2011; Medeiros & Medeiros, 2008; Ogbu, 1998). For example, Africans were forcibly taken from their families and lands only to be enslaved in the Western Hemisphere, particularly in the Caribbean and the United States (Davidson, 1998; Lindsay, 2007; Rediker, 2008; William, 2009). Likewise, many Jews and other marginalized groups such as the gypsies were forced to flee Hitler's Germany to avoid being tortured and murdered (Ash & Sollner, 2002; Lukas, 1994; Panayi, 2000).

Similarly, as a result of the genocide that occurred in Rwanda in 1994, many Rwandans were forced to leave their native land to immigrate to other African countries, like Somalia, Kenya, and Ethiopia, as well as the United States and Europe. In the same way, the genocide in Sudan, specifically in Darfur, forcibly caused the migration of many Sudanese to neighboring countries like Ethiopia. Likewise, the U.S./Iraq war forced many Iraqis to leave their land to migrate to neighboring countries, such as Syria and Jordan, as well as the United States. Also, many Mexicans, forced by poverty caused by internal political corruption and destructive economic effects of the North American Free Trade Agreement (Chomsky, 2011), have immigrated to the United States. Finally, Cubans and Haitians have left Cuba and Haiti for political and economic reasons. Many other examples can be given here to illuminate the root causes of human migration.

When people move from one region or country to another, they bring with them their languages and their cultural norms and values. These languages and cultural norms and values do not remain static; they evolve through interactions with people from different linguistic, cultural, and racial backgrounds and socioeconomic statuses. As a case in point, the native languages that immigrants, including students, speak are often influenced by accents coming from other languages to which they have been exposed. As a result of this exposure, they develop accents both in their native languages and other languages, which they have acquired as a second or third language (Lippi-Green, 2012).

Likewise, Africans, who were captured and forcibly transported to the Americas only to be enslaved, spoke various languages, for they belonged to different tribes. Through interaction with their masters and other slaves, their native languages evolved, borrowing words from other languages, including their masters' (Gilyard, 2011). Similarly, through interaction with the enslaved Africans, the native tongue of the masters evolved. In addition to their native tongues, the languages that the slaves acquired, English or French, through exposure to the masters' languages, were accented or, to be specific, were various forms of English or French (Gilyard, 2011).

Similar linguistic phenomena occur when refugees are forcibly moved from one region or country to another. Let's take the case of Iraqi refugees who migrate to Jordan or Lebanon. Arabic is spoken in these three countries, although the accent is slightly different. These Iraqi refugees, especially the younger ones, will mostly likely acquire a Jordanian or Lebanon Arabic accent after being exposed to it for a relatively long period of time, say, between five and 10 years, depending on the frequency level of the sociolinguistic exposure. Finally, in the United States, people from the South speak English with a different accent from those living in the North. However, if those living in the Southern part of the United States move to the Northern part and live there for a long period of time, say, 10 years or longer, they will most likely acquire a Northern type of English accent. The prime reason for this is that when languages enter in contact, they influence one another. This type of linguistic interexchange does not happen in a vacuum. It occurs through social interaction and cultural and linguistic encounters among people. In the following section, I further examine the conditions that have led to the birth and acquisition of various accents and the rise of accentism; these conditions include contacts between European languages and indigenous languages, the colonial encounters between the colonized and the colonizer, and the effect of the colonial legacy on historically marginalized groups.

Western Colonization and the Rise of Accents and Accentism

Imposing their languages on the colonized at the expense of the latter's indigenous languages was one of the ideological and political strategies of colonial powers (Chatterjee, 2012; Dei, 2010; Thiong'o, 1986; Young, 2006). At school, colonized children were forced to learn in the language of the colonized (Orelus, 2007, 2012; Thiong'o, 1986). By doing so, they were inadvertently indoctrinated; that is, they unconsciously grew to appreciate European culture and values entrenched in the language of the colonizers imposed on them (Thiong'o, 1986). Worse yet, because of linguistic domination and internalized oppression, the colonized started to dislike their own languages and culture while showing much more appreciation and respect for European culture and languages, which through institutions, such as schools and churches, they taught were superior to theirs (Memmi, 1965; Rodney, 1972; Thiong'o, 1986). Rodney notes,

> Schools of kindergarten and primary level for Africans in Portuguese colonies were nothing but agencies for the spread of the Portuguese language. Most schools were controlled by the Catholic Church, as a reflection of the unity of church and state in fascist Portugal. In the little-known Spanish colony of Guinea (Rio Muni), the small amount of education given to Africans was based on eliminating the use of local languages by the pupils and on instilling in their hearts the holy fear of God.
>
> (p. 249)

The encounters between European languages and indigenous languages as well as the contact among multiple languages spoken by the colonized have led to the emergence of a variety of accented Englishes, Frenches, or Portugueses. It is important to note that before the Europeans colonized Africa, Africans spoke and continue to speak many languages as they belonged to different tribes (Thiong'o, 1986). To divide and conquer, the colonizers put together colonized Africans belonging to diverse tribes and spoke different languages (Memmi, 1965). However, this "dividing to conquer" strategy could not be fully enforced because some level of verbal communication among the colonized was needed for the colonial machine to continue to be functional. That is, because the colonizers needed some form of verbal reports from the colonized they felt they could trust, they carefully allowed selected colonized workers speaking the same or similar tribal languages to work together in the same place (Memmi, 1965). Further, because the colonizers often had to communicate with the colonized, the latter was exposed to the language of the former. This linguistic encounter gave birth to a variety of accented Englishes, Frenches, or Portugueses that the colonized spoke and their children and grandchildren grew up speaking.

These accented forms of English, French, and Portuguese have been passed on from generation to generation. Structurally and linguistically, they had gone through different phases; they had evolved. In linguistic and sociolinguistic terms, they had moved from being called pidgins, which are the combined elements of two or more languages, to being called Creole, which is a much more evolved and refined version of pidgins (Chomsky, 2006). In African and Caribbean countries, like Cape Verde and Haiti, Creole is the primary language of communication. However, the Creole spoken in these countries is not the same. For example, Cape Verdean Creole is Portuguese based, whereas Haitian Creole is French based due to the fact that these countries were colonized by two different colonizing powers: Portugal and France, respectively.

In addition to Creole, people living in formerly colonized countries speak the inherited language of the colonizers, such as French, Portuguese, English, or Spanish, with an accent deviating from the accent of the colonizers. For example, in Cape Verde, Mozambique, and Guinea Bissau, Portuguese is spoken, and it is the primary language of instruction, used for socioeconomic and political mobility. Likewise, in Senegal, Guinea Conakry, and Haiti, French is spoken and tends to serve the same purposes. Finally, in Kenya, English is spoken, and it is the dominant language serving as the language of instruction. However, the types of English, French, and Portuguese spoken by Nigerian, Ghanaians, Haitians, Senegalese, Cape Verdean, and Guineans do not have the same social and political status as the French, English, and Portuguese spoken by white middle-class French, Portuguese, and British people because of unequal power relations existing between so-called standard accents and nonstandard ones (Macedo et al., 2003;

Phillipson, 2010). The refusal to place on the same equal footing these varieties of English, French, and Portuguese accents is the root cause of the linguistic discrimination Haitians, Senegalese, Ghanaians, and Cape Verdean speaking these languages with a nondominant accent often encounter when, for example, they travel to France, the UK, the United States, and Portugal.

Because of accumulative effects of language-and class-based oppression, which many minority groups have internalized, they have tried to emulate, for instance, the normalized, standardized accent spoken by dominant groups in society, with the hope of being accepted by these groups. As a case in point, in the United States many linguistically and culturally diverse groups, including students, have tried to speak standard English, hoping this would increase their chances to succeed academically, economically, and politically (Macedo et al., 2003). Likewise, in formerly colonized countries, the elite tends to embrace the language and cultural values of the colonizers for socioeconomic and political mobility (Thiong'o, 1986). The colonial or neocolonial system usually rewards members of the elite group who accept the status quo.

A prime historical and classic example of this is the late prominent Senegalese intellectual and politician, Leopold Senghor, who despite his great contribution to the Negritude Movement, accepted the colonial French status quo by embracing and talking about French culture and language as if they were superior to the languages and culture of his native land and compatriots. His calculated decision to not challenge the French colonial power enabled him to become the first Senegalese president after the independence of his native land. In addition, he was granted a place in the French Academy, a prestigious honor only granted to those who achieve excellence in mastering the French language and valuing French culture and history. In speaking about the French language and literature, Senghor stated,

> We express ourselves in French since French has a universal vocation and since our message is also addressed to French people and others. In our language [i.e. African languages] the halo that surrounds the words is by nature merely that of sap and blood; French words send out thousands of rays like diamonds.
>
> (Senghor, as cited in Thiong'o, 1986, p. 19)

Similarly, the prominent Martiniquais poet and politician, Aime Césaire, was rewarded for fully embracing the French culture and language. Despite his tireless dedication to the Negritude Movement, his great contribution to the struggle against Western racism, and his unshakable determination to defend and heighten African race, culture, and history, Césaire accepted the French colonial status quo in his native Martinique, where he was the mayor of Fort-De-France for almost half of a century. Unlike his former student, Frantz Fanon, who dedicated his entire life to the political struggle aimed at dismantling the Western colonial and imperialist power, Césaire never advocated for the total banishment of the French colonial establishment in Martinique. He realized that for him to be politically successful in the French colonized land, Martinique, he had to master the French language (mastering the language in this context means speaking or trying to speak nearly like the colonizer) and show great appreciation for French literature and culture. And, of course, he was rewarded for making this calculated political choice.

For example, in April 2008, the former French president Nicolas Sarkozy dedicated an official plaque in Césaire's memory at the French Panthéon. This has placed Césaire among the well-known figures of French writers, like Victor Hugo, Voltaire, and Rousseau. Although such an honorable act can be interpreted as a political move by the former French president, the reality is that such an honor would not have been ever given to Frantz Fanon and Check Ante Diop, for example, who were as intellectually and professionally accomplished as Césaire but decided to challenge the whole European colonial system until their deaths. Did Césaire's and Senghor's conscious choices to collaborate with the French colonial power benefit Martiniquais and Senegalese people as a whole? This question is subject to debate. However, I argue that the main objective of colonial powers is, and has always been, to ensure that colonized or formerly colonized countries and people remain in subordinate, dependent political and socioeconomic conditions so that the latter would not be able to compete with them.

I am not against one mastering a dominant language, nor do I oppose appreciation for European literature and culture. However, I am critical of those with a colonized mind trying to mimic the accent of their former colonizers, or their colonizers, or oppressive dominant groups, for professional advancement. Such action can only perpetuate the status quo and contribute to the discriminatory practices of accentism against those who have chosen to maintain their accents and fully embrace and value their native tongues and indigenous culture. As Lippi-Greene (2012) states, "When speakers of devalued or stigmatized varieties of English consent to the standard language ideology, they become complicit in its propagation against themselves, their own interests and identities" (p. 68). It is worth noting here that it is not speaking a language with an accent different from the so-called standard accent that is the problem; instead, it is people's prejudiced attitudes and discriminatory linguistic practices toward those who speak with a distinct nondominant accent.

The colonial legacy has not only caused many psychological scars in the minds of the colonized and their offspring but also accents-based divisions and inequalities among them. As I argued elsewhere (Orelus, 2007, 2012), in formerly French-colonized countries like Haiti, generally people who speak French, especially those who have mastered the language speaking it nearly with a Parisian French accent, tend to benefit of greater social and political prestige and mobility than those who do not. Consequently, younger generations of Haitian students who want to be successful and respected know early on that they have to strive to speak perfect French. But I ask: How about those who do not have the opportunity to attend well-resourced schools with highly trained teachers or, worse yet, who do not have the opportunity to attend school at all to receive quality education, which would enable them to speak perfect French? What would happen to their futures in a neocolonial-based school system and society?

Similar neocolonial linguistic phenomena have been happening in a formerly Portuguese colonized land, Cape Verde. Like in Haiti, Portuguese is seen and treated as a superior language, especially by the elite in that country (Macedo, 1991). At school, students are forced to learn in Portuguese, the language of their former colonizers. Those who manage to speak perfect Portuguese, that is, with the accent close to that of their former colonizers, receive higher socioeconomic, educational, and political awards (Macedo, 1991). And Cape Verdeans who do not are often denied educational and socioeconomic opportunities.

Macedo states,

> The sad reality is that while education in Portuguese provides access to positions of political and economic power for the high echelon of Capeverdean society, it screens out the majority of the masses who fail to learn Portuguese well enough to acquire the necessary literacy level for social, economic, and political advancement. By offering a literacy program conducted in the language of the colonizers with the aim of reappropriating the Capeverdean culture, these educators have, in fact, developed new manipulative strategies that support the maintenance of Portuguese cultural dominance.
>
> (Macedo, as cited in Mitchell & Weiler, p. 154)

Language and accent-based discrimination, or accentism for short, is a serious matter. People have been denied employment or job promotions because of their noticeable accents (Lippi-Green, 2012). Like any form of discrimination, accentism can be institutionally manifested in subtle ways. For example, just as someone is denied employment because of his/her race, gender, sexuality, or disability, a person who speaks with a noticeable accent deviating from the standard can be denied employment or a job promotion because of his/her accent. This explains the reason why many people have strived and spent money to reduce their accents in the hope of being able to speak with the accent valued and accepted in the mainstream society. The highly valued and so-called standard accent is the one with which privileged groups speak. One often hears expression such as Oxford, Sorbonne, or Cambridge types of accents. That is, the colonial-, class-, and race-based types of accents valued at these elitist institutions, which have historically earned the reputation of preparing elite groups, who have dominated the political and economic system of the world.

Because of accentism, in the United States little space in mainstream TV channels, for example, has been open to those who speak with an identifiable nondominant accent. TV hosts and anchors in this country tend to be those who speak with the so-called standard American or British English accent. Likewise, in institutions such as universities and colleges, rarely does one find people with a noticeable nondominant accent occupying top administrative positions, like being the president, the provost, or even the dean. Equally important to note, in the U.S. army it is rare to have high-ranking officers, like generals, who speak with an accent different from the so-called standard American English accent. Finally, in the high-ranking positions in the corporate world, dominated primarily by white males, it is not common to find someone who speaks with an accent deviating from the normalized types of accents, that is, the standard American or British English accent. What can be done?

Conclusion

Institutions such as schools and the army have been challenged and even penalized for discriminating against people because of their race, sexual orientation, disability, and gender. Policy makers and elected officials need to enact and enforce laws that penalize institutions where multilingual and multicultural diverse groups, including students, speaking with a noticeable, nondominant accent, have been victims of linguistic discriminatory practices, namely accentism. Discriminating against people because of their accents, something many do not have much control over, or do not have control over at all, should be considered a crime against their humanity. When this form of linguistic discrimination occurs, those who are victim of it deserve to receive some kind of restored justice; that is, they should be compensated for the linguistic injustice that has been long inflicted on them. However, the long-lasting solution to this will be to eradicate accentism. To this end, I propose social justice teachers create a learning atmosphere in their classrooms where students from various cultural, linguistic, social class, and racial backgrounds speaking nondominant languages with various forms of accents feel that their languages and accents are respected, valued, and cherished like dominant languages and accents. For this happen, teachers and school personnel must show genuine appreciation for and recognize the intrinsic cultural and historical values of the languages their students speak, for these languages constitute part of their community wealth (Yosso, 2006). Finally, they must make a genuine effort to be involved in the communities where their students live, reach out to their students' parents, try to know these parents, and invite them to be involved in the educational lives of their children at the school. Many social justice and community-oriented teachers have already been doing so; it is hoped many more teachers will follow this path.

References

Ash, M., & Sollner, A. (2002). *Forced migration and scientific change: Emigré German-speaking scientists and scholars after 1933*. Cambridge: Cambridge University Press.

Bessel, R., & Haake, C. (2011). *Removing peoples: Forced removal in the modern world*. Oxford, UK: Oxford University Press.

Canagarajah, S. (1999). *Resisting linguistic imperialism in English teaching*. Oxford: Oxford University Press.

Cetinish, D. (2003). *South Slavs in Michigan*. Michigan: Michigan University Press.

Chatterjee, P. (2012). *The black hole of empire: History of a global practice of power*. Princeton, NJ: Princeton University Press.

Chomsky, A. (2007). *They take our jobs: And 20 other myths about immigration*. Boston, MA: Beacon Press.

Chomsky, N. (2006). *Language and mind*. Cambridge: Cambridge University Press.

Chomsky, N. (2011). *Profit over people: Neoliberalism & global order*. New York: Seven Stories Press.

Cunningham, K. (2011). *Migration from Africa: Children's true stories*. London: Heinemann.

Davidson, P. (1998). *The African slave trade*. New York: Back Bay Books.

Dei, G. J. S. (2010). *Teaching Africa: Towards a transgressive pedagogy*. New York: Springer.

Gee, J. (2012). *Social linguistics and literacies: Ideology in discourses* (4th edition). New York: Routledge.

Gilyard, K. (2011). *True to the language game: African American discourse, cultural politics, and pedagogy*. New York: Routledge.

Goldin, I., Cameron, G., & Balarajan, M. (2012). *Exceptional people: How migration shaped our world and will define our future*. Princeton, NJ: Princeton University Press.

Harziq, C., & Hoerder, D. (2009). *What is migration history?* Oxford, UK: Polity.

Lindsay, L. (2007). *Captives as commodities: The transatlantic slave trade*. Upper Saddle River, NJ: Prentice Hall.

Lippi-Green, R. (2012). *English with an accent: Language, ideology, and discrimination in the United States*. New York: Routledge.

Lukas, R. (1994). *Did the children cry? Hitler's war against Jewish and polish children, 1939–1945*. New York: Hippocrene Books.

Macedo, D. (1991). The politics of an emancipatory literacy in Cape Verde. In C. Mitchell & K. Weiler (Eds.), *Rewriting literacy: Culture and the discourse of the other*. London: Bergin & Garvey.

Macedo, D., Dendrinos, B., & Gounari, P. (2003). *The hegemony of English*. Boulder, CO: Paradigm Publisher.

Medeiros, J., & Medeiros, J. (2008). *Migration North: African-American history*. New York: Weigl Publishers.

Ogbu, J. (1998, June). Voluntary and involuntary minorities: A cultural-ecological theory of school performance with some implications for education. *Anthropology & Education Quarterly, 29*(2), 155–188.

Orelus, P. W. (2007). *Education under occupation: The heavy price of living in a neocolonized and globalized world*. Rotterdam, The Netherlands: Sense.

Orelus, P. W. (Ed.). (2012). *A decolonizing encounter: Ward Churchill and Antonia Darder in dialogue*. New York: Peter Lang.

Panayi, P. (2000). *Ethnic minorities in nineteenth and twentieth century Germany: Jews, gypsies, poles, Turks and others: Themes in modern German history.* Upper Saddle River, NJ: Prentice Hall.

Pennycook, A. (1994). *The cultural politics of English as an international language.* Harlow: Longman.

Phillipson, R. (2003). *English-only Europe: Challenging language policy.* London: Routledge.

Phillipson, R. (2010). *Linguistic imperialism continued.* New York: Routledge.

Rediker, M. (2008). *The slave ship: A human history.* London: Penguin Books.

Skutnabb-Kangas, T. (2000). *Linguistic genocide in education—or worldwide diversity and human rights?* Mahwah, NJ: Lawrence Erlbaum.

Thiong'o, N. (1986). *Decolonizing the mind: The politics of language in African literature.* Portsmouth, NH: Heinemann.

Yosso, T. J. (2006). *Critical race counterstories along the Chicana/Chicano educational pipeline.* New York: Routledge.

Young, R. (2006). *Postcolonialism: An historical introduction.* Malden, MA: Blackwell Publishing.

William, S. (2009). *The door of no return: The history of cape coast castle and the Atlantic slave trade.* Katonah, NY: Bluebridge.

11 We Are the Stories We Share

A CDA and a Transformational Process

*Nancy Wasser, Romina Pacheco,
and Veronica Gallegos*

*Is it enough to leave the analysis of the social at the level of how talk and
texts function in social interactions or do we need to go further and consider,
as well, how talk and text function politically in social interactions?*
—*(Gee, 2011, p. 28)*

The dilemma Gee brings up in this question is of upmost importance for
scholars interested in the study of discourse and discourse analysis. If the
goal is to understand the relationship between text and society, why com-
plicate matters by adding politics into the mix? One could even ask what
politics has to do with discourse anyway. Gee (2011) responds to these
questions by arguing that "language-in-use is always part and parcel of, and
partially constitutive of, specific social practices, and that social practices
always have implications for inherently political things like status, solidarity, the distribution of social goods, and power" (p. 28). Thus, he continues,
"a full discourse analysis must discuss such matters and must, in that sense,
be critical" (Gee, 2011, p. 29).

In this study, we use CDA to unveil the workings of power in our situated
experiences as women with multiple identities. In accordance with CDA,
our purpose is to engage in a process of societal transformation in ways
that break with the constraining effects of sexism. We also attempt to contribute to the co-construction of roles for girls and women that give them
(us) real choices to participate in society with open eyes and full awareness
of what is detrimental to our general well-being and which roles allow us
to develop authentic relationships with our surroundings. In this sense, we
have chosen to do a discourse analysis from a critical feminist standpoint
because, as Lazar (2005) argues, "our central concern is with critiquing
discourses which sustain a patriarchal social order" (p. 5). Hence our purpose is to engage in a "radical emancipator agenda" (p. 6). Additionally,
as will be developed later, we feel that reducing the multiplicity of our
experiences to that of only "women" would be too simplistic; therefore, we
acknowledge that "gender as a category intersects with, and is shot through
by, other categories of social identity such as sexuality, ethnicity, social

position and geography" (Lazar, 2005, p. 1). Indeed, through discourse analysis, researchers can engage in critical inquiries of social problems that directly address the way social cognition and communication perpetuate oppression (van Dijk, 1987). This is due to the fact that CDA creates the possibility to study the relationship between language and social structures (Fairclough, 2010; Gee, 2011; van Dijk, 1987). As van Dijk (1987) points out, "[P]rejudice is socially reproduced through discourse" (p. 30); thus, "if we want to understand this important property of the social communication . . . we must examine the structures of such discourse in detail" (p. 30). Furthermore, "discourse is in many respects the central element in the processes of the interpersonal communication of prejudice, and discourse analysis is a key method for the study of the cognitive and social structures and strategies that characterize these processes" (van Dijk, 1987, p. 30). Certainly, CDA makes available the tools to examine the complexities that emerge from the dialectical relationship between discourse and the social world (Rogers, 2011).

As Gee (2011) explains, "discourse" can be understood either as distinctive ways of speaking/listening and writing/reading coupled with distinctive ways of acting, interacting, valuing, feeling, dressing, thinking, and believing that continue through time ("Big D"), or as simply language in use ("small d"). Furthermore, Fairclough (2010) reminds us that "discourse is not simply an entity we can define independently: we can only arrive at an understanding of it by analyzing sets of relations" (p. 3). Hence, for the purposes of this chapter as a *critical* analysis of *commonplace* discourses, we will use Gee's (2011) definition of the process as "Big D" discourse.

According to Fairclough (2010), "CDA has three basic properties: it is relational, it is dialectical, and it is transdisciplinary" (p. 3). That is, it is *relational* because it focuses on social relations. It is *dialectical* precisely because it studies the "relations between objects that are different from one another but . . . not fully separate in the sense that one excludes the other" (Fairclough, 2010, p. 4). And, it is *transdisciplinary* because the analysis of those relations crosses boundaries between disciplines (e.g. linguistics, politics, sociology, and education). In other words, CDA is the "analysis of dialectical *relations between* discourse and other objects, elements or moments, as well as the analysis of the 'internal relations' of discourse" (p. 4). Furthermore, Fairclough points out that CDA takes place in three dimensions. Namely, the linguistic description of the text, the interpretation of the relationship between the discursive processes and the text, and the explanation of the discursive processes and the social processes that are all embedded, simultaneously, at the situational, institutional, and societal levels.

The broad framework of CDA allows the researcher to connect critical social theories with theories of language in the process of inquiry to make visible what is not generally obvious to people, such as ideologies and power relations (Gee, 1996; Fairclough, 2010; Rogers, 2011). This is particularly important because "critical discourse analysts are generally concerned with a critical theory of the social world, the relationship of discourse in the construction and representation of this social world, and a methodology that allows them to describe, interpret, and explain such relationships" (Rogers, 2011, p. 3). This problem-oriented and transdisciplinary characteristic of CDA is relevant in research that seeks to analyze texts, talk, and other semiotic interactions across time and contexts (Rogers, 2011).

However, the ultimate goal of CDA is not limited to unveiling "unequal social arrangements sustained through language use" (Lazar, 2005, p. 1), but to take part in "social transformation and emancipation" (Lazar, 2005, p. 1). In fact, Fairclough (2011) asserts that one point critical discourse analysts must consider is "the social conditions of possibility for social transformation" (p. 126), which can be addressed "from a semiotic perspective in terms of latitudes for agents in social research to develop, recontextualize, and seek to enact and inculcate new discourses" (p. 126)—all of this in light of the saliency that discourse has gained in defining certain areas of social life "so that social and cultural changes *are* largely changes in discursive practices" (Fairclough, 2010, p. 131).

Another key aspect of CDA is that it takes into consideration how "discourse reflects and constructs the social world through many different sign systems" (Rogers, 2011, p. 1). In effect, "a shared assumption [in CDA] is that discourse can be understood as a multimodal social practice" (Rogers, 2011, p. 1) that goes beyond just the use of language. Kress (2011) refers to this as *multimodality* and states that "the term . . . draws attention to the many material resources beyond speech and writing which societies have shaped and which cultures provide as means for making [signs and symbols]," such as visual images, body language, music and sound effects (p. 208). A multimodal social semiotic approach offers a more complex view on the meaning-making process because it takes into consideration how socially made and cultural available material-semiotic resources can express thoughts, experiences, feelings, values, and attitudes (Kress, 2000).

A Model for Employing CDA to Analyze Multimodal Texts

Although this particular study draws on a number of theories of CDA, our major model for employing CDA to our narratives is through the model presented by James Paul Gee (2011) in his book *How to Do Discourse Analysis: A Toolkit*. This tool kit model provides specific directions as to what to look for when analyzing text along with explicit information regarding the method of analysis (Gee, 2011).

Gee (2011) references different types of tasks that discourse analysts may perform. *Utterance analysis* is dissected into two parts: "the utterance-type meaning task" and "the utterance-token meaning task" (p. 24). The former is concerned with the relationship between "form and function in language" at a general meaning level (p. 24). This discourse functions at the level of the sentence and dissects its grammatical parts for their communicative value.

However, the latter is the task we are concerned with in this analysis, that is, the "token" meaning task, also and hereafter referred to as the "situated meaning task" (p. 24). Additionally, Gee (2011) references another important task, that of employing a *critical form of analysis of social practices* (p. 28, in Rogers, 2011). We develop these tasks in what follows, and we also discuss other theories of the utterance as they relate to discourse analysis, notably that of Bakhtin.

Imagine the World Without Narrative

"All lives are narratives. We are not human without narrative. If you are alive, you cannot escape your own narrative. Whether we have the wit to fathom the structure within is another matter. Whether we personally are cognizant of our own journey is another matter."
—(Thompson, 2006, p. 327)

For the critical discourse analyst, narratives of personal experience provide powerful insights into the figured worlds that render experience meaningful. These narratives encode the different voices (Bakhtin, 1981) that make up a person's "space of authoring" (Holland, Lachicotte, Skinner, & Cain, 1998) and thus leave traces of discourses, positioning, and identities. "When someone narrates a personal experience, that person—not just her narrative—is now "available" for others and for one, all over again; our own discourse becomes an object and acquires its own-voice" (Bakhtin, 1986, p. 110). This new voice becomes everybody's voice; it no longer belongs to one individual. In other words, when we decide to share ourselves, our narratives, our personal experiences, in that breaking moment, we lose authorship (and the narrative "I" now belongs to everyone).

In her article *Narratives in Everyday Life*, Elinor Ochs (2011) posts the following reflection: "Imagine the world without narrative." The author invites us to stop for a moment and think deeply about this. We believe she makes a valid point: how would we feel going through life not telling others what happened to us and not recounting what we learned from our mothers and grandmothers . . . not being able to listen and learn from other stories? Imagine not even composing interior narratives to and for yourself. This whole idea is simply unimaginable, for it would mean "a world without history, myths or drama, and lives without reminiscence, revelation, and interpretive revision" (Ochs, 2011, p 64).

Many of us think of narratives as a form of genre and literary forms as narrative texts; narratives are more than this. A person's narrative is a fundamental genre that organizes the ways in which we think and interact with others. In *We Are the Stories We Share*, our narratives are composed of a variety of discourse forms, and our ordinary conversations are, we argue, the purist and most original form of narrative, that is, storytelling through speech.

Narrative is not only a genre; it is also a social activity involving different participant roles. Both Bakhtin (1981) and Goffman (1974) distinguish the narrative role of the author from that of the narrator. Bakhtin also inspired the perspective that the *narrative audience* plays a key role in the construction of narrative. He offers the concept of audience as coauthor of narrative form and meaning (1981). Wodak (2005) states that "narratives are particularly revealing indices of identity because they offer a sort of 'window' into how we evaluate our past experience and therefore position ourselves in our present world" (p. 101).

However, as noted, narratives are authored not only by those who introduce them but also by the many readers and interlocutors who influence the direction of the narrative (Bakhtin, 1981). This coauthorship is most evident in conversational narratives, where interlocutors will ask questions, comment, and otherwise overtly contribute to an evolving tale (Goodwin, 1984). At this point, the narrative will undergo changes and take on new directions; therefore, how we think about ourselves and others will be influenced by both the message content of jointly told narratives and the experience of working together to construct a new narrative (Ochs, 2011, p. 68). In terms of written text, readers function as coauthors of the narratives because they interpret the stories in light of their own "figured worlds," that Gee (2011) describes as "what counts as a typical story for people [in terms of] their social and cultural groups" (p. 70). Additionally, readers will continue the narratives in their imaginations and in conversation with other readers. From this perspective we invite readers of our following narratives to continue these stories in the vein of Bakhtinian utterances, that is, to ask "does this story relate to my/our own narrative, and if so, how?"

We Are the Stories We Share parts from the idea that how we choose to tell our stories displays only who we are to others. It also helps to construct for ourselves as individuals the range of identities that we bring together as different facets of "this is who I am." Our study draws from four different theoretical frameworks: discourse, identifying social languages, rooting out situated meanings, and identifying the figured worlds of the discourse of various social groups (Gee, 2011) to analyze how different facets of narratives project identities at gender, interactional, and cultural levels. The stories we tell deal with aspects of mother/daughter identity, the use of narrative data from life stories to compare relation-based identities, and the cultural aspect of time and place. As noted by Ochs (1997), the narrative is, among other things, "a tool for instantiating social and personal identities" (cited in Wodak & Chilton, 2005, p. 104). Through our study, we are establishing the relevance of sharing, discussing, and analyzing who we are within our narratives; we are inviting other women to find themselves in our stories as they position themselves in theirs.

Schiffrin (1997) argues that narratives can provide:

> A *sociolinguistic self-portrait;* a linguistic lens through which one discovers people's own views of themselves (as situated within both an ongoing interaction and a larger social structure) and their experiences.

> Since the situations that speakers create through narratives–the trans-
> formations of experience enabled by the story world–are also open to
> evaluation in the interactional world, these self-portraits can create an
> interactional arena in which the speaker's views of self and world can
> be reinforced or challenged.
>
> (cited in Wodak, 2005, p. 104)

Therefore, not only can narratives reveal footings, or substrata, which in turn reveal orientations to particular constructions of self, but they also infuse a *dynamic* aspect of identity construction within social interaction. It is this dynamism that we invite our readers and audiences to explore and participate in.

Labov and Waletsky (1967) discuss how basic narrative structures deal with the relationship between form and function. They also established two main functions of narratives: referential and evaluative. For the purpose of our study, we have not focused on form but rather on the function of our stories. The referential aspects include time, place, culture, religion, and the situated meanings (accepted cultural norms) of the stories. The function reveals the social message embedded in them.

Narratives are a method of recapitulating past experiences. The *referential* function refers to the sequence of events in the narrative; it makes reference to certain events, but then what? As Labov suggests, "[A] narrative that only carries this [referential] function may seem pointless and difficult to follow" (cited in Rogers, 2011, p. 49). It is the evaluative function that gives meaning to narrative. This becomes obvious even in ordinary conversations where we find ourselves creating the suspense that will keep our audience engaged in the narrative with the evaluative elements that reveal the desired attitude of the narrator toward the story being narrated. Gee (1999) sums it up by defining the evaluation in narratives as the "material that makes clear why the story is interesting and tellable" (cited in Rogers, 2011, p. 49).

This study investigates the relation between institutional stories—our stories and the ways in which we tell our own stories within this framework. *We Are the Stories We Share* examines the notions of intertextuality and textual communities, showing how stories are shaped in relation to narratives: positioning, identities, and figured worlds. This study argues that an individual's story is not only personal but is shaped as a response to earlier stories and the appropriate values and actions that those stories teach. This intertextuality of personal narrative means that one's presentation of the events and meanings of one's life is not only individual but rather is strongly shaped by the stories of the communities of which one is a member.

Our Theoretical Model Based on Gee's "Tools of Inquiry"

Gee (2011) has garnered four tools of inquiry from various academic disciplines concerned with language and social practices. The first, "Big 'D' discourses," introduced here, treats the notion that language is an ongoing phenomenon. Rooted in history, and practiced (spoken, written, acted out, drawn, symbolized, etc.) in the present, an utterance ripples out and affects the future as well as the present moment. In this manner, discourse relates to Bakhtin's (2005) notion of the *utterance* as the basis of language. "Let us call the meaning of the utterance as a whole its *theme* . . . [which, like the utterance] is individual and non-reiterative. . . . An essential feature of the theme, and therefore of the utterance, is that it is endowed with *values*" (cited in Todorov, 1995, p. 45). It is on the level of utterance, according to Bakhtin, that we need to study language, for it is in the utterance that "historical" meaning lies (p. 45).

Similarly, Gee (2011) approaches discourse as the use of language for "distinctive ways of acting, interacting with others, believing, valuing, dressing, and using various sorts of objects and tools in various sorts of distinctive environments" (in Rogers, 2011, p. 37). Discourse not only identifies us in the moment; it connects us to various social groups at various times and spaces. Discourses reflect our "kind" and "type." For example, one may be a teacher of mathematics interested particularly in geometry. As well, this teacher may be a member of a certain religious group, social club, service organization, political group, and so on. She may be a pianist and a hiker. She, therefore, will be engaged in many tasks of meaning employing many tools of expression of these various meanings. "Being in a Discourse is being able to engage in a particular sort of 'dance' with words, deeds, values, feelings, other people, objects, tools, technologies, places, and times" (Gee, 2011, in Rogers, 2011, p. 37). Put another way, being in a state of discourse could be construed as being able to "walk the walk and talk the talk."

Another task of CDA is that of identifying the *social languages* that people are using at any given time and space and, according to Gee (2011), "are an important aspect of the language part of Discourses" (in Rogers, 2011, p. 39). Social languages are many and vary according to context. They are "styles" of language embedded in other "styles." For example, in the math teacher example, she may also be a student of classical piano who will speak in that style and genre while studying. Perhaps she is also a member of a jazz group who performs at nightclubs. When referencing this work, she will employ another style of speaking. She is a mother with young children modeling speech in two languages. On her coffee dates with friends, she speaks a colloquial language and accent specific to the region where she lives. Often she and they *code switch* as their dialogue moves back and forth between the two prevailing languages of the region. Quoting Gee (2011), "The point just is that people must have some, however tentative, unspoken, and problematic, idea of who is speaking in the sense of what social identity is at play" (cited in Rogers, 2011, p. 40).

The *situated meaning* task of CDA is one emphasized heavily in this analysis study. Situated meaning of a discourse is based on a common agreement individuals have about the meaning of an utterance in a particular situation. Bakhtin (2007) explains an utterance as being anything from a nod of agreement to a word to a fully developed sign system, for example, a novel (pp. 42–43, 53). These semiotic expressions can have different meanings in different times, spaces, and situations. For example, the word "stoned" can refer to an archway, as in the "stoned" arch leading to the cathedral. It can refer to a person who is intoxicated by substance abuse, as in "He was stoned at the party." This word can refer to an abusive act, as in "They stoned the woman because she ran away from her husband." In each of these situations, there is common agreement among most speakers of English as to the "situated meaning" of each use of this word (Gee, 2011).

Why is CDA useful for teasing out the subtexts in these situated meanings? Using this example, we might ask, "Why is the woman being stoned because she ran away from her husband?" That question will refer us to a much deeper sociopolitical situated meaning that uncovers social/political situated meanings (agreements) about why the woman is being stoned. Situated meanings often reflect common historical agreements that CDA analysts want to call into question with the idea of transforming the agreements into other, more critical and life-affirming ones. For example, Stanley Aronowitz (2006) speaks of "global capitalism" in terms of the "new struggles that [have produced] a new discourse of human rights [that] . . . must be mediated by new conditions" in which both the "subaltern" together with the privileged who understand the challenges faced by the "subaltern" work together for transformation of the discourse" (cited in Apple & Buras, 2006, p. 177).

Finally, Gee (2011) asks us to consider the critical discourse task analysis of *figured worlds*. These figured worlds are "the reason we do not use words just based on their definitions or . . . their 'general meanings'" (p. 69). Figured worlds are "what counts as a typical story for people [in terms of] their social and culture groups" (p. 70). For example, a "windy day" in Louisiana means something very different than a "windy day" in New Mexico. In the semitropical, humid climate of Louisiana, where the weather can be hot, damp, and "airless," a windy day would probably indicate a severe weather front. It might very well mean a hurricane. In New Mexico, as high winds sweep across the desert vastness, a windy day might be a quite typical day. Thus, agreement about what is a "windy day" is determined by geographical location and climate conditions.

"What counts as a typical story for people differs by their social and culture groups" (Gee, 2011, p. 70). Gee (2011) gives as an example the different stories we have about children. In some social groups, for children to be assertive and self-seeking is a sign of independence. In other social groups, children should be reticent and obey their parents/caregivers in all things. These perceptions are a function of class as well as cultural background. "They are simplified theories of the world that are meant to help people go on about the business of life when one is not allowed the time to think through and research everything before acting" (p. 70).

In CDA, this tool is used to identify the "figured worlds" from which people are speaking and acting. It is a picture we have in our minds about, for example, what it is like to live on the borderland of the United States and Mexico. For some, it might be a scenario of drugs and a dangerous drug subculture. For others it may mean family members on either side of the border. For still others it may mean an opportunity for travel, for purchasing material goods, or for learning a second language. The critical discourse analyst uses this tool to determine what figured world or worlds are determining what is "taken to be typical or normal" [in these] 'simplified worlds'" (Gee, 2011, p. 71).

Thus, these four tools of inquiry: *"Big D" discourse*, identifying *social languages*, rooting out *situated meanings*, and identifying the *figured worlds* of the discourse of various social groups help the critical discourse analyst explore ways of transforming our commonsense ways of thinking, speaking about, and representing certain ideas to promote social justice for all groups. In our narratives, presented next, we will use these tools of inquiry to explore how the "commonsense" acceptance of our various "figured worlds" affected us in childhood.

Nancy's Story: Mothers, Don't Let Your Daughters Grow Up to Drive Tractors

Setting: *A July evening in central Kansas in the mid-1950s on a large Mennonite farm. The intense heat of the day slowly rises, and the farm cools. The uncles are gathered outside on the long, dirt driveway leading to the barn. We cousins are gathered around playing tag in the lingering light. Full of Aunt Sarah's fried chicken and chocolate cake, we duck and play among the laughing men.*

Suddenly Uncle Melvin appears on a big, bright-green John Deere tractor. Smiling his handsome smile, teeth lighting up his dark skin, he pulls to a halt among the gathering crowd. The aunts, finished with kitchen chores, wipe their hands on their aprons as they cross the yard to join us.

"Who wants to drive the tractor?" Uncle Mervin calls out. Choruses of "I do. I do. I do," are heard all around. I am one of them.

Cousin Ruben, the oldest among us, is the first to be favored. He can drive it all by himself, and he wheels around the farmyard with determined nonchalance.

Next come the "twin boys," from different families but the same age. Uncle Mervin instructs them about how to use the throttle. I listen intently. Then, each boy in his turn steers the tractor down the driveway and back.

"Would you like to try, Dylan?" my uncle inquires of my brother, whose eyes light up with anticipation. Hey, wait a minute, I think. My brother is not quite five years old, and I am already

six! Does this mean they are skipping over me? Does it mean they will let Dylan drive the tractor all by himself? Little Dylan?

Mommy clucks and chuckles as Dylan climbs aboard. "What a big lucky boy you are!" Uncle Mervin sets the throttle and Dylan takes off. He only goes a short distance, but he is driving the tractor all by himself!

My girl cousins stand around, smiling and looking on. Why have none of them asked to drive the tractor? Why have they not been invited to drive it by Uncle Mervin?

Dylan descends, hops off, and Uncle Mervin announces, "Well. I guess that's all for tonight!"

"Hey, wait a minute!" I call out. "I want a turn. I want to drive the tractor!"

"Oh, Nancy," Mommy disparages. "You can't drive the tractor!"

"Why not? Dylan drove it, and he's younger than I am!"

"But you're a girl!"

"So what?" I ask, knowing it's a useless question but asking it anyway. (How do they think?)

"Maybe she could have a ride with Mervin driving." Daddy steps up to the tractor and offers this as a solution. I know he's being kind, but I don't want to ride with Mervin. I want to drive the tractor.

"No," I say. "I want to drive myself!"

"Oh, Nancy." It's Mom again. "Don't be ungrateful."

I climb up onto the tractor and sit beside Uncle on the big seat. He drives down the road. I try to get into the spirit of the adventure, but the thrill is gone. Why does being a girl so restrict my activities? Why, why, why?

CDA Analysis: Nancy

I chose this piece of narrative data because it contains dialogue as well as including setting, both temporal and historical, plot, a strong narrative point of view, and also co-construction of the narrative through others' voices (Ochs, 2011). In the Bakhtinian sense of an utterance as an ongoing discourse whose beginning is historical and whose ending is never-ending or ongoing, this vignette represents multidimensional aspects of discourse (Gee, 1996) that can be analyzed in any number of ways. Thus I begin with Gee's advice to "[p]ick some key words and phrases in the data . . . and ask what [are the] *situated meanings*" (2011, p. 125).

Situated Meanings

Following Gee (2011), I look for the *situated meanings* to analyze the setting. The historical time is the Midwest of the United States in the mid-20th century. Since it is a large farm, one would expect that much work with many hands goes on. The fact that it is a Mennonite farm conjures images of women in long, plain dresses and a strict differentiation of tasks between men and women.

Bakhtin (1981), Todorov (1995) and others have "implored interpreters of narrative to embed [stylized] texts in the social and historical dialogues in which they participate" (Ochs, 2011, p. 68). The social setting, although embedded in the historical one, is important for defining the situated meaning of the setting. The division of labor is evident in the contrasting images of "Aunt Donna's chicken and chocolate cake" and "laughing men." Equally, "laughing men" can be juxtaposed with "aunts," "kitchen chores," and "aprons." The men have finished their work for the day, eaten a tasty meal, and are relaxing outside on the farm, laughing and talking among themselves. The women are just finishing their work. They are wiping their hands on their aprons as they finally finish their chores for the day.

Figured Worlds

Narrative Construction (A Scene From Everyday Life): *"who wants to drive the tractor;" "I do;" "I am one of them."*

Analysis of Narrative Construction

The utterance, in Bakhtinian theory, is not only an ongoing speech act but is semiotic. Therefore, written text "can be part of an ongoing communicative interaction" (Ochs, 2011, p. 67). Ochs (2009) goes on to explain that written text can be "strategic, stylized answers" to questions "posed by the situation in which they arose" (pp. 67–68, emphasis in original).

The motivating surface question that begins the plot construction in this vignette is: "Who wants to drive the tractor?" At this beginning point in the narrative, it is not known by Nancy that this question is politically charged. The answer to the question is where the plot begins to unravel and to become infused with situated meaning. The phrases, "I do." and "I am one of them" are quite loaded social ideas as will be seen as the plot evolves. They are *strategic* in Och's sense of the word because they set a tone for the plot turn which is to define the *figured world* (Gee, 2009).

According to Bakhtin (cited in Gardiner, 1992), "[I]deologies are practices which function symbolically, usually through the generation of utterances, subject to definite norms and constraints . . . [that] often . . . derive from the prevailing structure of class power. . . . [T]he study of ideologies must involve an analysis of the system of signs through which they are expressed" (p. 67). As will be seen, the plot of this narrative vignette turns on the "norms and constraints" derived from two prevailing ideologies of power, that is, age and gender.

Key Words/Phrases

Narrative Time: *"first to be favored;" "Next come the 'twin boys';" "each boy in his turn steers;" "not quite five;" "I am already six."*

Analysis of Narrative Time

Ochs (2011), referencing Heidegger's (1962) framework, informs us that "when we construct narratives about the past, we apprehend them in terms of what they imply for the present and future" (p. 70). Therefore, narratives of events that happened in the past may serve as cautionary tales. At any rate, "narratives that touch on past events are always about the present and future as well" (p. 70). Ochs goes on to point out that sometimes narratives about the past help change and shape the future.

The key phrases here concern sequential time according to age and also treat the gender favoritism of boys. The phrase "not quite five" in the context of the younger brother to Nancy, when juxtaposed against the phrase, "I am already six," situates the meaning of the importance of age in light of gender. At this point Nancy is puzzled as to why she was skipped over as the tractor-driving privilege moved down the chronological age of the cousins. A figured world of age favoritism and gender bias is emerging.

Key Words/Phrases

Narrative Point of View and Plot Structure: *"I do;" "I am one of them;" "my uncle inquires of my brother;" "already six;" "skipping over me;" "all by himself;" "girl cousins stand around;" "I want a turn;" "he's younger;" "I want to drive myself."*

Analysis of Narrative Point of View and Plot Structure

The point of view of the narrative is six-year old Nancy. The phrase "I do" signifies a desire for active participation in the social activities of the group. A situated meaning arises from the phrase "I am one of them," which aligns Nancy with the social group wanting to drive the tractor. However, when "my uncle inquires of my brother," even though she is "already six," we see the emergence of conflict around which the plot pivots.

The next phrase predicates the plot turn from Nancy's point of view; they are "skipping over me." This is the complicating event that Aristotle (1962) speaks of (cited in Ochs, 2011, p. 75) or as Ochs (2011) refers to it, the *"key event that disrupts the equilibrium of ordinary, expected circumstances"* (p. 75, emphasis in original.). From then on Nancy's expectation to drive the tractor by herself changes the narrative story line from one of excited anticipation to one of disappointment.

When Dylan is allowed to drive the tractor "all by himself," we are aware of the looming presence of gender bias in the making. And, in fact, this is the overarching "theory of events" as Ochs (2009) explains it. From the point of view of "Nancy," the theory of events I construct in the narrative is that of male privilege.

Key Words/Phrases

Co-Construction of Narrative [many-voicedness (Bakhtin, 1981, 1986)]: *"like to try;" "Dylan;" "big lucky boy;" "You can't; you're a girl;" "So what?" "have a ride with Mervin;" "No," "Don't be ungrateful."*

Analysis of Co-Construction of Narrative

Bakhtin (1981) embraces the idea that a single subject cannot construct reality. Reality is dialogically constructed, or co-constructed, as polyphonic utterances shape not only the dialogue itself but, indeed, the social being. According to Voloshinov (1973), "Individual consciousness is not the architect of the ideological superstructure, but only a tenant lodging in the social edifice of ideological signs" (p. 87). Thus, although the consciousness of Nancy is demonstrated in her insistent pleas to drive the tractor by herself, a socially situated identity is being constructed for her through the voices of the others.

Uncle asks Dylan if he would "like to try" driving the tractor. The fact that Nancy is not being asked to drive the tractor is as symbolic as the fact that Dylan was asked. Similarly, as Dylan is dubbed by his mother as a "big lucky boy," there is an absence of that same signature for Nancy. She is *not* a big, lucky girl. In fact, she is told point blank, "You can't (drive the tractor). You're a girl." The situated meaning of this discourse is that Nancy, due to the fact that she is a girl, is not allowed to drive the tractor. Thus, her figured world at the historical moment goes from "I can" to "You can't," or to borrow an idea from Cope and Kalantzis (2000), her future social discourse is in process of being "designed" (2000) in that present moment. The tractor becomes a symbol for an unattainable figured world for Nancy—a world where men are ranked by age r to drive a tractor and women are skipped over and not even considered as potential tractor drivers.

Although Nancy protests this socially designed world in which she has no say, despite her utterance of "So what," and is invited to "have a ride with Mervin," she persists in her thwarted narrative goal by shouting, "No!" Moreover, she is symbolically placed by her mother in the position of being "ungrateful." Thus, she capitulates and agrees to a ride on the tractor with Uncle; however future possibilities have been established by her insistence on wanting to drive by herself. Although her identity was socially constructed in the narrative by polyphonic voices (Bakhtin, 1981; Todorov, 1995) of the co-narrators directing her thoughts and actions, she established a position that was duly noted by the key characters in the narrative. Ochs (2011) claims that "[w]hen storytellers' recount that a problematic event incited psychological responses or actions, the story appears to be capped in past time" (p. 76). This is indeed the case with the tractor story where Nancy capitulated to the social designs of the Mennonite farmers' adult group. "However," Ochs (2011) continues, stories have a way of edging into the future, and storytellers will often frame an inciting event . . . as *still unresolved*" (p. 76). Our future task is to test the opportunity for females to learn to operate machinery in the present historical time to determine if that particular Discourse is still problematic for little girls.

Veronica's Story: *Christmas 1975*

I knew I wanted a bicycle for Christmas. I also knew my mom (or Santa Claus) would do anything to make sure I and my brother and my sister would get the gifts that we asked for: vivid memories of layaways at K-mart and my dad putting bikes together on Christmas Eve. I also remember getting a doll; I'm almost certain I didn't ask for a doll.

We rose Christmas morning and like a typical Mexican family ran into the living room to see what Santa Clos had left us. There it was: my beautiful "purple" bicycle with the "flower seat." My brother also received a bike he hadn't asked for, but he acted surprised anyway:

¡Ah, que chida bici! Me voy a cambiar para salir a pasear ("Cool bike! I'm going to get dressed so I can go out for a ride"). This offered by my brother, Luis Pablo, who had always been an intellectual; he loved to read in both English and Spanish. He enjoyed sports—watching them and keeping up with the stats, but he was never really an outdoorsy person. That morning he went back to his room and didn't come out until lunchtime.

¡Mi bicicleta! Dije, ¡Qué bonita, que linda que está! También la de Luis Pablo está bonita, me gusta mucho ese color. . . . ("My bike!" I said. "It's so beautiful. It really is nice! Luis Pablo's bike is nice too, I like that color a lot.")

My mom, always attentive to whatever I say, walked over to where I was hopping on my brother's bike and handed me an opened box, exclaiming,

¡Mire que bonita muñeca! Yo no supe que le había pedido eso a Santa Clos! ("What a beautiful doll! I didn't know you had asked Santa for one!")

¡Yo no sé la pedí! Yo le pedí una bici y un radio; que raro que se haya equivocado. ¡Bueno, al menos recordó lo de la bicicleta! ¡Está padrísima! ¿Puedo salir a andar en mi bici? ("I didn't ask for it! I asked for a bike and a radio; I'm surprised he made a mistake. . . . Well, at least he remembered the bike! It's so cool! May I go outside and ride it?")

¡Claro que la pidió! Todas las niñas piden una muñeca, especialmente esta que come . . . se parece a usted en lo comelón, ¡jajaja! ("Of course you asked for it; all the girls ask for a doll, especially this one that eats. . . . She reminds me of you—a good eater, ha ha ha!")

I didn't think it was funny, but I was in a hurry to take that bike out for a ride, so I went along with the conversation.

Le voy a poner las baterías para que pueda jugar con ella; está haciendo mucho frio para que salga, mejor juegue aquí adentro con su muñeca. ("I'm going to put the batteries in the doll, so you can play with her. It's too cold to go out; its better you play with your doll in here.")

My dad, sitting in his recliner watching us, was tired after all the "assembling" he did the night before: my brother's bike, my bike, my sister's dollhouse. He usually didn't say much, but that day I remember him saying:

(Gesturing to my brother's bike): Esa bicicleta está muy alta para usted pero si le gustan altas, le puedo subir el asiento a la suya ("That bike is too high for you, but if you like it high, I can raise the seat on your bike").

Nomás estoy calando esta a ver cómo se siente; a mí me gusta más la mía ("I'm just trying this one to see how it feels; I like mine better").

¡Uuuy, esa bicicleta está más grande! ¿Es para niñas Mami? ("Uuuy, that bike is so big! Is it for girls, Mommy?")

Claro que no, no ve que es azul y tiene ese tubo en medio; es bicicleta de hombre. La morada si es de niñas, tiene florecitas y una canasta . . . usted también la puede usar cuando sepa andar sin las llantitas. ("Of course not, can't you see it's blue, and it has that tube in the middle; it's a boy bike. The purple one is for girls. It has flowers and a basket. . . . You can use it when you learn to ride without training wheels").

But I liked that blue bike. I have a scar above my right eye that reminds me how much I liked and rode that bike.

As I got off the blue bike, I turned to my mother, who was struggling with the screw on the back of my doll: Gracias Mami. ¡Mientras le pones las baterías a la mona, me voy a vestir para salir a pasear a mi muñeca en mi bici nueva! ("Thanks, Mommy. While you put the batteries in the doll, I'm going to get dressed to go outside, so I can give my doll a ride on my new bike!")

I got dressed, tied the doll to the back of the seat, and took off down the driveway and onto the street. My dad was dressed too; he was waiting for me outside. I was barely seven when I found out that Santa Claus was actually my parents—and that I didn't like dolls. My parents didn't find out until not so long ago about what else I didn't like.

CDA Analysis: Veronica

The above is a reconstruction of a personal event that occurred when I was seven years old. I chose this narrative because its phrases and certain words elicit *situated meanings* that, in turn, implicate *figured worlds*. At the same time, the situated meanings and the figured worlds, in conjunction with the *social language(s)* present in this particular text highlight the identities of the participants, the *relationships* among them, and the *politics* taking place in this *discourse*. As I analyzed this scene from what I thought happened in my *past*, I couldn't help but question myself: Is it really in my past? Is it possible that this ostensibly simple Christmas scene is an ongoing learning experience that commenced before me and continued after the event itself? Did it reflect, substantiate, and continue an already ongoing discourse that is really a "Big D" discourse?

"Big D" Discourse: Socially Situated Identities

Gee (2011) states, "To mean anything to someone else (or even to myself) I have to communicate who I am (in the sense of what socially situated identity I am taking on here and now)" (as cited in Rogers, p. 37). In *Christmas 1975*, the different roles portrayed are evident: *Mami*'s role is to educate her daughter as to what is "politically and socially" correct. *Dad's* role is to mediate without causing major altercations; and Veronica's role is that of a seven-year old trying to "communicate" who she is.

Situated Meanings

Gee (2009) points out that when interlocutors speak, they communicate with what they believe to be shared assumptions. When "Mom" says things like, "Of course you asked for it. All girls ask for a doll" or "It's a boy bike. The purple one is for girls," she is assuming that Veronica shares with her the same gender knowledge and beliefs about girls' gender identity. Veronica, however, is beginning to question that shared assumption.

Figured Worlds

This text e is a perfect example of a "typical" Christmas morning story. It is typical in that its value assumes a "commonsense" acceptance of the norm to get up early on Christmas morning, rush to the living room, and act surprised about gifts that magically appeared while you were sleeping. By statements such as "It's a boy bike. The purple one is for girls, (because) it has flowers and a basket" or "All girls ask for a doll," *Mami* is creating a "typical" (i.e. socially acceptable from her cultural perspective) world for her family. As Gee (2009) explains, figured worlds can often be considered as simplifications about the world, simplifications that leave out authentic identities of those who populate these worlds.

Social Languages

The *social languages* theoretical tool concerns what a speaker says and the listeners' ability to identify "who" is (really) speaking and what the subtext is she/he is trying to communicate. Gee (2011) defines social languages as "styles or varieties of a language that enact and are associated with a particular social identity" (cited in Rogers, 2011, p. 39). In *Christmas 1975*, *Mami*'s role, or identity, is that of the caregiver, the educator, the transmitter of values and beliefs. When she says, "It's too cold to go out. It's better you play with your doll in here," she actually means, *When it's cold, you play inside, and you are going to play with this doll because you are a girl.* Similarly, when she stated, "You can use it, too, when you learn to ride without training wheels," Veronica interpreted her meaning as, *You are still little, but when you are old enough you will ride this particular bike because it is a girl bike and you are a girl* (the gender identity being associated with a heterosexual female).

Political Discourses

Gee (2011) defines politics as "any situation where the distribution of social goods is at stake" (p. 31). By "social goods" Gee means "anything a social group or society takes as a good worth having" (p. 31). Language can be used to either build or destroy social goods. As a seven-year-old Veronica was already developing political discourses. She was careful with her choice of words to appear respectful of the unstated (normative) social agreements. However, her child mind was in conflict about these agreements and beginning to question whether or not they reflected her own beliefs about herself.

Key Words and Phrases

Key words and phrases that exemplify these political "Big D" discourses are: *"Juan Pablo's bike is nice too, I like that color a lot." "I'm just trying this one to see how it feels; I like mine better." "While you put the batteries in the doll, I'm going to get dressed to go outside so I can give my doll a ride on my new bike."* and *"That bike is too high for you, but if you like them high, I can raise the seat on your bike."* Here we see the plot begin to pivot as Veronica pretends and tries to like her new bike when, in fact, her attraction is to her brother's new bike. As well, her father has noticed that and attributes her attraction to the height of the seat rather than to the fact that it is a boy's bike. The unspoken figured worlds agreements are still intact on the surface, but just below those surface agreements, Veronica is strategizing ways she might be able to ride Juan Pablo's bike. It's possible her father is struggling with a dawning awareness of his daughter's gender identity, but he is certainly not ready to admit it to anyone, including himself.

Romina's Story: *Eat Your Onions!*

I was four years old; my grandmother, dying of cancer, motivated the entire family to spend many hours at her house. On one of those afternoons at Abuelita's house my brother, my cousin Freddy, and I were eating lunch at the dining table. The salad was laced with onions; I don't remember what the rest of the dish included, but I remember clearly those obnoxious onions. I found onions disgusting; hence, I was doing everything under my control to avoid eating them. My mother kept insisting that I eat everything on my plate: "They [onions] are good for you!" "It is a sin to waste food!" "There are many hungry children in the world!"

None of these homilies were convincing enough to make me eat those nasty onions. One of my mother's closest friends, Greta, in the kitchen listening to all the arguments my mother was making to no avail, decided to intervene. Greta approached me, and pressing her hand down on top of my head, thereby straightening my hair, intoned a mantra that 30 years later still echoes in my ear: "Eat your onions; they will make your hair straight."

I yearned for my hair to be long and straight just like my Barbie doll's hair; silky and shiny like the women in shampoo commercials; bouncy and flowing like one of my favorite cartoon characters; not short, lifeless, and nappy like mine. Confusion descended after learning such a curious "fact," because if Greta was saying it, it had to be a fact. It took me a few seconds, maybe a couple of minutes, to internalize her words. I clearly remember thinking and reflecting on her words and gesture.

"Onions? Really? They'll make my hair straight?" The solution to my problem had danced in front of me all along and I all unaware. "How could it be?" Finally, my compulsion to get rid of my cursed, nappy, ugly hair was about to become true. I gobbled up every single piece of onion on my plate.

CDA Analysis Romina

I chose to analyze this vignette because it represents an example of how the intersecting effects of oppression (i.e., racism and sexism) are perpetuated through discourse in everyday interpersonal communications (Jiwani & Richardson, 2011; Van Dijk, 1985). These interactions between speakers and listeners form "microsocieties," based on Bakhtin's argument that discourse is interindividual. He states, " 'Society' begins with the appearance of the second person" (cited in Todorov, 1984, p. 30). Therefore, discourse does not belong to the speaker alone, but also to the listener, and to those whose voices resound in the words used by the author.

Van Dijk (1987) points out that these interactions are a key in the reproduction of racial prejudice as they facilitate production, interpretation, and transformation of ethnic/racial representations, beliefs, and attitudes. Jiwani and Richardson (2011) discuss how discourse has the power to shape and define the lives of minoritized groups in society as manifested in everyday talk through discursive repertoires that include jokes, stories, and arguments. As I will discuss in the analysis of the vignette, the microsociety formed by Romina, her relatives, and Greta illustrate how racist and sexist discourses intersect in everyday talk to reproduce oppression against girls of African descent. This narrative elicits *situated meanings* in the context of particular *figured worlds* (Gee, 2011) and is analyzed based on the assumption that "language-in-use is a tool" (p. 30) and as such it builds *identities*, *relationships*, and *politics*.

Situated Meanings:

onions;" "pressing her hand down on top of my head thereby straightening my hair;" "mother's closest friend, Greta;" "hair; long and straight, silky and shiny, bouncy and flowing, short, lifeless, and nappy;" "problem;" "solution;" " curse;" "fact."

The situated meaning that I internalized that day was that black girls don't have beautiful hair; therefore, they must change it to straight hair, even if it means doing something detestable, that is, eat nasty-tasting onions.

Figured Worlds

"Barbie," hair commercials, cartoon characters, and straight hair equal good, what an Afro-Venezuelan girl wants to have beauty. Girls should have long, straight, shiny, flowing hair. Nappy hair equals bad, ugly, lifeless: hair that one wants to get rid of.

A   Identities: How are these situated meanings and figured worlds being used to enact and depict identities (i.e., to determine who and what are socially significant kinds of people)?

B   Relationships: How are these situated meanings and figured worlds being used to build and sustain (or change or destroy) social relationships?

C   Politics: How are these situated meanings and figured worlds being used to create, distribute, or withhold social goods or to construe particular distributions of social goods as "good" or "acceptable" or not good and unacceptable?

Keep in mind:

• Many black girls/women have internalized oppression as a result of a white supremacist ideology that refers to straight hair as "good" and nappy hair as "bad" (Harris & Johnson, 2001; hooks, 1988).

• The underlying implications of Greta's words are that nappy hair is a problem that needs to be addressed right from childhood. In fact, the literature indicates that when many black women give birth to their children, one of the main concerns they have, after the health of their newborn, is the baby's skin tone and hair texture (Harris & Johnson, 2001).

• "Good hair" among people of African descent is synonymous with beauty, acceptance, status, professionalism, and success (Dash, 2006;

hooks, 1988; Thompson, 2009; Walker, 2001). It is broadly defined as hair that is straight, silky, and flowing (Harris & Johnson, 2001; hooks, 1988). bell hooks (1988) asserts that in the African American community "good hair" is "hair that was fine, almost straight . . . hair that had no nappy edges, no 'kitchen,' that area close to the neck that the hot comb could not reach." (p. 535). In other words, good hair equals white people's hair or at least as close as it can get to that (socially accepted) standard.

- An analysis of the sociopolitical roots of this issue speaks to the long history of colonialism and oppression in the forms of racism, sexism, and classism sustained by a sophisticated system of discipline and punishment (Foucault, 1995; Frye, 1995) and now imprinted in black women's psyche that goes beyond simply wanting to "look good." As a result, "for the vast majority of Black women, hair is not just hair; it contains emotive qualities that are linked to one's lived experience" (Thompson, 2009, p. 831). Such lived experiences are connected to a collective memory that goes back hundreds of years to precolonial Africa and the enslavement of African people (Drewal, 2001).
- In Latin America, Spanish colonial powers came up with a system in which " 'constructive miscegenation' (racial mixing) would ultimately eliminate the 'lower races' in a few generations. That is, instead of claiming more whites were needed to replace non-whites, Latin American leaders claimed that *mestizaje* would ultimately produce the desired whitening of the population" (Bonilla-Silva, 2009, p. 1077). It is precisely this ideology that informs popular expressions such as *mejorando la raza* (improving the race) when a dark-skin person gets romantically involved with a light-skin person of the opposite sex in the hopes that their offspring are born a shade lighter and with hair "less" nappy.
- TV and printed ads, women's magazines, cosmetic products, fashion, and cartoons are all examples of how whiteness is synonym of beauty and blackness, particularly in its natural state, with ugliness. Most magazine covers have white models on them, and those that have black models (such as those exclusively centered on African Americans) often display women with long, shiny, flowing, straightened hair.
- Part of the problem with these portrayals is that "media and social interactive processes mediate one's grooming choices while simultaneously ascribing an aesthetic value on one's body" (Thompson, 2009, p. 831). In other words, these images are informing the value we give to our bodies, which in the case of black females' hair would be ascribed a value of "less than." Certainly, *all* women in this society are pressured by a patriarchal system and sexist practices to look a certain way, but the intersectionality of race makes it more complex (Thompson, 2009).
- Black women's hair goes beyond "just hair" and connects to larger systems such as patriarchy and capitalism as well as to various forms of oppression (i.e. racism, sexism, and classism). According to Western

beauty ideology hair should be at a certain length and texture for women to be considered feminine, physically attractive, and sexually desirable (Thompson, 2009). This puts particular pressure on black women because their natural nappy hair does not fit into those standards, pushing them to conform to practices that are detrimental to the natural state of their hair, health, and finances (hooks, 1988; Lester, 1999; Thompson, 2009).

• Deeming black hair as "bad" was a deliberately constructed notion that contributed toward the colonization of African peoples. Moreover, by keeping an unattainable standard of beauty, black women's bodies become more vulnerable to power that seeks to control their minds as well as their bodies and keeps them at the bottom of society. Not surprisingly, "black hair continues to be eyed as a threat to the dominant hegemonic beauty ideal" (Thompson, 2009, p. 832).

Reflecting on Transformation: CDA and Research as Praxis

CDA + RAP = Transformation

> "Word is not the privilege of some few persons, but the right of everyone. Consequently, no one can say a true word alone—nor can [she] say it for another, in a prescriptive act which robs others of their words."
> —(Freire, 2000, p. 88)

> "Dialogue is the encounter in which the united reflection and action of the dialoguers are addressed to the world which is to be transformed and humanized."
> —(Freire, 2000, pp. 88–89)

When discussing the theoretical framework of our study, *We Are the Stories We Share*, we mentioned that we part from the idea that how we choose to tell our stories not only helps to display who we are to others, but it also helps to construct the range of identities that we bring together as different facets of "this is who I am." Because narratives, among other things, serve to represent social and personal identities (Ochs, 2009), in this study, our own lived experiences, in the form of narratives, are used as data to compare relation-based identities and the cultural aspect of time and place. We draw from CDA concepts such as social languages, situated meanings, and figured worlds as tools of analysis (Gee, 2011) to unpack our gendered experiences as they intersect with multiple social identities and systems of oppression.

In CDA, narratives of personal experience provide powerful insights into the figured worlds and situated meanings that render experience meaningful. These narratives encode the different voices (Bakhtin, 1986) that make up a person's "space of authoring" (Holland, Lachicotte, Skinner, & Cain,

1998) and thus leave traces of discourses, positioning, and identities. Furthermore, when someone narrates a personal experience, that person—not just her narrative, is now "available" for others and for that person all over again in a process of objectification; "our own discourse becomes an object and acquires a second [objectification]—its own—voice" (Bakhtin, 1986, p. 110). This new voice comes to be everybody's voice; it no longer belongs to that one person. Thus, the *audience* plays a key role in the construction of narrative as coauthor of form and meaning. In other words, narratives are authored not only by those who introduce them but also by the many readers and interlocutors who influence the direction of the narrative (Bakhtin, 1986). This coauthorship is most evident in conversational narratives, where interlocutors will ask questions, comment, and otherwise overtly contribute to an evolving tale (Goodwin, 1984). When this happens the narrative suffers changes and takes on new directions that influence how we think about ourselves and others. As a result, when we conceptualized *We Are the Stories We Tell* and decided to share our personal experiences with various audiences, we were well aware that we were losing authorship and our narratives would now belong to those with whom we share them. For that reason, we consider our engagement in this process a critical collective dialogue that has the purpose of transforming and humanizing ourselves as well as those that come in touch with our stories (Freire, 2000). That is, as we embarked on this journey, our hope was to establish the relevance of sharing, discussing, and analyzing who we are within our narratives and in that process invite other women to find themselves in our stories as they position themselves in theirs.

As we mentioned in our theoretical framework section, the ultimate goal of CDA is not limited to unveiling "unequal social arrangements sustained through language use" (Lazar, 2005, p. 1) but to take part in "social transformation and emancipation" (Lazar, 2005, p. 1). In this particular study, we use CDA to unveil the workings of power in our situated experiences as women with multiple identities, but again, our purpose is to engage in a process of societal transformation in ways that break with the constraining effects of sexism. We consider our contribution to be the co-construction of roles for girls and women that represent real choices to participate in society with open eyes to what is detrimental to our general well-being.

We agree that CDA is a good framework for academics to participate in emancipatory processes whose ultimate goal is societal transformation; we appreciate and see its value. However, we consider that the very nature of CDA represents a top-down approach that places most of the power in the hands of the academic. We were interested in a methodology that gave space for power sharing, where girls and women could be active participants from beginning to end in deciding the direction of the course of action. As a result, we decided to incorporate Research as Praxis (RAP) (Torres & Reyes, 2011) into our work as its radical participatory democratic principle offers the grounding we need to work with girls and women of all conditions.

Notwithstanding, we would like to emphasize that by no means do we see CDA and RAP as mutually exclusive or competing methodologies; quite the contrary, we see them as complementary to each other; hence, CDA is our framework to unveil power, and RAP is our philosophical foundation to work with others in transforming the system.

RAP is a paradigm shift rooted on radical democracy, transformation, and social justice that challenges traditional ways of understanding research. RAP represents what Torres and Reyes (2011) label "a counter-hegemonic research paradigm grounded on the idea that people of all conditions have the right to participate in generating knowledge and benefiting from it" (p. 51). Based on that, they identified three principles of RAP: (1) radical participatory democracy, (2) collective action for transformation toward a better world, and (3) commitment to work for social justice in solidarity with the marginalized. In following these principles, our hope is to continue engaging in a systemic process that gives light to new realizations of how to work toward the improvement of oppressive conditions along with other girls and women (Romero, Cammarota, Dominguez et al., 2008). Ginwright (2008) suggests the creation of collective spaces where radical imagination is shared to open the possibility for historically disenfranchised communities to "describe and name joy, pain, frustration, and hope" (p. 20) while reclaiming what has been systemically denied to them on the basis of inequity and oppression. While the actions the community takes might respond to an immediate need, the philosophical driving force "is led by the collective hope of a better world as dreamed of by participants and guided by public interest or common good" (Torres & Reyes, 2011, p. 59).

Moreover, RAP validates our commitment to identify and honor what is known as *vivencias,* " 'inner-life experience' linked to finding fulfillment as human beings committed to social justice and civic responsibility" (Torres & Reyes, 2011, p. 53). By doing so, we can, along with the girls and women with whom we work, reappropriate, develop, and socially produce our own knowledge in our own contexts (Gaventa, 1991). This represents an alternative to the control that positivist/ hierarchical "science" has possessed over what is recognized as valid and superior (Gaventa, 1991). Further, engaging in a "vision and view of the world that is produced by the many will be more humane, rational and liberating than the dominating knowledge of today that is generated by the few" (p. 131). For us, as researchers, committing to a collective vision creates a "convergence between academia and people in the communities . . . [that] might make academic work more socially responsive and down to earth" (Torres & Reyes, 2011, p. 54) and community work more "reflective and intellectual" (Torres & Reyes, 2011, p. 54). A reciprocal relationship such as this brings out benefits for everyone participating because the knowledge generated is equally valued and assumes that outside (academics) and inside (people from the community) participants are all subjects engaging in political action, growth, and transformation "toward the improvement of human conditions at local and wider levels" (p. 57).

In light of this our guiding questions included: How can we use narratives to take action, correct social wrongs, and mobilize? What are some ways in which we can connect with girls and women in constructing narratives about their own gender experiences? As educators, what is the role of narrative in social transformation in the classroom (and elsewhere)? Until this day our focus remains the transformation of social practices that directly and indirectly affect girls and women of all conditions. Our hope is that by critically analyzing the discourses that impact girls and women, starting with ourselves, we can contribute to a more socially just society. In what follows we each reflect on our learning these past few months after taking the first steps in our critical collective dialogue, particularly as they connected to two live presentations we gave to academic communities. We first performed the "skits" with dialogue, and then we opened up the floor to the audience to help us transform and reconstruct these narratives to serve a goal of gender, social, and racial transformation to a new commonsense agreement of the roles we play and the identities we choose in our personal and social lives.

Bringing CDA Narrative Into the Classroom
Through RAP: Nancy's Reflection

All of our performance presentations of our narratives were very different one from another. The first one was attended mainly by university faculty. They were an enthusiastic audience and asked many questions during the Q&A after our performance. One of the questions was a good segue for discussion of how we employed RAP/participatory action research (PAR) principles to facilitate personal transformation: "Why did you present the vignettes in the order in which they were presented?

Importantly for the critical analysis of this study, the various processes of transformation that transpired in the skits revealed various facets of the experience of growing up female at various historical and geographical intersections. To what destination did this crossroads point the way?

In Nancy's vignette, she is a six-year-old child living in the Midwest United States in the mid-1950s. She experiences a moment of lucid awareness when she proclaims, "So what!" in response to being told she can't drive a tractor because she is a girl. Many common agreements from Mennonite culture in the 1950s fall into place in that brief moment about the role of women and girls in her society. Her attempt to protest her frustration at this new awareness is further thwarted by her mother remarking that she is ungrateful.

In Veronica's vignette, which takes place in the Borderland region of Texas and Mexico, in the mid-1970s, she experiences a dawning awareness that she is not identified with traditional/dominant culture (i.e. straight) definitions of gender. She ponders the possibility, suggested by her mother's remark, "Girls like to play with dolls," and examines her affinity for her brother's new bike as opposed to her unexpressed distaste for her "girly" version of a bike. Perhaps she is turning into a boy? This is an interesting possibility for her and one that she had not thought of before. However, her dawning transformation of her gender identity was not allowed to come to light so that with a concerned adult, she might examine her feelings and experience authentication for the reality of them. The real issue of gender identity was not presented to her as a possibility. Again, as in Romina's case, that transformation needed to happen later in life, because it was thwarted by a definition of gender appropriateness bequeathed as a stock story by dominant (straight) culture.

Romi's vignette treated a childhood experience in coastal Venezuela in the early 1980s of being cajoled into eating onions because her mother's friend told her it would make her hair straight. In her little girl mind, she pictured women she had seen in advertising situations with long, straight, silky hair. She pondered her own very curly hair and wondered if perhaps her hair would magically straighten if she ate her onions. So she did. This vignette demonstrates a number of important psycho-emotive processes. First of all, it is the magical thinking of childhood, thus a transformation of sorts did take place in her mind. However, and importantly to the research on iden-tity and self/group transformation, this transformation was only in her mind and that mind had already been hugely affected by the dominant culture's (i.e. white culture) idea of beauty. So her transformation was directed by outside dominant forces into a channel that later in life needed to be redi-rected. Fortunately it was, but for how many young Afro Latino children is it not? This is the question the vignette was addressing.

Considering all three vignettes, we see clearly the intersectionality of gen-der stereotypes with issues of racism and homophobia. Present as well are intertextual discourses about cultural expectations as they play out in very different cultural settings with similar outcomes. All three vignettes demon-strate a transformation of personal consciousness that cannot be exterior-ized due to the strength of the prevailing cultural discourses. As we traveled forward in time, through the 1950s, then the 1970s, and finally the 1980s, we uncovered many strands of similar discourses of the roles and places of and for girls in society. Although the cultural settings were vastly different, the figured worlds of girls bore striking similarities from the perspective of nonacceptance of who we were/are. Our goal is to continue this critical study with younger generations of girls and, through critical discourse, reach a larger goal of social transformation of personal and/or group "conscien-tization" (Freire, 1970). This is the point at which PAR enters our study.

When we presented our vignettes on gender/racial discrimination the sec-ond time, our audience was a group of practicing teachers who were inter-ested in using transformative narrative as a teaching pedagogy for writing for social transformation in the classroom. This audience was alert to strat-egies they could bring to their own classrooms. After our performance we engaged in a Q&A with the audience participants and also distributed a handout by Linda Christensen (2009, p. 91) on "Acting for Justice." Participants wrote notes about a personal story in which they were part of an action for justice, after which they shared some of their experiences, thoughts, and ideas. Most of the ideas shared were concerned with experiences of teachers using similar strategies in their own classrooms. Some of the questions concerned logistics in terms of the standardized teaching and testing agenda that loomed large on their teaching/learning horizons. "How can we fit this into our already over-filled schedule?" or variations of this theme were a great concern. There was a general consensus that writing/dialoguing about social justice issues with a view to transformation was an important pedagogical piece of the instructional day. Participants lamented their perceived powerlessness in the face of standardized testing controls on their curricula. We offered suggestions, mainly in the form of courageous risk taking and personal stance on the behalf of the importance of transformational curriculum in schools. Also, we suggested taking standardized exercises geared for testing skills and transforming them into narrative writing/performance exercises as a participatory and transformational action.

Trap of Essentialism and RAP

According to Torres and Reyes (2011), an inherent danger of postmodernism is to fall into the trap of essentialism (p. 32). We wanted this project to avoid falling prey to the sometimes enticing lure of setting up binaries: Women are this and men are that; people of color are this way, and white people are that way, and so on. Torres and Reyes (2009) discuss the essentialist framework in regard to Lather's (1998) postmodern feminism (p. 32) and warn RAP practitioners that "[m]ainstream postmodern and post structural critique goes against what constitutes the emancipatory goals and tenants of Research as Praxis (RAP)" (p. 33). Keeping this in the forefront of our consciousness, the question became: How do we seek to establish projects using our narratives as we continue to dialogue, act, and write using RAP strategies to move our CDA into the realm of transformation? As RAP researchers, we believe that knowledge is co-constructed, that research is never neutral, that academic "experts" are not experts in all fields of knowledge, particularly when it comes to grassroots knowledge, and that the role of language, indeed all semiotics, plays a huge part in "understanding all human activity" (Torres & Reyes, 2011, p. 39).

The principle of *vivencia*, embedded in the RAP process, implies a research paradigm that is living, existential, and experiential. Torres & Reyes (2011) explain it as an "open system", "which is conducive to authentic participation to achieve not only growth but power" (p. 55). RAP does not seek to prove theories, nor does it aim to isolate practices from their social realities. Its goal is "to gain knowledge in a collective dialogical process aimed at transformation of reality toward the improvement of human conditions at local and wider levels" (Torres & Reyes, 2011, p. 56).

Our purpose for this project was to examine issues of discrimination by gender, race, gender preference, and culture through personal written narratives that are then transformed into skits and performed for interested educational groups. The resulting discussion and dialogue would, in turn, engender classroom projects and teaching pedagogies presenting social justice issues as transformational possibilities. It is to be hoped that we are creating a ripple effect by presenting our narrative creations, promoting them as a dialectical process with semiotic (symbolic) elements that question existing social structures and seek to change them.

RAP connection/conclusion

Particularly with our second presentation, we were able, through this multimodal format, to make a connection with RAP research principles to achieve an, albeit ever-changing, state of praxis. We, as research presenters and assembled educators, examined questions of how we could engage our students in our classrooms through transformational narrative writing, dialogs, and theatrical presentations of social justice issues relevant and important to students. An extension of this practice would be to emphasize the use of these personal narrative practices for healing. We begin with our own classrooms, and the transformational, healing effects spread. By employing the processes of transforming narrative and dialogue, we slowly begin to transform our schools.

What Is Transformation? Romina's Reflection

I began this journey convinced that the purpose of conducting any kind of research is to contribute to societal transformation (Torres & Reyes, 2011). In the past I have taken part in research projects where no meaningful engagement has been made, and the process seemed to have been filled with academic vanity. I quickly grew wary of those kinds of projects where the ultimate agenda seemed to be individualistic goals of moving up in the academic ladder. Thus, I have promised myself not to participate in projects that do not have a social justice agenda at the forefront. Nonetheless, at the beginning of *We Are the Stories We Share*, I only understood *transformation* from a theoretical standpoint; when it came to the practical aspects, it all seemed like a mystery to me. While engaging with the literature, I would often ask myself, "What does transformation look like?" "How will I recognize it when I am standing in front of it?" "How will I know I am engaging in a transformative process?"

Rogers (2011) asserts that in CDA, "the end goal is to hope, to dream, and to create alternative realities that are based in equity, love, peace, and solidarity" (p. 5). Furthermore, she emphasizes that beyond just "resisting, critiquing, and reacting to domination, those inspired by critical social theory, seek, in addition, to design and forge alternative ways of representing, being, and interacting in the world with the goal of creating a society free of oppression and domination" (p. 5). That is, in *We Are the Stories We Share*, it was not enough to simply uncover the sexism, racism, classism, and the oppression against gender nonconformance embedded in our narratives; we needed to go beyond and seek alternative ways of representation that lead to equity, love, peace, and solidarity. That, by itself, put forward a major challenge for both our group as well as for me as an individual. How could our stories push for the creation of a society free of oppression? Do we even have that power? Isn't it arrogant to think that my single narrative could inspire change?

As we moved along in our process, I became more in tune with the sense and spirit of collectivity. Slowly, but surely, I realized that it was not my single experience that was going to create change but the united voice that all of our stories represented and their echo in the ears of other women who came in touch with them. As I see it, the work in which we engaged is only the beginning of what has yet to come. Our first step was to come together as a community if our goal was to engage with other girls and women to work toward the elimination of sexism and other forms of oppression. Our CDA/PAR work was precisely that "coming together," connecting our ideas and negotiating roles.

On reflection, I notice that our process has not followed a straightforward path. In an article that discusses ways of developing a collaborative culture, Zubizarreta (2006) points to the importance of letting *opportunity-driven creative design* take place when working in groups. That is, Zubizarreta (2006) recommends giving space for the design to follow a nonlinear progression "where early attempts at solutions help test the design requirements for the problem" (271). I am certain that what we have done so far is to test a design that will later enable us to participate in the creation of real choices for girls and women that move away from the oppressive ones our narratives reflect. There is no control of what is to come, except from our desire for transformation and our endless thirst for knowledge.

In discussing Bush and Folger's (2005) work on transformative mediation, Zubizarreta (2006) points out that an alternative paradigm in mediating group conflict consists on not focusing on the end product or "achieving a resolution" but "supporting participants in the process of empowering themselves and in finding their own way to a greater sense of human connection with one another" (p. 273). My own growth and development thus far resonates with this notion of transformative mediation as my greatest achievement (in this project) was feeling self-empowered to own my story, to deconstruct the workings of power embedded in it, and to connect it to larger discourses of race, class, and gender. For instance, immediately after our presentation at New Mexico State University, I had a deep sense of pride of myself and of our group. It was a feeling of "Yes, we did it. We pulled it off, and we did a good job!" For me it was the fact that we could actually come together, push and support each other in our process, and take action in meaningful ways. The small but important success of our presentation was manifested through the immediate feedback we received from our audience. Our stories moved people; many were able to connect with them and in return shared their own stories.

Nonetheless, I am very aware of the fact that our work is far from being done, and our process is far from being over. If anything, the steps we have taken are only the beginning. When speaking about liberating pedagogy, Paulo Freire (2000) compares liberation with childbirth pains, "The man or woman who emerges is a new person, viable only as the oppressor-oppressed contradiction is superseded by the humanization of all people" (p. 49). He goes on to say that liberating pedagogy has two stages; in the first "the oppressed unveil the world of oppression and through the praxis commit themselves to its transformation" (p. 54), and in the second, "the pedagogy ceases to belong to the oppressed and becomes a pedagogy of all people in the process of permanent liberation" (p. 54). Looking at our own process from a Freirean perspective, this project engaged the first stage; we are not yet at the second stage. We are still going through that process of birth, trying to become new women in our full humanity.

As an individual, I am still asking myself the same question I started with: *How do I recognize transformation when I'm standing in front of it?* The difference between then and now is that today, I can say that transformation looks different depending on the context, the goals, and the needs of those involved. Though I still cannot answer that question in concrete ways, I am certain that as we move forward, I will be able to recognize transformation when I see it. For now, I am able to recognize the changes in me in the form of my knowledge expansion as well as the growth of confidence in what I know. The sense of empowerment left by presenting our work in front of different audiences has given us the encouragement to continue to move forward; my hope is that in future, we will experience transformation that goes beyond the self.

As we continue the process of finding solutions to larger issues connected to the oppression our group has experienced, collectively and individually, our next steps need to be negotiated. An invitation I would extend to my colleagues is to pay attention to Barat's (2005) call for self-reflexivity. Barat asks her fellow Hungarian feminist researchers to ask themselves: "How far does our own theoretical discourse participate in the reification of this hetero-gendered sexual identity?" (p. 222). I would ask our group: *How far does our own theoretical discourse participate in the reification of oppressive research that just seeks the advancement of individuals? What do we have to do to continue engaging in what Freire calls a liberating pedagogy? And what direction should we take next?*

CDA for Transformation: Veronica's Reflection

Two key concepts arose from the context of this endeavor for me: making meaning and making change. The project propelled me to develop an awareness of the power of discourse analysis in culture and in society. I discovered the power of language to control individuals, communities, and societies in general. CDA has multiple meanings but for language and for the purpose of our study, CDA focused on the social/political facet of language. To my way of understanding, CDA functioned as both theory and method that helped interpret, describe, and explain the relationship between the sociocultural and the political.

Among the eight principles of CDA that Fairclough and Wodak (1997) address are three that are relevant to my analysis: (1) CDA addresses social problems, (5) discourse is historical, and (8) CDA is a socially committed scientific paradigm. I posit that as educational researchers, we are looking for the relationship between language and the social configurations of education. My colleagues and I chose CDA as a means to critically theorize our own social worlds, to understand the relationship between language and discourse, and to discover our own methodology to help us describe, interpret, and explain the intersectionality of our social worlds and to employ the relationship of language to discourse as a cautionary tale. In truth we are the stories we share, and how we tell them can promote or discourage analysis and discourse.

CDA is not a simple concept; its complexity is what makes it a valid tool for researchers. CDA is an analysis of not only what is said but what is left out. Through our vignettes, we tried to develop a sense of reflection that goes beyond our words and our personal experiences; the idea was to create an awareness of our stories as they stand as testament to our experiences of a gendered world but also to promote the unstated subtexts that touch each person in the audience as they relate to their own experiences. For the classroom teacher the idea is to trigger these stories and then find the teaching moments in the story that advance a new contextual awareness that moves us ever forward toward a socially just society.

In my process of appropriating CDA, it becomes clear that the methodology requires action, which because it is complex and time demanding, causes a degree of *conscientization* (Freire, 2000) to impact both researcher and participant audience, it is to be hoped. Thus, this kind of research is invaluable since its transformational properties and purpose are intrinsic and arise at the beginning stage of the research.

Nancy posited the question, "How do we seek to establish projects using narrative vignette presentations to continue to dialogue, act and write using RAP strategies to move our CDA into the realm of transformation?" Wertsch (1998) states, "The task of a sociocultural approach is to explicate the relationships between human action, on the one hand, and the cultural, institutional, and historical contexts in which action occurs, on the other" (p. 24). As educators, our goal must be not only to transform personal consciousness but to "go beyond the individual agent" (Wertsch, 2011, p. 24) to begin transforming our schools, that is, the cultural, institutional, and historical contexts in which actions occur.

CDA assists us in addressing, that is, naming and explaining, oppression by gender, race, and culture. RAP provides a medium by which we can both present our research and invite our "audience" to be participants in both analysis and action in their own lives. By linking dialectics and action, we develop a process of transforming social practices by transforming discourses. Through acting out our stories, and inviting audience analysis and reflection, we hope to impact women and girls to become critical thinkers and actors in the world.

Romina questioned the intent of our study, that sharing our stories may bring social change, as perhaps being arrogant. I feel it is not arrogant and that we made and will continue to make a difference. I say this after presenting on a number of occasions and witnessing the impact made upon our participant audience. Considering the audience participants—university professors, doctoral students, public school teachers, and family members—and the input we received after the presentations, I believe what other types of audiences, for example, teenage girls, would be equally receptive and would bring another dimension to both the analysis and to becoming thoughtful change agents.

"Engaging in action is more than just 'doing things', it is doing them as intellectual, ethical and political activities aimed at transforming consciousness, life, material, and social conditions toward building a better world from the bottom up" (Torres & Reyes, 2011). There is a strong connection between CDA and RAP, and that is the collective research part in both. CDA provides the vessel for analysis and RAP the container for collective action for transformation and social justice. Therefore, CDA and RAP are both compatible and complimentary.

Romina is correct that our work is far from being done, and our process is far from being over. Nancy stated, "[I]t is to be hoped that we are creating a ripple effect by presenting our narrative creations, promoting them as a dialectical process with semiotic (symbolic) elements that question existing social structures and seek to change them." Bakhtin (1981) stated that "the word in language is half someone else's. It becomes one's own when the speaker populates it with his/her own intention" (p. 293). From this perspective, discourse inherently involves a process of appropriating the words of others and making them, at least in part, one's own (Wertsch, 1998). *We Are the Stories We Share* are everyday stories of common life experiences. It is to be hoped that they are one-half of the stories that those who participate with us may share.

References

Apple, M. W., & Buras, K. L. (Eds.). (2006). *The subaltern speak: Curriculum, power, and Educational struggles*. New York: Routledge.

Aristotle (1962). *Poetics*. New York: Norton.

Aronowitz, S. (2006). Subaltern paradise: Knowledge production in the corporate academy. In M. W. Apple & K. L. Buras (Eds.), *The subaltern speak: Curriculum, power and education struggles* (pp. 177–96). New York: Routledge.

Bakhtin, M. (1981). *The dialogic imagination: Four essays by M.M. Bakhtin*. (M. Holquist, Ed., C. Emerson and M. Holquist, Trans.). Austin: University of Texas Press.

Bakhtin, M. (1986). *Speech genres and other late essays*. Austin, TX: The University of Texas Press.

Barat, E. (2005). The "terrorist feminist": Strategies of gate-keeping in the Hungarian printed media. In M. Lazar (Ed.), *Feminist critical discourse analysis, gender, power and ideology*. Basingtoke: Palgrave Macmillan.

Bonilla-Silva, E. (2009). Are the Americans "sick with racism" or is it a problem at the poles? A reply to Christina A. Sue. *Ethnic and Racial Studies*. 32(6), 1071–1082.

Bush, R. A. B. and Folger, J. P. (2005). *The promise of mediation: The transformative approach to conflict*. San Francisco, CA: Wiley and Sons.

Christensen, L. (2009). *Teaching for joy and justice: Re-imagining the language arts classroom*. Milwaukee, WI: Rethinking Schools.

Cope, B., & Kalantzis, M. (2000). Designs for social futures. In B. Cope & M. Kalantis. (Eds.), *Multiliteracies: Literacy learning and the designs of social futures*. New York: Routledge.

Dash, P. (2006). Black hair culture, politics, and change. *International Journal of Inclusive Education*. 10(1): 27–37.

Fairclough, N. (2010). *Critical discourse analysis: The critical study of language* (2nd edition) New York: Pearson.

Fairclough, N., & Wodak, R. (1997). Critical Discourse Analysis. In T. A. van Dijk (Ed.), *Discourse studies: A multidisciplinary introduction: Vol. 2. Discourse as social interaction*. London, UK: Sage.

Fals-Borda, O., & Rahman, M. A. (1991). *Action and knowledge: Breaking the monopoly with participatory action-research*. New York: The Apex Press.

Foucault, M. (1995). *Discipline and punish: The birth of the prison*. Vintage.

Freire, P. (2007). *Pedagogy of the oppressed*. New York: Continuum.

Frye, M. (1995). Oppression. In Andersen, M., and Hill Collins, P. *Race, class, and gender*. Boston: Wadsworth.

Gardiner, M. (1992). Bakhtin's carnival: Utopia as critique. *Utopian Studies*. 3(2): 21–49.

Gaventa, J. (1991). Toward a knowledge democracy: Viewpoints on participatory research in North America. In O. Fals-Borda, & M. A. Rahman (Eds), *Action and knowledge: Breaking the monopoly with participatory action-research* (pp. 121–133). New York, NY: The Apex Press.

Gee, J. P. (1996). *Social linguistics and literacies: Ideology in discourses*. New York: The Falmer Press.

Gee, J. P. (2011). *How to do discourse analysis: A toolkit*. New York: Routledge.

Ginwright, S. (2008). Collective radical imagination: Youth participation action research and the art of emancipatory knowledge. In J. Cammarota & M. Fine (Eds.), *Revolutionizing Education: Youth participatory action research in motion* (pp. 13–22). New York: Routledge.

Goffman, E. (1974). *An essay on the organization of experience*. Cambridge, MA: Harvard University Press.

Goodwin, C. (1984). Notes on story structure and the organization of participation. In M. Atkinson and J. Heritage (Eds.), *Structures of social action* (pp. 225–246). Cambridge: Cambridge University Press.

Harris, J., & Johnson, P. (2001). *Tenderheaded: A comb-bending collection of hair stories*. New York: Washington Square Press.

Harris-Johnson, D. (2001). *The African American guide to personal growth, health, safety, sex and survival: Living and learning in the 21st century*. Phoenix, AZ: Amber Books.

Heidegger, M. (1962). *Being and time*. New York: Harper & Row.

Holland, D., Lachicotte, W., Skinner, D., & Cain, C. (1998). *Identity and agency in cultural worlds.* Cambridge, MA: Harvard University Press.

hooks, b. (1988). Straightening Our Hair. In *Talking back: Thinking feminist, thinking black.* Toronto, Ontario: Between the Lines.

Jiwani, Y., & Richardson, J. E. (2011). Discourse, ethnicity and racism. In T.A. van Dijk. (Ed.), *Discourse studies: A multidisciplinary introduction* (2nd edition) (pp. 241–262). Los Angeles, CA: Sage.

Kress, G. (2000). Multimodality. In B. Cope & M. Kalantis (Eds.), *Multiliteracies: Literacy learning and the designs of social futures* (pp. 179–200). New York: Routledge.

Labov, W., & Waletsky, J. (1967). Narrative analysis: Oral versions of personal experiences. In M. McCabe (Ed.). *Journal of Narrative and Life History.* Mahwah, NJ: Lawrence Erlbaum.

Lather, P. (1998). Critical Pedagogy and Its Complicities: A Praxis of Stuck Places. *Educational Theory.* (48): 487–498.

Lazar, M. (2005). Politicizing gender in discourse: Feminist critical discourse analysis as political perspective and praxis. In M. Lazar (Ed.), *Feminist critical discourse analysis: Gender, power and ideology in discourse* (pp. 1–30). Houndmills: Palgrave Mcmillan.

Lazar, M. M. (Ed.). (2005). *Feminist critical discourse analysis: Gender, power and ideology in discourse.* New York: Palgrave Macmillan.

Lester, N. (1999). Roots that go beyond big hair and bad hair day: Nappy hair pieces. *Children's Literature in Education.* 30(3): 171–183.

Ochs, E. (2011). Narratives in everyday life. In T. A. van Dijk (Ed.), *Discourse studies: A multidisciplinary introduction* (2nd edition) (pp. 64–84). Los Angeles, CA: Sage.

Rogers, R. (Ed.). (2011). *An introduction to critical discourse analysis in education* (2nd edition). New York: Routledge.

Romero, A., Cammarota, J., Dominguez, K., Valdez, L., Ramirez, G., & Hernandez, L. (2008). "The opportunity if not the right to see": The Social Justice Education Project. In J. Cammarota and M. Fine (Eds.), *Revolutionizing education: Youth participatory action research in motion* (pp. 131–151). New York: Routledge.

Shields, C. M. (2007). *Bakhtin primer.* New York: Peter Lang.

Thompson, C. (2009). Black women, beauty, and hair as a matter of being. *Women's Studies.* 38(8): 831–856.

Todorov, T. (1984). *Mikhail Bakhtin: The dialogical priniciple.* Manchester, UK: Manchester University Press.

Todorov, T. (1995). *Mikhail Bakhtin: The dialogical principle.* Minneapolis, MN: University of Minnesota Press.

Torres, M. N., & Reyes, L. V. (2011). *Research as praxis: Democratizing education epistemologies.* New York: Peter Lang.

van Dijk, T. A. (1987). *Communicating racism: Ethnic prejudice in thought and talk.* Thousand Oaks, CA: Sage.

Voloshinov, V. N. (1973). *Marxism and the philosophy of language.* L. Matejka and I. R. Titunik, (Trans.). Cambridge, MA: Harvard University Press.

Walker, A. (2001). Oppressed Hair Puts a Ceiling on the Brain. In J. Harris & P. Johnson (Eds.), *Tenderheaded: A comb-bending collection of hair stories.* New York: Washington Square Press, pp. 283–287.

Wertsch, J. (1998). *Mind as action.* New York: Oxford University Press.

Wertsch, J. (2011). Beyond the archival model of memory and the affordances and constraints of narratives. *Culture & Psychology.* 17(1): 21–29.

Wodak, R. (2005). Gender mainstreaming and the European Union: Interdisciplinarity, Gender Studies and CDA. In M. Lazar (Ed.), *Feminist critical discourse analysis: Gender, power and ideology in discourse.* New York: Palgrave Macmillan.

Wodak, R., & Chilton, P. (Eds.). (2005). *New agenda in (critical) discourse analysis.* Amsterdam: John Benjamins.

Zubizarreta, R. (2006). Practical dialogue: Emergent approaches for effective collaboration. In S. Schuman (Ed.), *Creating a culture of collaboration: The International Association of Facilitators handbook.* San Francisco: Jossey-Bass.

12 CDA
Dichotomous Reality From a Polish Immigrant's Perspective

Ewa Krawczyk

Introduction

Before the story of my life in the Communist, post-Communist Poland, and the United States is presented and analyzed from the critical discourse and emancipation perspective, terms such as "discourse" and "emancipation" need to first be addressed. What is a discourse? Gee (1989) defines discourse as an "identity kit" (p. 7) that comes complete with appropriate costume and instruction on how to act, talk, and often write. Thus, discourse is a registrar, a specific environment and examined reality for a specific group of people that they happened to live in. The people have a common understanding of issues that are characteristic for their particular environment/registrar and use similar patterns such as language, ideology, political affiliation, dress code, manners, and such, which make up their culturally and historically conditioned discourse.

Gee (1989) explains the initial discourse as acquired through socialization in the home and peer group. He refers to it a discourse with a capital "D." It is our primary discourse that we use to make sense of the world and interact with others, and "[w]e acquire this primary Discourse, not by overt instruction, but by being a member of a primary socializing group (family, clan, peer group)" (p. 7). After we are initially socialized to our home community within our primary discourse, we interact in nonhome based social institutions such as schools, community groups, and churches. Such discourses are referred to as secondary discourses (Gee, 1989).

Discourse is culturally and historically conditioned. It comprises social distance, hierarchy, status, and rules that members of a particular discourse are expected to follow. Mismatch in a discourse is one of the elements that can cause friction or even break communication in a discourse culture or society. Wearing an appropriate "identity kit" (Gee, p. 7) minimizes frictions among members and their relationships within a given discourse. However, friction in a discourse, particularly in a political discourse, is often necessary and leads to a political change in society that people might benefit from. When awareness of social issues and change in society take place, emancipation follows. Rosaldo (1989) asks how much tension or conflict is present between any two of a person's discourses. Gee (1989) adds,

> The various Discourse which constitute each of us as persons are changing and often are not fully consistent with each other; there is often conflict and tension between the values, beliefs, attitudes, interactional styles, uses of language, and ways of being in the world which two or more Discourses represent. (p. 7)

Emancipation concerns social groups that suffer from oppression, exclusion, discrimination, imperialism, dictatorship, and colonization. Emancipation is liberation from oppression, segregation, injustice, discrimination, gaining equal rights and access to information, education, religion of choice, and private ownership. The term "emancipation" plays a vital role in the left-wing ideology. It means equality in the face of the law. As a result of emancipation, discrimination is excluded from social groups to gain their full citizen status (Benton, 2001).

As it is known from history, even if full status is guaranteed for all the citizens, in practice citizens are frequently divided by social inequalities, social hierarchy, socioeconomic status, levels of education, and equal access to it. According to the liberal view, the core of emancipation is the tenet that human beings have in-born autonomy, which cannot be violated (Benton, 2001). However according to the radical perspective, the autonomy must be created, and it requires interference from outside. Therefore, emancipation is connected with changes of awareness and an action following it. My dual life experiences in Poland and the United States contributed to my personal discourses and ultimate emancipation.

My Life in Poland in the 1970s and the 1980s

I was born in 1969 in a country of a 1,000-year history situated in the middle of Europe. Because of its central locality, it has been a country plagued by frequent wars for centuries. As Lourie (1998) mentions, it is a country that has a tragic history in the true Aristotelian sense, and "was erased from the map of Europe at the end of the eighteenth century and did not reappear until after the First World War" (p. vi). Nonetheless, Poland is a country that despite being landless during that 120-year period, had a vibrant culture and language, survived the years of colonialism and oppression, and continues to thrive today. The reality of my native country could be described as a juxtaposed discourse of Communism and Catholicism. One might ask how it is possible since Communism's philosophy is purely atheistic and Catholicism believes in God. One must have lived in my native country of Poland in Eastern Europe to comprehend the dichotomy of the Polish reality between 1945 and 1989.

I was born in Mysłowice, a heavily industrialized region called the Upper Silesia known mainly for its coal-mining industry. Mysłowice is located about 50 kilometers/30 miles from Oświęcim-Brzezinka. The name of the city might not reveal much to the majority of my readers; however, if the name is translated into the German version: Auschwitz-Birkenau, the majority of my readers will have correct connotations with the Nazi regime during the World War II and human extermination of powerless Jews and other European nationalities. Even though I did not live during the time of World War II, my entire life in Poland was influenced by painful stories of other people who experienced it. These stories and reenactments were passed on from generation to generation, which shaped my image of the tragic historical discourse in my native country as well as the specific World War II historical discourse.

Family Discourse

My father was a member of the Communist Party, even though he was a practicing Catholic who attended mass in church every Sunday. He worked as a supervisor at a coal mine. My mother never joined the Communist Party. She worked as an accountant in the coal-mining industry as well. I have an older half-sister and a younger brother. We lived in the reality of Communism until its fall in 1989. During that time many political conversations took place in my family discourse that I personally witnessed as a child. Even when I was very young, I was aware of the reality's limitations. There were no democratic presidential elections in Communism. The government wanted me to be proud of the Communist system, but most Polish people, including myself, were never really socialized to the idea. We felt that there was a better world out there where we could feel and spread our wings. However, we could not travel to the countries of our choice, and even when traveling to the Soviet Bloc, countries required a lot of bureaucracy with less-than-favorable results. As Braudel (1981) comments, we were confined to "the limits of the possible in human life" (p. 27). We were conditioned and limited in the political Polish discourse in the era of Communism.

My secondary school discourse was developed through being forced to learn a language that was not native to me. I had to start learning the Russian language at the age of 11. No one liked that language, even though it was relatively easy, as it is similar to Polish. Mainly we hated the Russian language because of the context, which symbolized oppression and power coming from the Soviet Union. I attended a private Catholic secondary school between 1984 and 1988. Ironically, I also had to learn Russian, the language of the Communist oppressor, in a high school run by Catholic nuns.

Growing up as a child, a teenager, and young woman, I witnessed and participated in the historical Polish discourse in the 1970s and 1980s. The reality and everyday life was not what the Communism system promised. People worked extremely hard for very little money. There were attempts to abolish Communism. There were protests sparked by a sudden increase in prices of food and other basic everyday items in December of 1970 (Lukowski & Zawadzki (2006). As pointed out by the Department of State (DS) (2012), because of the riots, brutally put down by the Polish People's Army and the Citizen's Militia, at least 42 people were killed and more than 1,000 wounded. Fueled by large infusions of Western credit, Poland's economic growth rate was one of the highest in the world during the first half of the 1970s. Unfortunately, much of the borrowed capital was misspent, and the centrally planned economy was unable to use the new resources effectively. Even though I did not witness the riots personally, I was exposed to the heated political discussions at home in my primary discourse, where my parents often gathered with other family members and their friends.

In 1976, my family moved to a city called Rybnik, also situated in the Upper Silesia. I remember as a child that for the first time, my family was using ration stamps to purchase minimum portions of sugar. Then starting from the early 1980s, all of the products were rationed. We were not starving, but we just had the basic necessities: even school supplies for students were rationed. There were long lines to purchase everything from food and clothing to cleaning supplies. Otherwise, store shelves were sadly empty. I remember green oranges imported from Cuba as a rare delicacy. This set of circumstances affected me personally because I felt constant tension and fear of the unknown political and economic future in my country. With time passing by and me growing up, I became more aware of the situation in the economic and political discourse I lived in.

As mentioned by Lukowski and Zawadzki (2006), in early July of 1980, with the Polish foreign debt at more than $20 billion, the government attempted to increase meat prices. Workers responded with escalating work strikes in big cities. Following the successful resolution of the largest labor confrontation in Poland's Communist history, a new national union movement "Solidarność" (Solidarity in translation) swept the country (Kemp-Welch, 2008). As mentioned by *Time Magazine* (1978), in October of that year the Cardinal Archbishop of Cracow, Karol Wojtyła, was also elected to be the Catholic Pope John Paul II. The election meant that Poles fighting against the Communist regime were not alone and could not be controlled locally by the Communist government any longer. It gave Poland's people hope for the political emancipation, a better future, and motivation to cope through the challenging political and economic situation in the oppressing Communist discourse.

According to the Department of State (2012), political and economic problems continued in Poland with widely spread corruption and galloping inflation and mismanagement within the Polish state and party leadership. As mentioned by Kemp-Welch (2008), on December 12–13, 1981, the regime declared martial law, under which the army and Motorized Reserves of the Citizens' Militia (ZOMO) known for their brutal and sometimes lethal actions of quelling civil rights protests and riot control were used to crush the union. Virtually all anti-Communism leaders and many affiliated intellectuals were arrested or detained. The United States and other Western countries responded by imposing economic sanctions against Poland and the Soviet Union. Unrest in the country was subdued but continued (Olecki, 1993). Until this day, I remember the frosty night of Saturday/Sunday December 13–14, 1981. I woke up in the middle of the night and pressed my nose to the window, observing dozens of tanks passing through our street, one of the busiest streets in my hometown. I looked on with fascination, not understanding the implication of what I was witnessing.

After some semblance of stability had been achieved, the Polish regime in several stages relaxed and then rescinded martial law. Martial law was suspended. Hope, joy, relief, the feeling of liberation, and faith in a stable, democratic and prosperous future entered the Polish discourse.

My Life in the Post-Communist Polish Discourse of the 1990s

In the early 1990s, Poland made substantial progress toward achieving a fully democratic government and a market economy. The process of emancipation from political oppression had begun. The Russian language was removed from Polish schools. The English language entered the Polish institutions, and English-language colleges mushroomed all over the country in the 1990s. From 1990 to 1993, I attended Foreign Language Teacher Training College in Racibórz, southern Poland, to become a teacher of English. The college education enabled me to become exposed to political ideas and concepts of Western countries. Through open access to information and my newly acquired college education, I felt emancipated.

From 1993 to 1999, I was a teacher of English as a foreign language in a public high school. My students came from a very specific secondary discourse. They were all males, all Polish, and Catholic for the most part and came from a very similar socioeconomic status, resulting from the just-abolished era of Communism. I saw that particular discourse as one dimensional in the sense that Poland is monocultural, mono-racial, monolingual, and mono-religious.

The era of capitalism began in Poland, which I saw in a very positive light at that time. The first non-Communist president, Lech Wałęsa, was elected after more than 40 years of the Communist regime in 1990. In 1992 Hanna Suchocka, the first woman ever was elected to be a prime minister of Poland ("Walesa Seeks," 1992). In those times, capitalism equated to liberty and emancipation. It opened the door to competitive markets, freedom of speech, access, flow of information, and perspectives from the Western bloc. Having a traumatizing experience of living under the Communist regime on the one hand, and the romanticized and overly positive vision of the political, economic, and cultural situation in in post-Communist Poland and the United States on the other hand, I relocated to the United States in 1999, where I have been residing ever since.

CDA of the Polish Discourse Through the Author's Lenses

Life under the Communist regime was a very difficult time. It was a limiting and challenging environment. Polish people's right to democracy and freedom of speech were violated. The Polish citizens felt "boxified": hopeless, helpless, and downtrodden by the Communist regime. We, as a group felt like citizens of the lowest category. Even though we were able to bear the political oppression, most were not able to bear the economic oppression in situations where prices of food skyrocketed astronomically and the people could not afford to purchase the bare minimum basics. When people are pushed to their limits and do not have the basic necessities provided, such as proper nourishment, they begin to fight the system. It was the dramatic climax where the oppressed in the Communist dictatorship shifted their mind-set from being resistant to exercising their rights in open battle against Communist oppression.

In a political crisis, a leader is needed who will unite people in their fight for the common good against their oppressive government. The Polish nation found that leader in the person of Lech Wałęsa, who first as a leader of the Polish liberation movement Solidarność and then the president of the Republic of Poland freed his nation from the chains of oppressing Communism. There could have been no better time than 1978 when a Polish cardinal was elected to be the pope. It gave Polish citizens hope for liberty and for a better future for themselves and their children. As pointed out by Zamoyski (2001):

> To the Poles the election of Pope John Paul II was not only a solace in their misery, as well as a great national honor, it was also the final breach in the wall behind which they had been kept since 1945. The Pope's visit to Poland in June 1979 was an extraordinary event, and it had a profound effect in reaffirming the Poles in their spiritual and cultural values. . . . It brought to a head the growing sense of the power of that society in the face of coercion. . . . It brought millions together at rallies and open-air Catholic services. The Papal visit had opened new channels of communication, and it is no exaggeration to say that Polish society was transformed by it.

(p. 389)

The freedom from the Communist regime was finally achieved. However, it created economic chaos. Polish society was not prepared for a new reality. It is undeniable that Poland made headway toward achieving a free market economy and a fully democratic government: Nevertheless, economic chaos and destabilization of society ensued. Guaranteed jobs and the equalization of society in Communism were lost, and the wide division between the poor and the rich arose. After the fall of Communism, there was an expectation of an economic miracle, which did not take place. People realized that free market was not so free after all. It was free and accessible for businesspersons and entrepreneurs with substantial financial resources in the right place at the right time, but it was off limits for average citizens, who became swiftly dependent on the financial tycoons. Therefore, people losing hope in open new capitalism chose in the second free elections a president who represented a left-wing party. When the Polish people experienced an after-emancipation shock, they began asking themselves, "What is going to happen now?" My optimistic perspective of the reality in Poland also began to shift.

My Life in the United States

I immigrated to the United States in 1999; thus as of 2014, the year this chapter was written, I have lived in the country for the last 15 years. My experience in the United States has been significantly shorter than the experience in my native country of Poland. At the beginning of my immigration journey, I had an idealized vision of the political, economic, and cultural situation in the United States. The picture of the reality became crystallized with time as I continued being a member of various discourses in the United States. From 1999 to 2000 and 2003 to 2010 I was a member of a faith-based Christian communities called L'Arche, established by Jean Vanier, a prolific Christian from Canada (Vanier Website, n. d.), who believed that "to work for community is to work for humanity" (Vanier, 1989, p. 100). The awareness and opposition to institutionalization led Vanier to his purpose in founding a family, a community with and for those who are weak, poor, and marginalized and who feel alone and abandoned (Vanier, 1989). Attracted to Vanier's philosophy, I resided with adults with developmental disabilities who were removed from various public institutions and lived in homes with people without disabilities, creating together a community. From 2000 to 2003 I was a part of a different discourse, and I worked as a codirector of an emergency shelter for homeless women with children run by Catholic nuns. I served to protect women and their children who, for various reasons, needed temporary shelter.

In 2006 I entered the academic discourse. In 2007, I graduated with a bachelor's degree from the University of Massachusetts in Boston, majoring in American studies. The courses that focused on American history, culture, and society were very enlightening to me and awoke my curiosity about the education of minorities, social justice, poverty, economics, inequality, suppression, asymmetrical power relations, globalization, and democracy in this country. As a result, I decided to pursue my education even further by entering the graduate program in applied linguistics, majoring in teaching

English as a second language at the University of Massachusetts in Boston. I obtained my master's degree in May of 2009.

I continued deepening the knowledge through my educational and cultural experiences as I became a doctoral student in the Department of Curriculum and Instruction at New Mexico State University in Las Cruces, New Mexico in 2011. In 2012 I became a teacher at the same university. Progressively, I merged into the discourse of higher education. I have been studying and teaching in the area of bilingual education, English to speakers of other languages, content area literacy, and multiculturalism in a very culture-specific location situated only 40 miles from the border of Mexico.

CDA of the American Discourse Through the Author's Lenses

Being a member of a faith-based community, my secondary discourse, I experienced a life under a protective umbrella despite the fact my status shifted from national majority in Poland to immigrant minority in the United States. It felt as if there were a wall osmosis between my life and the outside world in the United States. However, the experience in the particular community discourse sharpened my understanding of the social justice issues and marginalization of people with disabilities on the one hand and an alternative approach toward people with disabilities, who were valued as human beings and were able to enjoy their lives with dignity in home setting communities created with people, both with and without disabilities.

While working with homeless women in an emergency shelter in the post-September 11 reality, another discourse I entered, I became increasingly aware of notions such as racism, poverty, classism, and social justice. My idealized image of the political and economic situation in the United States began to shift.

I continued deepening my knowledge on racism, poverty, classism, and social justice through my college and university education. From being a part of the academic discourse through students' and a faculty perspective, I understood more profoundly the complexity of American society, which I view now as a hybrid of multiculturalism and multilingualism. I have come to realize the disproportions in economic and class status, political situation, and limited access to education. Living in Las Cruces and being a part of its university as a student and a teacher exposed me to the uniqueness of the New Mexican culture. New Mexico is heavily influenced by its historical culture and Spanish language contributing to the dynamism, diversity, and liveliness of the New Mexican culture.

The fact that I immigrated to the United States became a significant change in my life. It gave me a whole new perspective into my personal life, as well as it impacted my educational and professional goals and aspirations. While living in Poland, I belonged to the demographic majority. However, the moment I set my feet upon American soil, I felt that I was instantly classified into the category of "the other." It was not only a mind-altering experience to me, but by shifting from a homogenous, monocultural, mono-linguistic, and mono-religious discourse into a very diverse, multidimensional, heterogeneous, complex, and dynamic hybridized discourse, I underwent a process of personal transformation and awakening.

Through this process of being a part of various discourses, my work with people pushed to the margins of society, people with learning disabilities, homeless individuals, and refugees in the United States, and my experience as a student and university teacher, I gained new perspectives, new experiences, new opportunities, and new challenges, factors that have decidedly made me a better person, more tolerant, open, empathetic, understanding, and compassionate. I can only describe this as a shift in my entire being. Through membership in various discourses and being exposed to their multiple issues and beliefs, I underwent a process of personal emancipation as an immigrant in the United States.

Conclusion

Human beings come in and out of discourses through life constantly. We are born into culture and become a part of it whether we want to or not. We first become participants in the culture and the discourse of our parents and caregivers. With time and age, we are able to make changes and adjustments and become members of other various cultures. We are predestined to live in our primary discourse involuntarily and accidentally, and we are not given a choice as the time or place where we are born.

With time and increased knowledge, we are able to some extent make our own choices in terms of discourses that we want to be a part of or not. We become parts of secondary discourses consciously and voluntarily for the most part. Some of us have more freedom in our political choices than others. We then choose to follow our own selected views, ideologies, and political orientations. Individuals from different countries fundamentally vary in their values and beliefs, also within a nation, such as the American nation. There are numerous intercultural and even intra-cultural differences and diversity so that it becomes impossible to place everyone within the same perspective.

We are all parts of different discourses and identity groups that we enter, influence, shape, and exit constantly throughout our life cycles. It is a never-ending process in society that contributes to the creation and transformation of a hybrid that is culture, where humans mingle, change, and transform. How we define our own culture depends on our unique circumstances, origins, and the society in which we grow.

Numerous discourses with cultures are never just innocent, neutral, indifferent, or apolitical. Claiming to be nonpolitical is a political act. Discourse is never static either as it is shaped by people whose thoughts, ideologies, and actions fluctuate and shift. According to Foucault (1976/1980), "[P] ower is neither given, nor exchanged, nor recovered, but rather exercised, and . . . it only exists in action" (p. 89). I experienced changes in my Polish discourse leading to political emancipation and later a voluntary change of discourse from the Polish discourse to the American discourse, which provided me with empowering personal liberation through experience, informal education, and formal institutional education.

Blommaert (2005) points out that people have different capabilities to incorporate chunks of history in their discourses. Depending on one's place in the world, history has a different meaning; the world is a different place depending on the point of view from which you look at. In the discourse analysis all of this is usually gathered under the label of " 'context'—the context, a singular point, but a nexus of layered simultaneity, for in every context we shall find features of different orders operating at different speeds and scales" (p. 134).

Discourses within cultures are also very complex concepts that are never static. It is a powerful dynamic, a constantly changing system with multiple layers that inform our ways of life. We need to realize that cultures and discourses exist in ideological and political spaces and that our values and beliefs may not coincide with those of others. Therefore, to achieve smoothness in cultures and discourses, we as individuals need to be flexible, understanding, friendly, selfless, willing, compromising, enthusiastic, positive, tolerant, and empathetic while still maintaining our most deeply held principles. This can be a very difficult task to accomplish; thus, there are frequent clashes and frictions within cultures and discourses. However clashes are sometimes inevitable and inexorable to create a change that can benefit a majority of a discourse member and lead to a desired emancipation.

References

Benton, T. (2001). Emancipation. In P. B. Clarke & J. Foweraker (Eds.), *Encyclopedia of democratic thought* (pp. 332–337). New York: Routledge.

Blommaert, J. (2005). *Discourse: Key topics in sociolinguistics*. New York: Cambridge University Press.

Braudel, F. (1981). *The structures of everyday life: The limits of the possible (civilization and capitalism vol. 1)*. New York: Harper & Row.

A foreign pope. (1978, October 30). *Time Magazine*. Retrieved from http://content.time.com/time/magazine/article/0,9171,912229–4,00.html

Foucault, M. (1980). *Power/knowledge: Selected interviews and other writings, 1972–1977* (C. & K. Soper, Trans., C. Gordon, L. Marshall, & J. Mepham, Eds.). New York: Pantheon. Gordon, (Ed.), L. Marshall, J. Mepham (Original work published 1976).

Gee, J. P. (1989). Literacy, discourse, and linguistics: Introduction. *Journal of Education, 171*(1), 5–17. Boston, MA: Boston University.

Jacobs, D. (2011). Occupy Wall Street and the rhetoric of equality. *Forbes*. Retrieved from http://www.forbes.com/sites/deborahljacobs/2011/11/01/occupy-wall-street-and-the-rhetoric-of-equality/

Kemp-Welch, A. (2008). *Poland under communism: A cold war history.* Cambridge, UK: Cambridge University Press.

Lourie, R., & Konwicki, T. (1998). *The polish complex.* Normal, IL: Dalkey Archive Press.

Lukowski, J., & Zawadzki, H. (2006). *A concise history of Poland.* Cambridge, UK: Cambridge University Press.

Olecki, O. (1993). *History of Poland.* New York: Barnes and Noble Books.

Rosaldo, R. (1989). *Culture and truth: The remaking of social analysis.* Boston, MA: Beacon.

Sleeter, C. (2000). Multicultural education, social positionality, and whiteness. In E. M. Duarte & S. Smith (Eds.), *Foundational perspectives in multicultural education* (pp. 118–134). New York: Longman.

U.S. Department of State. (2012). *Poland profile: History.* Retrieved from http:// www.state.gov/outofdate/bgn/poland/197879.htm

Vanier, J. (1989). *Community and growth.* Mahwah, NJ: Paulist Press.

Vanier, J. (n. d.). *Personal website.* Retrieved from http://www.jean-vanier.org/en/ home

Walesa seeks approval for 1st woman Prime Minister. Poland: Hanna Suchocka's formation of a seven-party coalition breaks weeks of political deadlock. (1992, July 9). *Los Angeles Times.* Retrieved from http://articles.latimes. com/1992–07–09/news/mn-2363_1_prime-minister

Zamoyski, A. (2001). *The polish way: A thousand-year history of the Poles and their culture.* New York: Hippocrene Books.

13 Emergent Bilinguals in the Curriculum

Adriana Goenaga Ruiz de Zuazu

Introduction

This chapter is informed by CDA as a critical tool to analyze the ways in which ELLs are viewed in the curriculum. In this essay, I substitute the term "ELLs" that is commonly used and only refers to students' English proficiency, with "Ofelia," García's (2009) term of emergent bilinguals that instead gives validity to the linguistic skills of bilingual speakers. Emergent bilinguals are students who are becoming bilingual, acquiring English in school but also maintaining their home language (García, 2009). Throughout the chapter, I refer to a selection of readings analyzed with a critical perspective to extend my conceptualization of bilingualism, biliteracy, and emergent bilinguals.

At the beginning, I show an analysis of curriculum, curriculum development, and briefly of immigration over the course of history. In this analysis, I want to present how emergent bilinguals have been viewed historically and how they have been impacted by issues of curriculum development in a general sense as well as in the hidden curriculum. Later, I reflect on deficit-thinking perspectives (Valencia, 2010) and two other negative attitudes toward diversity and, particularly, toward emergent bilinguals. Next, I present the funds of knowledge approach in accordance to multicultural education. At the end and with an aim to shift from traditional deficit-thinking views toward valuing a pluralistic society, I suggest fundamental ideas for teacher education programs to implement.

My thoughts are with emergent bilinguals attending schools with a dominant ideology and being taught by teachers with personal perceptions toward them and their families, which highly affect teaching and their learning. In this chapter, I emphasize the complexities and richness of being bilingual and biliterate, and I make a call for this to be shown in the curriculum and in daily teaching-learning processes.

Curriculum and Curriculum Development Along History

History is essential in which to conceptualize issues regarding immigration and bilingualism in the present. Many of our bilingual students are descendants of immigrants or are immigrants themselves; thus, we should consider how language issues are indeed related to immigration issues. Schools have been structured around immigration and language issues, and according to many, educational institutions function as structures of control through hegemonic relations (Apple, 2004). Immigration movements into the United States happened highly in the 20th century (Zinn, 2007), which could have provoked anti-immigrant sentiment against language diversity and a learned nationalism.

In consideration of making curriculum, Apple (2004) states that schools aimed Americanization through acculturation and standardization in the late 1980s and economic reproduction through inculcating traditional moral values at the beginning of the 1990s. Then, homogeneity and stability in ideology was achieved by implementing a differentiated curriculum to prepare immigrants, those with low socioeconomic status (SES), and people of color to "follow," differentiating also an education for leadership versus education for "followership." Curriculum and curriculum making act as tools to manage ideological, political, professional, and public matters in schooling (Westbury, 2007); otherwise, what ideas, values, or norms get represented behind standards, or what knowledge, attitudes, and competences are seen as appropriate in schools? (Westbury, 2007)

School knowledge needs to be analyzed here. Schools teach a consensus of selective knowledge, which relates and belongs to the middle class and aims to a form of consciousness, which also permits social control of dominant groups (Apple, 2004). Thus, whose knowledge is in the curriculum? Whose knowledge is not apparent in the curriculum (Sleeter, 2005)? Specifically, textbooks gather valuable knowledge, pertinent of certain groups and not others (Apple, 1988, 2000; Apple & Buras, 2006; Apple & Christian-Smith, 1991; Cornbleth & Waugh, 1995, as cited in Apple, 2007) and mostly represent the dominant race and social class in pictures (Sleeter, 2005). Pictures might perpetuate stereotypes such as linking poverty with people of color and portraying Latinos as farmworkers, gang members, or from single-parent households (Sleeter, 2005). Further, textbooks arrive into the schools where teachers will use them at their convenience: being fully transmitted to students, selected or transformed, or neglected in relation to the way teachers and students read and receive them, that is, in dominant, negotiated, or oppositional manners (Apple, 2000, as cited in Apple, 2007). Belonging to this selection of knowledge also conforms to a form of cultural capital, called "habitus" by Pierre Bourdieu (1977) that indeed shows differences in access and a reproduction of hegemonic and power relations (as cited in Apple, 2004). Schools do not provide minoritized students with the cultural capital they lack outside the school context, and therefore, public institutions such as schools magnify the effects of societal inequities.

Additionally, the development of curriculum is being impacted by technical knowledge, this being both teachable and testable, for teaching and learning skills and how to do things, and in opposition to the interdisciplinary curriculum (Apple, 2004). Even more, the aspect of making school knowledge technical has brought the focus on considering curriculum and learning as instrumental and "accountable" (Habermas, as cited in Apple, 2004), reducing world knowledge to measurable knowledge (Sleeter, 2005). Explaining this further, technical knowledge is more concerned on production than on distribution, being a "commodity," with those with access to high-status knowledge leading to economic expansion (Apple, 2004). Ultimately, the decision-making process regarding teaching and learning has been passed from teachers, educators, and practitioners to technical people attending a political agenda, widening the gap of performance between majority and minority students and creating even more inequalities (McNeil, 2009).

Curriculum as Colonizer

The curriculum can be seen as colonizer in which it neglects immigrants' and bi(multi)lingual and bi(multi)cultural students' home languages, traditions, and cultural norms; generalizes students by ethnicity group; and tests, evaluates—on reading and mathematics—labels, and punishes them for not being proficient or on grade level. The curriculum actually reinforces, values, and privileges a Eurocentric dominant culture, the books focus on white people, and history is taught referencing white supremacy (Hyland, 2010). Goodwin (2010) refers to three of the major reforms in the United States to claim that curriculum defines, "labels," silences, and marginalizes, which highly affects emergent bilingual and other minoritized students like Asian Americans and Pacific Islanders (APIs). The three reforms are the No Child Left Behind (NCLB) legislation, focusing on accountability and reading; the culturally relevant pedagogy, vaguely representing diversity in the curriculum; and the "model minority" mythology, placing and marginalizing. Goodwin refers specifically to APIs, as the "Other Other" (Talmy, 2005). Historically, these reforms have highly impacted emergent bilinguals, immigrants and their children, people of color, the poor, and APIs. In this sense, school is "not to liberate but to limit, not to intellectually expand but to sort or classify, not to transform but to conform" (Goodwin, 2010, p. 3113). I find it also important to mention that schools are organizations that have a hierarchical structure, a political nature, and their cultural assumptions about students' abilities and merits (Buttaro, Catsambis, Mulkey, & Steelman, 2010). As we see, curriculum can acculturate, socialize, emancipate, or colonize if we look at the U.S. nation and whose cultural ideals it values and serves.

Hidden Curriculum

Schools exercise a social and economic control, mainly through the apparent selected school knowledge and through the nonapparent hidden curriculum (Apple, 2004). Ideology, related to class and ability, is purposefully infused through covert teaching, or hidden curriculum, assuming the economical but also cultural and ideological role of schools and reproducing a cultural and ideological hegemony (Apple, 2004). Understanding hegemony, the lived meanings, values, practices, and actions incorporated without even being conscious hegemony (Gramsci, 1975; Williams, 1989 as cited in Apple, 2004) acclaim some and exclude others through school knowledge and through the privileged ideology taught in schools. Thus, the hidden curriculum reproduces a distribution of cultural and ideological hegemonies to students. These cultural and ideological norms, or habitus and doxa (Bourdieu, 1977), transcend school knowledge to control outside schools and power relations (Apple, 2004). The hidden curriculum also negates students' historicities and diverse linguistic and cultural backgrounds (Freire, 1987). As an example, there is a part of the curriculum, which can be called "tourist curriculum" (Derman-Sparks, 1989, as cited in Sleeter, 2005), that permits students to visit heroes and heroines to get to know the "other" groups' general characteristics as a whole and to celebrate multicultural festivals for later returning to the classroom and the dominant curriculum. Through the hidden curriculum and these practices, the emergent bilinguals are often and indirectly reminded of their non-belonging status, in bilingual classrooms infused with a mainstream curriculum and more so in English-only classrooms, where monolingualism and monoculuralism are the norm.

In practice, Apple (2004) argues that the hidden curriculum seems natural due to a special treatment of the concept of conflict in schools, especially in the subjects of science and social studies. Science is usually presented as objective empirical data not influenced by personal or political matters. In science, therefore, students understand that people—students included—do not have any responsibility in how institutions work. They are taught that scientists do not create or recreate values and that the conflict is negative and does not lead to change and/or progress (Apple, 2004). Social studies are usually presented through a collaborative view of society that denies conflict; therefore, instead of creating new values, it receives and transmits those accepted by the collective. However, progress comes from conflict or from disagreement among scientists, not from conformity and denial of social issues (Apple, 2004). In schools, students are used to accepting authority, socializing under certain basic rules, and behaving according to an established reward system (Apple, 2004; Jackson, 1968, Giroux, 1983, as cited in Kentli, 2009) as part of a hidden curriculum. Students are expected to be passive (Lynch, 1989, as cited in Kentli, 2009) and to internalize norms, values, and principles to conform to the system (Bourdieu, 1977), giving consent, and moving away from conflict, taking a stand, and taking action. The latter significantly affects all students and specifically emergent bilinguals who are persuaded to adapt and to feel ashamed of their essence.

Deficit Thinking

The deficit thinking model has been current since long ago. We can understand deficit thinking as "the process of 'blaming the victim.' It is a model founded on imputation, not documentation" (Valencia, 2010, p. xiv). The deficit thinking model is misused in the education field to explain school failure of students of color, Native Americans, low-SES students, and emergent bilinguals. Present equalities and inequities are indeed consequences of a historical legacy of hierarchies consciously established and embedded in political structures maintained and transferred in schools (Valencia, 2010). Politicians, administrators, and people of power do not examine educational structures and systemic inequalities/inequities (Pearl, 1997, as cited in Valencia, 2010), or do not question class domination (Bourdieu, 1977, as cited in Valencia, 2010), but instead presuppose white superiority, blame the victim, support racial differences in individual intellectual ability, promote racial segregation (Valencia, 2010), and establish compensatory programs to "fix" and change the victim (Ryan, 1971, as cited in Valencia, 2010).

In fact, with segregation, language and culture exclusion, inequities in school financing, teacher certification, and special education programs, schools sustain these conditions and replicate the linkage between the victim and his/her unsuccessful school outcomes. As an example, Mexican American students are blamed for their high drop-out rates and low enrollment in college (Valencia, 2010). Segregation in schools start in the early ages with homogeneous grouping practices, which is called, "second generation" segregation (Mickelson, 2001, as cited in Buttaro, Catsambis, Mulkey, & Steelman, 2010). According to Buttaro, Catsambis, Mulkey, and Steelman (2010), within-class grouping is most common in elementary education, and between-class grouping and tracking in secondary education, both with lasting effects on self-perceptions as well as academically.

The tem "minority," according to Freire (1987), is used to hide—to ignore— the negative effects of a cultural dominance and the fact that those "minoritized" groups represent a major section of the population; however, to be labeled a "minority" is to be placed outside of the political and economic center. Furthermore, the "cultural difference" framework (Baratz & Baratz, 1970; Labov, 1970; Valentine, 1971) also views the differences of children of color and their families as deficits to assume a disconnection between school and home culture and consequently to justify students' learning problems (e.g., Hale-Benson, 1986; Ramirez & Castañeda, 1974, as cited in Valencia, 2010).

Additionally, it is surprising to know there is not more research about the establishment of programs for ELLs being highly influenced by political ideologies (Welner & Escamilla, 2002, as cited in Welner & Oakes, 2007), aside from the already-known negative view toward bilingualism in the United States, some authors argue (Welner & Oakes, 2007). In relation to bilingual programs, Two-Way Immersion (TWI) programs are the ones that focus on maintaining and valuing biliteracy in contrast to Second Language Acquisition (SLA) or ESL, transitional bilingual programs, or dual-language education (Welner & Oakes, 2007). In schools, emergent bilinguals are taught with a lack of instructional quality over linguistic quantity and systemically tracked as a homogeneous group (Callahan, 2005). Even so, due to the increased number of emergent bilinguals, more attention is being given to language-proficiency levels and specifically, English fluency. This is provoking a bigger linguistic achievement gap, comparing the difference in academic performance between mainstream students and emergent bilinguals (Thomas & Collier, 2002, as cited in Callahan, 2005). Also, the curriculum has been simplified in content and language for emergent bilinguals, who become long-term English learners. Moving away from a deficit-thinking perspective, we should view emergent bilinguals not with a linguistic impairment but with a rich linguistic repertoire and background knowledge and view bilingual programs not compensatory but rather as a setting for gaining linguistic competence, academic knowledge, and critical thinking.

Apart from the deficit-thinking model, two other attitudes also neglect linguistic and cultural diversity: "colorblindness" (Nieto, Bode, Kang, & Raible, 2007) and "cultural neutrality" (Ladson-Billings, 2000). The term "colorblind racism" (Bonilla-Silva, 2003, as cited in Nieto, Bode, Kang, & Raible, 2007) might appear in discourses, views on curriculum, and teaching practices, reflects historical amnesia—conscious or "unconscious" ignorance, and perpetuates "the myth of colorblindness" (Nieto, 2003, as cited in Nieto, Bode, Kang, & Raible, 2007). Cultural neutrality in teaching and in literature supports the dominant group, delegitimizing cultural diversity, disregarding students' distinctive characteristics, and categorizing them as "other" (Ladson-Billings, 2000).

I have become aware of the necessary turn in the discourse from calling students as being at risk to considering schools and the educational system as being at-risk (Valencia, 2010). Additionally, a call for a transformation is urgent, avoiding quantitative responses (standardization, high-stakes testing and accountability) and top-down solutions. This transformation will also bring preservice teacher education, parent engagement, educational leadership, social justice conceptions and promoters, and school communities together (Valencia, 2010).

Funds of Knowledge

To start off, the curriculum is "a reflection of what people think, feel, believe, and do" (Smith, Stanley, & Shores, 1957, as cited in Schubert, 2007, p. 408), "a reading and writing of the self in relation with the world" (Graham, 1991; Grumet, 1980; Pinar & Grumet, 1976, as cited in Schubert, 2007, p. 409), and an experiential process (Dewey, 1916, 1938). Thus, the notion of curriculum should include not only materials, the learning environment, and teacher-student interactions but also intentional and unintentional messages coming from the school, the community, and the students themselves (e.g., students' expectations and demands) (Nieto, Bode, Kang, & Raible, 2007). Indeed, a holistic view of the curriculum relates to multicultural education, including equal curriculum for all, textbook content and curriculum relevant for all, curriculum transformation for social improvement (Sleeter, 2005), and funds of knowledge for teaching that require getting to know the students and households and to incorporate those home knowledges and skills (Moll, Amanti, Neff, & González, 1992) into the classroom curriculum.

The curriculum should fully consider issues of language, culture, identity, and power, these being at the core of immigrant students' experiences of school curriculum (He, Phillion, & Chan, & Xu, 2007). Issues of language and culture should be situated within identity issues; identity is fluid and changing (He, 2003), developed within one's ethnicity (Lee & Zhou, 2004; Olsen, 1997) in the relation with others (Chan, 2003, 2004; Lei, 2003), and is affected by sociopolitical and cultural contexts (Cummins, 2001; Nieto, 2000b). In my opinion, curriculum should be developed by the community, learning should happen through valuing and building on students' connections to their cultural and linguistic roots and community-based identities, and such learning should be accountable—go back— to the community (Sleeter, 2005).

Primarily, I strongly believe that diversity should be regarded as real, vivid, and reflecting people's lives and their different perspectives (Ladson-Billings & Brown, 2007). Second, students should require and use spaces for self-empowerment, with teaching pedagogies that sustain and acknowledge their language, ideology, and different perspectives (Freire & Macedo as cited in Freire, 1987). Agreeing with Gutiérrez, Rymes, and Larson (1995), classrooms are reflective of three instructional discursive spaces: The first space is controlled by the teacher, the second is controlled by students in contraposition to the teacher's agenda, and the third space is, ideally, mutually controlled. The third space involves students' funds of knowledge in classroom discursive practices and in the curriculum. The existence of counter-discourse spaces, called "third spaces" by Gutiérrez, Rymes, and Larson (1995, as cited in Nieto, Bode, Kang, & Raible, 2007), are necessary for cultural discussions to happen, to acknowledge nondominant discourses, and for all voices to be heard. *Testimonios* and the production of students' "counterstories" in the classroom are therefore critically linking their home, their community, and their bi(multi)lingualism and culturalism with social change purposes (Delgado, 1989).

Teacher Education

Ladson-Billings (2006) suggests teachers have a change of attitude and change their way of being (instead of what they are doing). "Being" for Ladson-Billings means informed empathy, a term that describes solidarity in union with doing democracy and having high expectations. In this manner, "love" encompasses dignity, freedom, and equal opportunities for students, and "hate" represents their opposite (Boutte, 2008). In the same direction, Sleeter (2005) recommends that teachers should reflect on their assumptions, stereotypes, ideologies, and where they stand (Freire, 1998, as cited in Sleeter, 2005) in terms of teaching a prescribed curriculum to a diverse classroom and in terms of multicultural education. This is very important for emergent bilinguals because teachers will value the cultural and linguistic diversity that they bring and will implement it into the curriculum. Teachers should definitely deconstruct, construct (Dewey, 1997), and reconstruct (Shujaa, 1994) the curriculum to promote students' success. In the case of emergent bilinguals this is more critical because teachers should have high expectations, scaffold and provide an individualized instruction, and require higher-order thinking from them. Implementing a challenging curriculum for emergent bilinguals and their counterparts is crucial.

In a context of reform spurred by high-stakes standards and testing, school administrators and teachers should reject taking an assimilative stand and take an affirmative one with students, diversity, and equity at the front (Nieto, 2000a). Teachers should be curriculum makers (Schwab, 1969) in the way that they have the experience and the space to connect theory and practice, and curriculum and pedagogy, with lessons leading to reflection and action. Also, teachers are knowers, inquirers, and learners (Schwab, 1970). Teachers should be seen as curriculum activists, with agency, because they can and should recuperate and gain empowerment to take control of the curriculum for the benefit of the students.

Starting small with equity pedagogy is essential. Beginning in early childhood, teachers should purposefully plan lessons and activities to raise consciousness (Freire, 1970) and to specifically work against injustices (Hyland, 2010) with students. According to Boutte (2008), there are two true illusions. One is that children are color-blind, and the other is that diversity is valued nowadays. Small children indeed internalize messages about differences among people, comparing themselves to others in terms of race and other aspects of diversity. Omitting, "sins of omission" for Greenberg (1992, as cited in Boutte, 2008), or providing the wrong information, "sins of commission" for Greenberg, will support injustices and perpetuate stereotypes and biases in the students. Division, ethnocentrism, and injustices might start with girls versus (against is more used) boys, cheering one team and not the other, and so on (Boutte, 2008). Teachers should then incorporate into the curriculum racial justice, cultural power, and gender issues, which are critical in identity development and sexual orientation (Hyland, 2010). Also, I am aware of the responsibility that the entire society—and all teachers—has to confront discriminative practices and to work toward justice not only for people of color, poor people, other marginalized people but in schools and bilingual teachers (Boutte, 2008).

Additionally, teacher education programs need to be transformed toward being centered on social justice (Nieto, 2000b). I totally agree with considering diversity as a resource; this promotes a reaffirmation of identities, acknowledgment, and valuing of all languages, cultures, people, and types and paths to learning. Thus, we as teachers—and teacher-researchers—should look at our own privileges and reflect on our identity, take a stand, make social justice our priority, and promote learning as a lifelong transforming process. We must also learn with and from our students and become multilingual and multicultural.

Conclusion

In this essay, I started by giving a brief overview of curriculum and curriculum development throughout history. It is obvious that in its beginnings, curriculum was highly influenced by the view of immigrants as a threat and diversity as a deficit—and still is. The curriculum and the schools were used to both achieve homogeneity and to reproduce a cultural and ideological hegemony within the diverse students of color, low-SES students, emergent bilinguals, and students from nondominant cultural backgrounds—and still are. School knowledge pertains to the dominant social class, textbooks reproduce stereotypes, and technical knowledge becomes the goal of education because of being both teachable and testable. Curriculum can be viewed as a colonizer since it negates diversity and it only emphasizes dominant values and a white supremacy. Even more, the hidden curriculum establishes hierarchies within students by only giving one side of the story and showing diversity as nonexistent or stereotypical. It is interesting to me how students are taught in science and social studies to understand change as something not negotiable but, instead, to assimilate that they cannot change how things are and they should just accept and behave accordingly to the socially accepted norms.

Schools offer remedial programs or lower-leveled courses, segregate students, and base their programs on the funding they receive. Schools have structures such as the latter ones as different forms of discrimination. Deficit-thinking perspectives justify them and see the students as "at risk," "not trying hard," or "coming from difficult backgrounds." These thoughts blame the students and/or their families for not being successful in school, dropping out, and not going to college. Instead, we should blame the system and its systemic structures, which position diverse students that do not conform to the norm as "behind" and "failing." Deficit thinking views consider emergent bilinguals with a linguistic impairment and promote a simplification of curriculum for them.

Understanding how the history supported current negative and discriminative views on diverse and, specifically, immigrants and emergent bilinguals saddens me. It also reminds me of a call for a transformative curriculum and multicultural education with an emphasis on social justice. I highly believe that teaching should start by structuring lessons around students' funds of knowledge. I negate the way the additive curriculum approaches multiculturalism and "food, fun, and festivals" to encourage students to accept diversity. Acceptance, or tolerance, does not embrace acknowledgment or valuing diversity. Therefore, I support a change of attitude of pre- and in-service teachers to look at their privileges, prejudices, and stereotypes to challenge the curriculum and to recuperate a humanized and democracy education. I see teachers as curriculum makers, professionals, and researchers in their own classrooms. I encourage all teachers to own the school curriculum and to promote discussions on controversial issues with their students. They should view them as knowledgeable and full of valuable lived experiences and as inquirers and curriculum makers along with them. As a final thought, curriculum must definitively relate and build on emergent bilinguals' experiences and background knowledge, pursue critical thinking, and exist toward transformation. Ultimately, teachers must aim for our students to take action against injustices and inequities and all unite for a better world.

References

Apple, M. W. (1988). *Teachers and texts: A political economy of class and gender relations in education.* New York: Routledge.

Apple, M. W. (2000). *Official knowledge: Democratic education in a conservative age* (2nd edition). New York: Routledge.

Apple, M. W. (2004). *Ideology & curriculum.* New York: Routledge.

Apple, M. W. (2007). Curriculum planning: Content, form, and the politics of accountability. In F. M. Connelly, M. F. He, & J. Phillion (Eds.), *The SAGE handbook of curriculum and instruction* (pp. 25–44). Thousand Oaks, CA: SAGE.

Apple, M. W., & Buras, K. L. (Eds.). (2006). *The subaltern speak: Curriculum, power, and educational struggles.* New York: Routledge.

Apple, M. W., & Christian-Smith, L. (Eds.). (1991). *The politics of the textbook.* New York: Routledge.

Baratz, S. S., & Baratz, J. C. (1970). Early childhood intervention: The social science base of institutional racism. *Harvard Educational Review, 40,* 29–50.

Bonilla-Silva, E. (2003). *Racism without racists: Color-blind racism and the persistence of racial inequality in the United States.* Lanham, MD: Rowman & Littlefield.

Bourdieu, P. (1977). *Outline of a theory of practice.* New York: Cambridge University Press.

Buttaro, A., Catsambis, S., Mulkey, L., & Steelman, L. C. (2010). An organizational perspective on the origins of instructional segregation: School composition and use of within-class ability grouping in American Kindergartens. *Teachers College Record, 112*(5), 1300–1337.

Callahan, R. M. (2005). Tracking and high school English learners: Limiting opportunity to learn. *American Educational Research Journal, 42*(2), 305–328.

Chan, E. (2003). OP-ED. Ethnic identity in transition: Chinese New Year through the years. *Journal of Curriculum Studies, 35*(4), 409–423.

Chan, E. (2004). *Narratives of ethnic identity: Experiences of first generation Chinese Canadian students.* Unpublished doctoral dissertation, University of Toronto, Ontario, Canada.

Cornbleth, C., & Waugh, D. (1995). *The great specked bird.* New York: St. Martin's Press.

Cummins, J. (2001). *Negotiating identities: Education for empowerment in a diverse society* (2nd edition). Los Angeles: California Association for Bilingual Education.

Delgado, R. (1989). Storytelling for oppositionists and others: A plea for narrative. *Michigan Law Review, 87*, 2411–2441.

Derman-Sparks, L. (1989). *Anti-bias curriculum.* Washington, DC: National Association for the Education of Young Children.

Dewey, J. (1916). *Democracy and education.* New York: Macmillan.

Dewey, J. (1938). *Experience and education.* New York: Macmillan.

Dewey, J. (1997). *How we think.* Courier Corporation.

Freire, P. (1970). *Pedagogy of the oppressed* (M. B. Ramos, Trans.). New York: Continuum.

Freire, P. (1987). The illiteracy of literacy in the United States. In *Literacy: Reading the Word and the World.*

Freire, P. (1998). *Pedagogy of freedom.* Boulder, CO: Rowman & Littlefield.

García, O. (2009). *Bilingual education in the 21st century: A global perspective.* Malden, MA: Wiley-Blackwell.

Giroux, H. A. (1983). *Theory and resistance in education.* London: Bergin & Garvey.

Goodwin, A. L. (2010). Curriculum as colonizer: (Asian) American education in the current US context. *Teachers College Record, 112*(12), 3102–3138.

Graham, R. (1991). *Reading and writing the self.* New York: Teachers College Press.

Gramsci, A. (1975). The theory of hegemony. *Journal of the History of Ideas,* XXXVI, 36.

Greenberg, P. (1992). Teaching about Native Americans? Or teaching about people, including Native Americans? *Young Children, 47*(6), 28–30.

Grumet, M. R. (1980). Autobiography and reconceptualization. *Journal of Curriculum Theorizing, 2*(2), 155–158.

Gutiérrez, K., Rymes, B., & Larson, J. (1995). Script, counterscript, and underlife in the classroom: James Brown vs. Brown of Education. *Harvard Educational Review, 65*(3), 445–471.

Hale-Benson, J. E. (1986). *Black children: Their roots, culture, and learning styles* (Rev. edition). Baltimore, MD: Johns Hopkins University Press.

He, M. F. (2003). *A river forever flowing: Crosscultural lives and identities in the multicultural landscape.* Greenwich, CT: Information Age.

He, M. F., Phillion, J., Chan, E., & Xu, S. (2007). Immigrant students' experience of curriculum. In F. M. Connelly, M. F. He, & J. Phillion (Eds.), *The SAGE handbook of curriculum and instruction* (pp. 219–239). Thousand Oaks, CA: SAGE.

Hyland, N. E. (2010). Social justice in early childhood classrooms what the research tells us. *Young Children, 83*, 82.

Jackson, P. W. (1968). *Life in classrooms.* New York: Holt, Reinhart & Winston.

Kentli, F. D. (2009). Comparison of hidden curriculum theories. *European Journal of Educational Studies, 1*(2), 83–88.

Labov, W. (1970). The logic of nonstandard English. In F. Williams (Ed.), *Language and poverty* (pp. 153–187). Chicago, IL: Markham Press.

Ladson-Billings, G. (2000). Fighting for our lives: Preparing teachers to teach African American students. *Journal of Teacher Education, 51*(3), 206–214.

Ladson-Billing, G. (2006). Yes, but how do we do it?. In J. Ladsman, and C. Lewis, (Eds.) (2006), *White teachers, diverse classrooms* (pp. 29–41). Sterling, VA: Styhes Publishers.

Ladson-Billings, G., & Brown, K. (2007). Curriculum and cultural diversity. In F. M. Connelly, M.F. He, & J. Phillion (Eds.), *The SAGE handbook of curriculum and instruction* (pp. 153–175). Thousand Oaks, CA: Sage.

Lee, S. J., & Zhou, M. (Eds.). (2004). *Asian American youth: Culture, identity and ethnicity*. New York: Routledge.

Lei, J. L. (2003). (Un)necessary toughness? Those 'loud Black girls' and those 'quiet Asian boys.' *Anthropology & Education Quarterly, 34*(2), 158–181.

Lynch, K. (1989). *The hidden curriculum: Reproduction in education*. New York: Pergamon Press, 41–42.

Mickelson, R. A. (2001). Subverting Swann: First- and second-generation segregation in Charlotte-Mecklenburg schools. *American Educational Research Journal, 38*, 215–252.

Moll, L., Amanti, C., Neff, D., & González, N. (1992). Funds of knowledge for teaching: Using a qualitative approach to connect homes and classrooms. *Theory into Practice, XXXI*(2), 132–141.

Nieto, S. (2000a). *Affirming diversity: The sociopolitical context of multicultural education* (3rd edition). New York: Longman.

Nieto, S. (2000b). Placing equity front and center some thoughts on transforming teacher education for a new century. *Journal of teacher education, 51*(3), 180–187.

Nieto, S. (2003). Afterword. In S. Greene & D. Abt-Perkins (Eds.), *Making race visible: Literacy research for cultural understanding* (pp. 201–2015). New York: Teachers College Press.

Nieto, S., Bode, P., Kang, E., & Raible, J. (2007). Identity, community, and diversity. In F. M. Connelly, M. F. He, & J. Phillion (Eds.), *The SAGE handbook of curriculum and instruction* (pp. 176–197). Thousand Oaks, CA: Sage.

Olsen, L. (1997). *Made in America: Immigrant students in our public schools*. New York: The New Press.

Pearl, A. (1997). Cultural and accumulated environmental deficit models. In R. R. Valencia (Ed.), *The evolution of deficit thinking: Educational thought and practice* (pp. 132–159). The Stanford Series on Education and Public Policy. London, UK: Falmer Press.

Ramirez, M., III, & Castañeda, A. (1974). *Cultural democracy, bicognitive development, and education*. New York: Academic Press.

Ryan, W. (1971). *Blaming the victim*. New York: Random House.

Schubert, W. H. (2007). Curriculum inquiry. In F. M. Connelly, M. F. He, & J. Phillion (Eds.), *The SAGE handbook of curriculum and instruction* (pp. 399–419). Thousand Oaks, CA: Sage.

Schwab, J. J. (1969). The practical: A language for curriculum. *School Review, 78*, 1–24.

Schwab, J. J. (1970). *The practical: A language for curriculum*. Washington, DC: National Education Association.

Shujaa, M. W. (Ed.). (1994). *Too much schooling, too little education: A paradox of Black lives in White societies*. Trenton, NJ: Africa World Press.

Sleeter, C. E. (2005). *Un-standardizing curriculum: Multicultural teaching in the standards based classroom*. New York: Teachers College Press.

Smith, B. O., Stanley, W. O., & Shores, J. H. (1957). *Fundamentals of curriculum development* (Rev. edition). New York: Harcourt, Brace, and World.

Talmy, S. (2005). The other : Micronesians in a Hawaii high school. In C. C. Park, R. Endo, & A. L. Goodwin (Eds.), *Asian and Pacific American education:*

Learning, socialization, and identity (pp. 19–50). Greenwich, CT: Information Age Publishing.

Thomas, W. P., & Collier, V. P. (2002). *A national study of school effectiveness for language minority students' long-term academic achievement.* Santa Cruz, CA: Center for Research on Education, Diversity and Excellence.

Valencia, R. R. (2010). *Dismantling contemporary deficit thinking: Educational thought and practice.* New York: Routledge.

Valentine, C. A. (1971). Deficit, difference, and bicultural models of Afro-American behavior. *Harvard Educational Review, 41,* 137–157.

Welner, K. G., & Escamilla, K. (2002). *The unintended consequences of Colorado's antibilingual education initiative.* Boulder, CO: Education and the Public Interest Center.

Welner, K. G., & Oakes, J. (2007). Structural curriculum: Technical, normative, and political considerations. In F. M. Connelly, M. F. He, & J. Phillion (Eds.), *The SAGE handbook of curriculum and instruction* (pp. 91–112). Thousand Oaks, CA: Sage.

Westbury, I. (2007). Making curriculum: Why do states make curricula, and how? In F. M. Connelly, M. F. He, & J. Phillion, (Eds.), *The SAGE handbook of curriculum and instruction* (pp. 45–65). Thousand Oaks, CA: Sage.

Williams, R. (1989). *Resources of hope.* New York: Verso.

Zinn, H. (2007). *A young people's history of the United States.* New York: Seven Stories Press.

Contributors

Nancy Wasser: University of New Mexico

Romina Pacheco: Smith College

Veronica Gallego: New Mexico State University

Giselle Martinez Negrette: University of Wisconsin-Madison

Donna-Marie Cole-Malott: Pennsylvania State University

Paulo A. Oemig: New Mexico State University

Debasmita Roychowdhury: New Mexico State University

Loretta H. Wideman: New Mexico State University

Lihua Zhang: University of China

Adriana Goenaga Ruiz de Zuazu: New Mexico State University

Susana Ríos: New Mexico State University

Ewa Krawczyk: College of the Marshall Islands

Karen R. Trujillo: New Mexico State University

Index

Iraqi refuges 129, 130
Islam 48, 82

Jamaica 77–9
Jordan 129

Kress 2, 3, 140

Labov 143
language 1, 4, 6–8, 12, 15, 17–19,
  20–1, 23, 25–6, 105–6, 116–9,
  120–5, 134, 138, 143–4, 154, 167,
  171–3, 175, 178; colonial language
  116, 120; colonized language 122;
  dominant language 127, 131, 133,
  135; European language 130, 131;
  foreign language teacher 175; home
  language 182, 184; indigenous
  language 130, 131; language in
  action 61, 68; language discourse
  175; language diversity 183; language
  ideology 3, 5; language issues 183;
  language proficiency 187; language
  use 4, 159; language in use 4, 15,
  21, 138; languages 129; minority
  language 127; native languages 118,
  122, 129; power of language 167,
  171; social/political facet of language
  167; uses of language 172
Latin America 157
Latino 104, 109; Latinos 109, 111
Lebanon 129
learning community 100; learning
  communities 93; learning
  environment 187; learning process
  128, 182
Left-wing ideology 172
liberating pedagogy 166
linguicism 4; applied linguistics 177;
  linguistic 1, 2, 5, 7, 11, 12, 128–9,
  130–1, 142, 187, 188, 190; linguistic
  achievement gap 187; linguistically
  1, 2, 8, 9, 127, 128, 131; linguistic
  and cultural diversity 187;
  linguistic description 139; linguistic
  discrimination 127, 132, 134;
  linguistic diversity 189; linguistic
  domination 130; linguistic encounter
  130, 131; linguistic ideology 68;
  linguistic interexchange 130;
  linguistic repertoires 21; linguistic
  skills 182; linguists 7; monolingual
  175; monolingualism 185;

mono-linguistic 179; multilingual
  1, 4–5, 8, 127, 135, 181, 190;
  multilingualism 12, 178
literacy 7, 178, 180
long-term English learners 187
Luckmann 61

macro-level 70
marginalized groups 1, 4, 5, 7, 11,
  128–9, 130
María Estela Martinez de perón 64
Martin, Lockheed 48–9
Marxism 17
Marxist 63
materialism 71
Max-Neef, Manfred 47
meaning-making process 140
measurable knowledge 184
media 8
melting point 15
Mennonite culture 146, 148, 151,
  161
Mestizos 105
micro-level 70
microsocieties 155
Middle East 48
Midwest United States 161
military 63, 64, 65; military coup 63;
  military dictatorship 60, 63, 64, 68,
  72; military domination 60; military
  junta 63, 64, 65, 66, 67, 68, 69;
  military-ruled country 66
minoritized group 155, 186;
  minoritized students 183–4
minority 184, 186; minority groups
  128, 132; minority language 127;
  minority students 184, 194
Mobilize 161
model for employing CDA to analyze
  multimodal texts 140
model minority mythology 184
mother tongue 119, 120, 122, 125
Mulattos 105
multimodality 140
multimodal social semiotic approach
  140

narrative 2, 7, 142, 147–8, 152, 159,
  161; basic narrative structures 143;
  narrative construction 148; narratives
  7–9, 141–3, 146, 149, 150, 159,
  161, 163, 165; narrative vignette
  148; personal narrative practices

Made in United States
North Haven, CT
06 September 2022

23722202R00122